Also by Dexter Masters:

THE ACCIDENT (1955; REVISED EDITION, 1965)

This is a Borzoi Book, published in New York by Alfred A. Knopf

The Intelligent Buyer

and

the Telltale Seller

Drawings by Christina Malman

The Intelligent Buyer
and
the Telltale Seller

by

DEXTER MASTERS

◄◄◄◄◄◄◄◄◄◄◄◄◄◄◄◄◄◄◄◄◄◄◄◄◄►►►►►►►►►►►►►►►►►►►►►►►►

New York : Alfred · A · Knopf

1 9 6 6

Most of the text of this book appeared, in different form and under a different title (*The Intelligent Buyer's Guide to Sellers*), in a special 1965 edition published by Consumers Union for its subscribers. The Preface and Chapter 13 of the present book are entirely new, as are the illustrations; several chapters and the Postscript have been extensively revised and enlarged; a great many changes and additions have been made throughout.

L. C. catalog card number: 66–11345

THIS IS A BORZOI BOOK,

PUBLISHED BY ALFRED A. KNOPF, INC.

FIRST BORZOI EDITION

Manufactured in the United States of America

Acknowledgment is hereby made for permission to quote from the following:

Catch-22, by Joseph Heller, copyright © 1955, 1961 by Joseph Heller; reprinted by permission of Simon & Shuster, Inc.

The Grapes of Wrath, by John Steinbeck, copyright 1939 by John Steinbeck; reprinted by permission of the Viking Press, Inc.

Death of a Salesman, by Arthur Miller, copyright 1949 by Arthur Miller; reprinted by permission of the Viking Press, Inc.

Absentee Ownership, by Thorstein Veblen, copyright 1923 by B. W. Heubsch, Inc.; all rights reserved; reprinted by permission of The Viking Press, Inc.

Antic Hay, by Aldous Huxley, copyright 1923, 1950 by Aldous Huxley; reprinted by permission of Harper & Row.

The Boss, by Roy Lewis and Rosemary Stewart, copyright © 1963; reprinted by permission of the authors.

Preface

◀◀◀◀◀◀◀◀◀◀◀◀◀◀◀◀◀◀◀◀◀◀◀◀◀◀◀▶▶▶▶▶▶▶▶▶▶▶▶▶▶▶▶▶▶▶▶▶▶▶▶▶

THE FINAL FLOWERING of the increasingly standardized culture of our technical civilization will come, as Jacques Ellul wrote in *The Technological Society*, "when psychological techniques, in close cooperation with material techniques, have at last succeeded in creating unity." In the bloom of that time, Ellul notes, "all possible diversity will have disappeared and the human race will have become a block of complete and irrational solidarity." Among the psychological techniques thus implicated is one which Ellul calls "a striking phenomenon of involuntary psychological collectivization," by which he means that exercise of the commercial spirit known generally as advertising.

Ellul's elegantly structured analysis of contemporary civilization does not spend much time on advertising. Still, some of the central facts emerge. As Ellul points out, the inevitable consequence of his involuntary psychological collectivization is the creation of a new mass man, who finds in Elsie the Cow, for example, an ideal type; and he notes the corollary truth that "we can get a general impression of this new human type by studying America, where . . . advertising enjoys universal popular adherence, and the American way of life is fashioned by it."

A general awareness of the workings of advertising linked to a rather surface treatment of them is often found in the writings of social critics whose eyes are on larger game. It is as though the workings of advertising are assumed to be of such a simple nature that they may be taken for granted; as though advertising's debasements of American life are thought to be so self-evident that anyone who understands anything will understand this; as though one has to do little more than mention the word for his readers to nod their heads in approval of the criticism that need hardly be made. There have been many detailed critiques of the frauds and excesses of advertising on a relatively straightforward, muckraking plane. But the social critic who stops at advertising on his way to larger considerations tends to take only nominal note of the heavy hand of the seller and usually discusses its manipulations just enough to tap the public's consciousness of them but not enough to add to it. Those individuals who make their living at advertising and have chosen to write about their business—several recent examples of this odd genre are looked into in the pages that follow—have done so uniformly at such a low level as to illuminate little beyond themselves.

The present volume is an attempt to enlarge public comprehension of the commercial spirit as it thrives in America. I have laid myself open, I suppose, to the charge that I have simply attacked advertising once again and am just putting on display once more some of the visible manifestations of its boisterous irresponsibility. The first thing to be said in answer to such a charge is that every little bit helps; no matter how much awareness of the workings of advertising is assumed, it never turns out to be up to the need; and no matter how extensive the critiques, they never quite cover the subject. One more critique won't carry the day for reason, but it may spread the light a little further. The second thing to be said is that this volume, certainly in intention and I trust in execution, goes beyond the charge.

The approach in the pages that follow is to the base nature of modern commercial pressures, to their origins and development, and to something of what they may hold for the future. In part, this undertaking has involved me in tracking the soul of the trader through time, through the words of a number of wise and innocent practitioners and observers, through some conscious and unconscious confessions of the greedy. The resultant litany is, I think, a novel one and I believe and hope the reader will get some amusement out of it. But with respect to this as well as to other areas of the book's contents, moral indignation is possible, too, and one can only hope that things are not too far advanced for the effective exercise of that.

DEXTER MASTERS

New York
May 1966

Author's Note

◄◄◄◄◄◄◄◄◄◄◄◄◄◄◄◄◄◄◄◄◄◄◄◄◄◄►►►►►►►►►►►►►►►►►►►►►►►►►

A FEW YEARS AGO, on the occasion of the twenty-fifth anniversary of Consumers Union, that curious and perverse byproduct of the commercial spirit, John Kenneth Galbraith wrote to wish the organization well and to note the danger that "it might settle into comfortable middle-age." As an "interested reader and well-wisher," he wrote, "I can only hope that what is inevitable may in this instance be avoided." It was avoided during my years as the Director of Consumers Union, if only because of the presence of the late Mildred Edie Brady, my very close friend and the highly respected colleague of half a lifetime, who knew more about the front-line economics of the buyer's life than anyone, and enough about keeping a middle-aged organization from settling down to save it, at least until her most untimely death last year, from the administrators and policy makers who are always around and ready to abandon an organization to comfort and prosperity. I am in her debt as a hundred times before, this time for her careful and intelligent review of most of what follows, and I gratefully dedicate this book to her memory.

I am indebted to Colston E. Warne, professor of economics at Amherst and President of Consumers since its beginning, for suggesting several lines of inquiry and for his own detailed review. (And of course I relieve him of all responsibility for numerous expressions with which he may not agree.)

My debt to all the authors of all the books I quote is obvious, and I most humbly acknowledge it. And to all the editors of all the trade journals cited I express my appreciation for their illumination of their specialities. The numerous excerpts from these journals were taken in large part from the files of Consumers Union covering the period 1958–1965.

To the indispensable person who went over every word, provided insights and perceptions beyond counting, helped in the composition, and set all to paper—namely, Joan Masters—I reaffirm feelings of which she is well aware. Among many other things, she knows how far beyond these pages the subject reaches. It is the book thus broadly viewed that the drawings of the late Christina Malman Masters illustrate, to the great gain of reader and author alike.

DEXTER MASTERS

Contents

ONE REASON why modern life is so uncomfortable is that we have grown self-conscious about things that used to be taken for granted. Formerly people believed what they believed because they thought it was true, or because it was what all right-thinking people thought. But since Freud exposed to us our propensity to rationalization and Marx showed how our ideas spring from ideologies we have begun to ask: Why do I believe what I believe about what it is that makes me believe it? So we remain in an impenetrable fog. Truth is no longer true. Evil is no longer wicked. "It all depends on what you mean." But this makes life impossible—we must find a way through.

"Backward or forward, it's just as far. Out or in, the way's as narrow." "Who are you?" "Myself. Can you say as much?" "What are you?" "The great Boyg . . . Go round about, go round about."*

JOAN ROBINSON, *Economic Philosophy*

* Ibsen, *Peer Gynt*, Act II, Scene 7

Part One

‹‹‹‹‹‹‹‹‹‹‹‹‹‹‹‹‹‹‹‹‹‹‹‹‹‹‹‹‹‹‹›››››››››››››››››››››››››››

The Record

of an

Immoral Relationship

1

‹‹‹‹‹‹‹‹‹‹‹‹‹‹‹‹‹‹‹‹‹‹‹‹‹‹‹›››››››››››››››››››››››

In Explanation of
One-Sidedness

THIS will be, of course, a one-sided discussion. It could hardly be otherwise, although the reasons for that may not be at once apparent and a brief word of explanation may therefore be useful to start matters going. First of all, a practical reason, which cannot fail to win the indulgence of any fair-minded reader, is at work. Sellers are by nature a talkative and gregarious species; they are given to setting forth and justifying their notions in many books, innumerable articles, and speeches beyond counting. It is a further mark of their kind that they are inordinately fond of coming together for conventions and meetings, at which they spend much time drawing up statements, codes, programs, and the like, all designed to be expressive of the seller view of things (this is a particularly noticeable trait of sellers and as good a one as any for the intelligent buyer to make first note of). In short, sellers may be counted on to speak for themselves, however badly, and any one-sidedness or seeming immoderation in the present study should properly be taken as no more than a simple redressing of a balance very much in want of that.

Despite the foregoing, it will be observed that sellers are referred to very frequently and their statements quoted, often at length, in the pages that follow. It seems not only fair but, in all honesty, useful to my project to provide this additional forum to those already possessed of so many. For, unquestionably, the things that sellers say sometimes do throw light on the buyer-seller relationship, and the seeking of such light is, as will be increasingly clear, the objective of this study. One would expect and even hope that steady reference to the words of the seller would also help to mitigate one-sidedness. But, in a curious and interesting way, the very opposite turns out to be the case.

This comes about because of another trait of sellers—what may be considered their realism. It always makes a seller very happy to be told that he is realistic—hard-nosed, hard-headed, down-to-earth, and other such euphemisms please him greatly, too—and the truth is that he really is some of these things, at least some of the time, at least in part, and at least when he is talking in his native habitat (a convention hotel or the pages of a trade journal circulated among his own kind) and is not in danger of being quoted too publicly. But the irony that goes with this truth is that realism about the buyer-seller relationship tends to indict the seller. Moreover, hardly anyone is so simply abusive of the seller, so rather mopingly condemnatory of the seller's practices, as a seller.

The trade journals are filled to overflowing with abuses and condemnations, presumably because sellers like to write and read them, possibly as a counter to the mechanical smile mouthing the often ridiculous words of the seller in his official guise. One can sense the legitimate puzzlement and groping worry of the author of this *mea culpa* in the trade journal *Printers' Ink*, where *mea culpa*'s appear regularly:

A strange malady seems to come over many an advertising man when he sits before his typewriter. A man who is morally straight in his personal life will write half-truths

when he would never dream of making the same statements to friends or acquaintances.

Here is the authentic voice of the small boy who stopped
Shoeless Joe Jackson in the stadium after the White Sox had
become the Black Sox, and sobbed his heart out into that im-
mortal cry: "Say it ain't so, Joe!" And here, too, is Biff dis-
covering Willy Loman with the woman in the hotel room.

More self-conscious and less honest than that seller's view
of sellers is this one, also from *Printers' Ink:*

> Some evening, when your stomach is feeling particularly
> strong and your senses a little blunter than usual, sit down
> with some current magazines and newspapers . . . steal an
> occasional glimpse at your television screen. I think you
> may be surprised at the amount of sheer cheapness that is
> creeping into advertising.

Surely this is naïve beyond all reason; surely a seller above
all must know that cheapness has been creeping into advertising since there has been advertising, although it just may
be that some sellers, viewing matters from in where the creeping is, can still be surprised at the amount. What is interesting about this particular *mea culpa* is the hint of corruption
even here; this breast-beater is beating his breast because that
has become a rather faddy thing to do among the sellers; it
bespeaks sophistication and it embodies a kind of plea that
this seller be thought of not as a clever man with low values
but as a simpleton with high ones, however they may be
aggrieved. The intelligent buyer should note that many sellers
(although not all) do not like to be thought clever in public.

For all that it is endless, there is really little more for the
intelligent buyer to learn from the literature of *mea culpa*,
almost all examples of which follow in the line of one or the
other of the two cited. He should know of this literature's existence, and from time to time might buy a copy of *Printers'
Ink* or *Advertising Age* or *Sales Management*, or one of the

hundreds of trade journals for particular product categories, such as *Women's Wear Daily, Tobacco, Merchandising Week, Home Furnishings Daily*, and the like. He can hardly fail to find from any reading therein the testimony of one or two sellers worrying over the nature of selling, this one with a heavy frown upon his words as he tries to penetrate its mysteries, that one with a well-contrived mask of earnestness around his—although both would rise as one to defend this ailing, cheapened calling which gives them these bothersome though transient moments.

In the interests of common courtesy, and to keep one-sidedness from getting out of hand, I have chosen to minimize my use of many of the more outrageous declarations by sellers of principles which they hold dear and of practices in which they engage—such pronouncements as the recent one by the executive vice-president of Fuller & Smith & Ross, one of the country's largest advertising agencies. A trade journal quoted him as follows:

> In new business, if you engage in anything short of a direct assault on the jugular vein, you're in the Mickey Mouse league.

This is instructive (the intelligent buyer will be reminded at once of the ironic instruction given by the German economist Werner Sombart many years ago: "Search out the customer and attack him"). But it does fall rather harshly on the ear so early in the game, and the reader will not be asked to dwell on it at this stage.

On the other hand, it may be conducive to the greater good, however one-sided it might seem in a narrow interpretation, to keep alive the information, found in the semi-private pages of *Supermarket News*, that a survey conducted not long ago by the National Bureau of Standards in Arkansas showed that "more than 80% of pre-packaged foods were found to be of short measure." Assuredly the intelligent buyer finds the buyer-seller relationship illuminated by this small bit of information, and even the seller who has always referred such simple cheating to "a small minority" of his kind will be happy to learn the dimensions that the "minority" may take on occasion.

Similarly, the understanding of all of us is plainly nourished by knowledge of a recent merchandising symposium for funeral directors which, as the *Wall Street Journal* noted, "wound up with a talk entitled: 'As Ye Price, So Shall Ye Reap.' " For surely, after all, it is through an open and friendly contemplation of the truths by which we live and die that we learn to know each other.

 With this consideration in mind, the intelligent reader will appreciate that the present undertaking is not to be thought of as just one more attack on selling or advertising, of the kind that has been quite common in years past. The frauds, cheats, and other sins associated with the selling area of life have been set down by many able researchers and, as we shall see, by many good writers, beyond the need of simple embellishment from me. The issue for this inquiry runs more to the seller himself and the institutions he commands; and it is my aim to examine the character and customs of these for the edification and possible advantage of the buyer.

It was in something of this broad and tolerant spirit that the late Calvin Coolidge, the distinguished thirtieth president of the United States, averted his eyes from the frauds, cheats, etc., to give his assessment of the seller and his greatest institution, advertising; he spoke in the 1920's to an audience of advertising men, who listened with rapt attention, and we should do no less:

> Advertising ministers to the spiritual side of trade. It is a great power which has been entrusted to your keeping, which charges you with the high responsibility of inspiring and ennobling the commercial world. It is all part of the greater work of regeneration and redemption of mankind.

It may be that neither the intelligent buyer nor, for that matter, the intelligent seller will wish to follow one-sidedness quite that far. Assuredly there are some things left hanging between the late president's conception of the seller's world and such conceptions as the one advanced by the adman who described the getting of business so graphically. But even so, let none suppose that Mr. Coolidge's words were strung on such a simple thread only because of the saintliness of Mr. Coolidge or the pure moral tone of life in the 1920's. "Advertising is like praying . . ." said W. Noel Eldred, vice-president of marketing for the Hewlett-Packard Company of Palo Alto, California, as quoted in *Advertising Age* only a couple of years ago.

To whatever extent Mr. Eldred speaks for other modern sellers, it is reasonable and even imperative to ask to whom the prayers are being said. Prayer is a very private thing, and the intelligent buyer seeking to understand the seller must remember that, all evidence to the contrary, including TV commercials and billboards, sellers must have at least occasional moments of privacy, even as other people, and have been reported to hold some things sacred.

Is "calling for" like praying? Perhaps there is an important clue for buyers in the words of a former editor of *Printers' Ink,* one Woodrow Wirsig, who was quoted as "calling for" built-in obsolescence in all new products and a law compelling everyone to spend a specified minimum each year for consumer goods. He was quoted further as saying, and one can only be thankful that Calvin Coolidge was not here to listen:

> Thrift is no longer a virtue. A dollar saved may cost us our jobs.

The intelligent buyer should listen, however.

In the jungle of the marketplace, indeed, the intelligent buyer must be alert to every commercial sound, to every snapping of a selling twig, to every rustle that may signal the uprising arm holding the knife pointed toward the jugular vein. Beyond the gregariousness, the articulateness, and the private realism of sellers, we must take notice of another trait; this trait is contempt for the buyer, and, for the buyer, this trait is possibly the most dangerous of all, although it may come to be equally dangerous for the seller. The carefully listening buyer will hear both the snapping and the rustle in something the president of the American Association of Advertising Agencies told a meeting of his association a year or so ago: "Stop worrying about every piddling criticism of our business," the *San Francisco Chronicle* reported him as saying. "If there is any collective quality of the public, it is indifference."

Still, man is an animal that likes to bargain—the only one, as Adam Smith has pointed out—although it may be questioned that the trait comes built-in, like obsolescence. It is more probable that it is something learned, and certainly an aptitude for bargaining is the product of procedures which, like hate and fear, have to be carefully taught. Man's distinction, or at least the average man's distinction, is that he can and does respond to such teaching.

But, by the same token, if men have to learn these things, it follows that some men are going to fail in the process. The discovery that things are sold, even beautiful things like candy and flowers, provides undoubtedly one of the first looks into the imperfections of life, and this look comes very early. Some do not recover from it. They may go on to become non-buyers, who are the anti-heroes of the commercial world. Others may start or end up with gaps or wounds in their intelligences, may eventually recoil from the corrosive intensity that modern bargaining often takes on, may be victimized into submissiveness by the sellers, and may come to indifference as a ship comes to founder on a reef, there to be buffeted by endless forces until it wears away.

A buyer in this state is, of course, the seller's dream, and the president of the American Association of Advertising Agencies, in his reassurance to his fellows, is thus expressing not only what he surely considers to be the truth, or some reasonable facsimile of the truth, but a deep wish fulfillment as well. It is quite important that the intelligent buyer know this in particular about sellers: they want him heart and soul, but they do not want his mind thrown in.)

There are a thousand evidences of the seller's love for the mindless buyer. Almost the entire packaging industry, with its near total confusion of sizes and shapes and weights, is a labor of love on the seller's part for the mindless buyer. What buyer, unless he has a mind, can fail to be moved by the hand lotion manufacturer who issued a news release to the trade from which *Modern Packaging* quoted this proud sentence:

> A relatively tall, graceful bottle was modeled that in a 5-ounce size actually gives the appearance of being larger than the old 10-ounce size.

And what a triumph of mindlessness, linking seller and buyer together in one great vibration, shone forth in *Time* Magazine's report that

> Chicago's Alberto-Culver was so eager to beat Procter & Gamble's Head and Shoulders shampoo to market that it filmed the TV commercials for its Subdue shampoo even before it had developed the product.

In the mindless world, to be sure, *Time*'s arrow points both ways, and a seller working backwards is doubtless unaware of it—or at least, to borrow the thought of our friend in the American Association of Advertising Agencies, indifferent to working that way. Moreover, in the mindless world the loved one and the lover tend to run together. Thus, the president of the Polaroid Corporation, as quoted in *Product Engineering*, can solemnly avow:

> New products here at Polaroid are never developed because of market research or questionnaires to customers. Industry must have insight into what are the deep needs of people that they don't know they have.

This is heady stuff, ready-made for the mindless buyer, although the intelligent buyer, one trusts, can see the raised hand and hear the warning rustle. He can certainly hear the rustle and see the hand in such a statement as this by Alfred Politz, one of the country's leading market researchers, as set forth in the *Wall Street Journal*:

> The solution to marketing problems is not necessarily one of giving consumers what they want, but rather to make consumers want what we, the marketers, want them to want.

The concern of sellers for needs and wants that people do not know they have can become all too quickly a concern for needs and wants they do not have. And the seller's arrival at this point is the consummation of his affair with the mindless buyer, although a whole array of dalliances goes on before the point is reached. It is one of the purposes of this book, in searching for the light, to help the intelligent buyer learn to identify this point, and to acquaint him better with the dalliances as they have been identified and written of throughout history and must be identified and written of anew from time to time.

The general area where the seller's lust despoils the buyer was laid out perfectly clearly by ben Sirach long ago in these lines from Ecclesiasticus (as translated by Edgar Goodspeed):

Over two things my heart is grieved . . .
A merchant can hardly keep himself from doing wrong,
And a storekeeper cannot be acquitted of sin.
Many sin for the sake of gain,
And the man who is intent on increasing what he has, has to shut his eyes.
A peg will stick between the joints of stones,
And between buying and selling, sin is ground out.

Directing his attention to the locale of the process so graphically described by ben Sirach, Diogenes Laertius gave the marketplace perhaps the most straightforward, simplest description ever conferred on it:

> The market is a place set apart where men may deceive each other.

Within this marketplace the seller is under a pressure that he cannot very well withstand and remain a seller, and his manner of responding to it was put plainly enough by Cicero:

> ... For the dealer will gain nothing except by profuse lying, and nothing is more disgraceful than untruthful huckstering.

A little later, and more philosophically, Marcus Aurelius contemplated both a kind of huckstering and one of man's natural defenses against it:

> When we have meat before us and such eatables, let us receive the impression that this is the dead body of a fish, bird or a pig; and again, that this Falerian is only a little grape juice, and this purple robe some sheep's wool dyed with the blood of a shell-fish. These impressions . . . recall the things themselves, and penetrate them, so we see what kind of things they are. Just in the same way we ought to act all through life, and where there are things which appear most worthy of our approbation, we ought to lay them bare and look at their worthlessness, and strip them of all the words by which they are exalted. For outward show is a wonderful perverter of the reason. . . .

But by the time of Shakespeare the concept of the market as a place of deceit and the seller as a deceiver had become so common that it could be used in passing to embroider other references:

> Let me have no lying: it becomes none but tradesmen.

It was shortly after Shakespeare's lifetime that advertising as the seller's arm took shape. By the middle of the eighteenth century it was already somewhat confounding Dr. Johnson, who noted in *The Idler* in 1758 the old familiar essence of the technique:

> Advertisements are now so numerous that they are very negligently perused, and it is therefore become necessary to gain attention by magnificence of promises and by eloquence sometimes sublime and sometimes pathetick. Promise—large promise—is the soul of advertising. . . .

By Disraeli's day the pressures of the marketplace had hardened as the commercial revolution that was new to Shakespeare and casual to Johnson had intensified. Thus spoke Disraeli:

> It is well known what a middle man is: he is a man who bamboozles one party and plunders the other.

And of Disraeli's cynical observation Dickens made a rule for cynics—that is to say, for intelligent buyers:

> Here's the rule for bargains: 'Do other men, for they would do you.' That's the true business precept.

The mordant Ambrose Bierce summed it up in *The Devil's Dictionary* as the twentieth century got under way:

> Don't steal; thou'lt never thus compete
> Successfully in business. Cheat.

This small set of observations, be it noted—and it would be no difficult thing to present a hundred others of the same sort—runs a range of two thousand years or more. Not the inconstancy of the human heart is a more durable element in man's view of himself than the low estate of his values under the tension of the buyer-seller relationship. We must approach closer to what constitutes this tension, the better to understand it and the better to become intelligent buyers. And we have guides without number, as we shall see.

2

<<<<<<<<<<<<<<<<<<<<<<<<<<<<<<<>>>>>>>>>>>>>>>>>>>>>>>>>>>>

" . . . a Place
Set Apart"

THERE has sometimes been an imputation that the bargaining process is a contest almost between equals. This is not remotely true, as we will all surely agree by the time this book is done. But there was a little more of truth in it once than there has come to be. Oliver Goldsmith conceived matters thus in Letter LXXVII from *The Citizen of the World*, a collection of newspaper columns on eighteenth-century English life. Here is how Goldsmith and a silk mercer dealt with each other in the London of the early 1760's:

> I was this morning to buy silk for a nightcap; immediately upon entering the mercer's shop, the master and his two men, with wigs plastered with powder, appeared to ask my commands. They were certainly the civilest people alive; if I but looked, they flew to the place where I cast my eye; every motion of mine sent them running round the whole shop for my satisfaction. I informed them that I wanted what was good, and they showed me not less than forty

pieces, and each was better than the former, the prettiest pattern in nature, and the fittest in the world for nightcaps. "My very good friend," said I to the mercer, "you must not pretend to instruct me in silks; I know these in particular to be no better than your mere flimsy Bungees."—"That may be," cried the mercer, who I afterwards found had never contradicted a man in his life; "I cannot pretend to say but they may; but I can assure you, my lady Trail has had a sack from this piece this very morning."—"But friend," said I, "though my lady has chosen a sack from it, I see no necessity that I should wear it for a nightcap." —"That may be," returned he again, "yet what becomes a pretty lady, will at any time look well on a handsome gentleman." This short compliment was thrown in so very seasonably upon my ugly face, that even though I disliked the silk, I desired him to cut me off the pattern of a nightcap.

While this business was consigned to his journeyman, the master himself took down some pieces of silk still finer than any I had yet seen, and spreading them before me, "There," cries he, "there's beauty, My lord Snakeskin has bespoke the fellow to this for the birth-night this very morning; it would look charmingly in waistcoats."—"But I don't want a waistcoat," replied I.—"Not want a waistcoat!" returned the mercer, "then I would advise you to buy one; when waistcoats are wanted, you may depend upon it they will come dear. Always buy before you want, and you are sure to be well used, as they say in Cheapside." There was so much justice in his advice, that I could not refuse taking it; besides, the silk, which was a really good one, increased the temptation; so I gave orders for that too.

As I was waiting to have my bargains measured and cut, which, I know not how, they executed but slowly, during the interval the mercer entertained me with the modern manner of some of the nobility receiving company in their morning gowns; "Perhaps, sir," adds he, "you have a mind

to see what kind of silk is universally worn." Without waiting for my reply, he spreads a piece before me, which might
be reckoned beautiful even in China. "If the nobility,"
continues he, "were to know I sold this to any under a Right
Honorable, I should certainly lose their custom; you see, my
lord, it is at once rich, tasty, and quite the thing."—"I am
no lord," interrupted I.—"I beg pardon," cried he; "but be
pleased to remember, when you intend buying a morning
gown, that you had an offer from me of something worth
money. Conscience, sir, conscience is my way of dealing;
you may buy a morning gown now, or you may stay till they
become dearer and less fashionable; but it is not my
business to advise." In sort, most reverend Fum, he persuaded me to buy a morning gown also, and would probably have persuaded me to have bought half the goods in
his shop, if I had stayed long enough, or was furnished
with sufficient money.

Upon returning home, I could not help reflecting, with
some astonishment, how this very man, with such a confined
education and capacity, was yet capable of turning me as he
thought proper, and molding me to his inclinations! I knew
he was only answering his own purposes, even while he attempted to appear solicitous about mine: yet, by a voluntary
infatuation, a sort of passion, compounded of vanity and
good-nature, I walked into the snare with my eyes open,
and put myself to future pain in order to give him immediate pleasure. The wisdom of the ignorant somewhat re-
sembles the instinct of animals; it is diffused in but a very
narrow sphere, but within that circle it acts with vigor,
uniformity, and success.

What the intelligent buyer should particularly consider in
Goldsmith's charming story is how one set of traits is pitted
against another. The "animal instinct" that gives "vigor, uniformity, and success" to the ignorant seller feeds on the "vanity
and good-nature" of Mr. Goldsmith, who has portrayed him-

self as a most unintelligent buyer. As such, he is, of course, outmaneuvered and taken. But an air of cheerfulness hangs over everything, and it is possible to assume that, as and when he wishes to, Goldsmith might handle matters differently.

In short, Goldsmith's seller is presented as a man acting at the peak of his limited capacity, while Goldsmith's buyer is seen as a rather tolerant fellow utilizing some fraction of *his* capacities. The deeper implication is that, so long as the buyer is an eighteenth-century gentleman, a real contest with a seller is beneath him.

The heart of the matter, which lies outside of Goldsmith's story, is that the seller always has an advantage over the buyer, however stubborn and stern and however lacking in vanity and good-nature the latter may be. The essence of the buyer-seller relationship is that the seller, as a professional, is in a position to know things about the product he is selling that the buyer cannot know or at the least cannot readily know. The seller may use his advantage sparingly or may abuse it to the hilt, but the fact that he has an advantage is not to be questioned.

For a cogent statement of this view of things the searching buyer may go to Bernard Mandeville's small classic of the early eighteenth century, *The Fable of the Bees.* In an essay quite as charming as Goldsmith's, almost as good-humored, but much tougher at the core, Mandeville observes the buyer-seller relationship from the inside out. He, like Goldsmith, addresses himself to a meeting between a mercer and his customer, in this instance a young lady:

> . . . Those who have never minded the conversation of a spruce mercer and a young lady, his customer, that comes to his shop, have neglected a scene of life that is very entertaining. I beg of my serious reader that he would for a while abate a little of his gravity, and suffer me to examine these people separately.
>
> His business is to sell as much silk as he can at a price by which he shall get what he proposes to be reasonable, ac-

cording to the customary profits of the trade. As to the lady, what she would be at is to please her fancy and buy cheaper by a groat or sixpence per yard than the things she wants are commonly sold at. From the impression the gallantry of our sex has made upon her, she imagines (if she be not very deformed) that she has a fine mien and easy behaviour and a peculiar sweetness of voice; that she is handsome, and, if not beautiful, at least more agreeable than most young women she knows. As she has no pretensions to purchase the same thing with less money than other people but what are built on her good qualities, so she sets herself off to the best advantage her wit and discretion will let her. The thoughts of love are here out of the case; so on the one hand, she has no room for playing the tyrant and giving herself angry and peevish airs and, on the other, more liberty of speaking kindly and being affable than she can have almost on any other occasion. She knows that abundance of well-bred people come to his shop and endeavours to render herself as amiable as virtue and the rules of decency allow of. Coming with such a resolution of behaviour, she cannot meet with anything to ruffle her temper.

Before her coach is yet quite stopped, she is approached by a gentleman-like man, that has everything clean and fashionable about him, who in low obeisance pays her homage, and as soon as her pleasure is known that she has a mind to come in, hands her into the shop, where immediately he slips from her, and through a by-way that remains visible only for half a moment, with great address entrenches himself behind the counter; here facing her, with a profound reverence and modish phrase, he begs the favour of knowing her commands. Let her say and dislike what she pleases, she can never be directly contradicted: she deals with a man in whom consummate patience is one of the mysteries of his trade, and whatever trouble she creates she is sure to hear nothing but the most obliging language and has always before her a cheerful countenance, where joy and respect seem to be blended with good humour and altogether make up an artificial serenity more engaging than untaught nature is able to produce.

When two persons are so well met, the conversation must be very agreeable as well as extremely mannerly, though they talk about trifles. While she remains irresolute what to take, he seems to be the same in advising her and is very cautious how to direct her choice; but when once she has made it and is fixed, he immediately becomes positive that it is the best of the sort, extols her fancy, and the more he looks upon it, the more he wonders he should not before have discovered the pre-eminence of it over anything he has in his shop. By precept, example, and great application, he has learned unobserved to slide into the inmost recesses of the soul, sound the capacity of his customers, and find out their blind side unknown to them: by all which he is instructed in fifty other stratagems to make her over-value her own judgment as well as the commodity she would purchase. The greatest advantage he has over her lies in the most material part of the commerce between them, the debate about the price, which he knows to a farthing and she is wholly ignorant of; therefore he nowhere more egregiously imposes on her understanding; and though. here he has the liberty of telling what lies he pleases as to the prime cost and the money he has refused, yet he trusts not to them only, but, attacking her vanity, makes her believe the most incredible things in the world concerning his own weakness and her superior abilities; he had taken a resolution, he says, never to part with that piece under such a price, but she has the power of talking him out of his goods beyond anybody he ever sold to; he protests that he loses by his silk, but seeing that she has a fancy for it and is resolved to give no more, rather than disoblige a lady he has such an uncommon value for, he will let her have it and only begs that another time she will not stand so hard with him. In the meantime, the buyer, who knows that she is no fool, and has a voluble tongue is easily persuaded that she has a very winning way of talking, and thinking it sufficient for the sake of good breeding to disown her merit and in some witty repartee retort the compliment, he makes her swallow very contentedly the substance of everything he tells her. The upshot is that, with the satisfaction of having saved ninepence per yard, she has bought her silk exactly at the same price as anybody else might have done, and often gives sixpence more than, rather than not have sold it, he would have taken.

Among the seller's repertoire of stratagems and advantages, Mandeville saw the big one; his greatest advantage over the buyer, as Mandeville put it, "lies in the most material part of the commerce between them, the debate about the price, which he knows to a farthing and she is wholly ignorant of." But the intelligent buyer must note well that a statement of general principle is involved here and not just a statement of particular fact. The buyer-seller relationship is shaped by many things other than the price of what is being sold, and with respect to all of them the seller, the professional, has the great advantage. Mandeville's spruce mercer, indeed, was dealing in an area where the seller's advantage in the "material part" of the commerce was apt to be at its least. The silk could be felt and examined, and the young lady, from her description, plainly was no tyro at buying silk.

On this head, as the intelligent buyer well knows, matters have greatly worsened since Mandeville's day. The same principle of advantage favors the seller, but the area of the buyer's ignorance has grown enormously. The modern housewife, who usually cannot describe even roughly how an electric motor functions, for example, owns a variety of motors upon which she and her family may depend for laundering, refrigerating, freezing, heating, cooling, mixing, beating, cleaning, ironing, can-opening, tooth-brushing, shoe-cleaning, shaving, and so forth. The materials from which such goods are made, as well as many other goods that families now live with—from detergents and clothes to automobiles and house insulation—are themselves also fabricated, and increasingly out of substances with which the average buyer has never had any experience. Moreover, the young lady may have known the mercer; but the sellers of today are generally unknown to the buyers and as remote to them as the chemicalized and mechanized products are mysterious in their origins. The home operates "Whizz! Whizz! all by wheels! Whirr! Whirr! all by miniature electric motors!"[1] But how many buyers know how the wheels and the motors operate?

Concerning one kind of product, the nostrum, the quack remedy, or what is known now more respectably as the proprietary drug, the buyer has seldom had a chance to know anything. It has been sold from time immemorial as it is sold today, stridently, backed usually by unsupportable claims, and with the idea of wearing the buyer down as much as trying to convince him of the product's merits. Any TV commercial for an indigestion serve-all or headache drug illustrates the point. Since the seller typically says nothing meaningful about a product of this sort and since the buyer as a rule has no way of knowing anything meaningful about it other than what the seller chooses to tell him (aside from what he might pick up from friends no better informed than himself), the relationship between seller and buyer in this area is and always has been marked by a kind of sanctimony on the one hand and a kind of desperation on the other. Daniel Defoe, a merchant himself who wrote a book in praise of the merchant's life (*The Complete English Tradesman*), captured both in a small incident that he set forth nearly 250 years ago in *A Journal of the Plague Year*. Defoe was not the most scrupulous of reporters, but this incident has the ring of truth to it. This is what he wrote:

> I cannot omit a subtility of one of those quack operators, with which he gulled the poor people to crowd about him,

[1] ". . . to adapt the famous observation of the Pasha to Kinglake," as Roy Lewis and Rosemary Stewart observe in their book *The Boss* (see pages 91 and 138).

but did nothing for them without money. He had, it seems, added to his bills, which he gave about the streets, this advertisement in capital letters, viz., "He gives advice to the poor for nothing."

Abundance of poor people came to him accordingly, to whom he made a great many fine speeches, examined them of the state of their health and of the constitution of their bodies, and told them many good things for them to do, which were of no great moment. But the issue and conclusion of all was, that he had a preparation which if they took such a quantity of every morning, he would pawn his life they should never have the plague; no, though they lived in the house with people that were infected. This made the people all resolve to have it; but then the price of that was so much, I think 'twas half-a-crown. "But, sir," says one poor woman, "I am a poor almswoman, and am kept by the parish, and your bills say you give the poor your help for nothing." "Ay, good woman," says the doctor, "so I do, as I published there. I give my advice to the poor for nothing, but not my physick." "Alas, sir" says she, "that is a snare laid for the poor, then; for you give them advice for nothing; that is to say, you advise them gratis, to buy your physick for their money; so does every shopkeeper with his wares." Here the woman began to give him ill words, and stood at his door all that day, telling her tale to all the people that came, till the doctor, finding she turned away his customers, was obliged to call her upstairs again and give her his box of physick for nothing, which perhaps, too, was good for nothing when she had it.

The buyer's desperation, when it comes to buying a product of this sort, carries right on into Defoe's own closing words, ". . . which perhaps, too, was good for nothing when she had it." There is always this doubt about the patent medicine. You never know for sure because you usually don't know what's in the product, and you wouldn't know how to assess it if you did, yet the product always holds a real hope which the seller always exploits—and that is where the desperation comes in.

Nobody ever got to the heart of a patent medicine better than H. G. Wells fifty years ago in that curious novel *Tono-Bungay*. For all the Edwardian flavor of the book, there is nothing quaint about the techniques that George Ponderevo's Uncle Teddy sets to work for the greater glory of his patent medicine. And in the process of telling about them Wells took the pulse beat of present-day selling and advertising in one astonishing passage after another. Defoe's anonymous "physick" of the early 1700's, Regimen and other drug frauds of recent years, and a few presently active occupants of television screens are all more than faintly visible in the background as Wells recounts Uncle Teddy's doings with Tono-Bungay. Here is George's report on what the elixir is:

"And what is it?" I pressed.

"Well," said my uncle, and then leant forward and spoke softly under cover of his hand, "it's nothing more or less than . . ."

(But here an unfortunate scruple intervenes. After all, Tono-Bungay is still a marketable commodity and in the hands of purchasers, who bought it from—among other vendors—me. No! I am afraid I cannot give it away.)

"You see," said my uncle in a slow confidential whisper, with eyes very wide and a creased forehead, "it's nice because of the" (here he mentioned a flavouring matter and an aromatic spirit), "it's stimulating because of" (here he mentioned two very vivid tonics, one with a marked action on the kidney). "And the" (here he mentioned two other ingredients) "makes it pretty intoxicating. Cocks their tails. Then there's" (but I touch on the essential secret). "And there you are. I got it out of an old book of recipes—all except the" (here he mentioned the more virulent substance, the one that assails the kidneys), "which is my idea. Modern touch! There you are!"

And here is George meditating some time later on certain broader aspects of Tono-Bungay:

You know, from first to last, I saw the business with my eyes open, I saw its ethical and moral values quite clearly. Never for a moment do I remember myself faltering from my persuasion that the sale of Tono-Bungay was a thoroughly dishonest proceeding. The stuff was, I perceived, a mischievous trash, slightly stimulating, aromatic and attractive, likely to become a bad habit and train people in the habitual use of stronger tonics and insidiously dangerous to people with defective kidneys. It would cost about sevenpence the large bottle to make, including bottling, and we were to sell it at half a crown plus the cost of the patent medicine stamp. A thing that I will confess deterred me from the outset far more than the sense of dishonesty in this affair was the supreme silliness of the whole concern. I still clung to the idea that the world of men was or should be a sane and just organization, and the idea that I should set myself gravely, just at the fine springtime of my life, to developing a monstrous bottling and packing warehouse, bottling rubbish for the consumption of foolish, credulous and depressed people, had in it a touch of insanity. . . . Do you realize the madness of the world that sanctions such a thing?

Here finally is George's friend Ewart, freewheeling with Uncle Teddy just like a Madison Avenue adman at a bar after work:

"We are artists. You and I, sir, can talk, if you will permit me, as one artist to another. It's advertisement has—done it. Advertisement has revolutionised trade and industry; it is going to revolutionise the world. The old merchant used to tote about commodities; the new one creates values. Doesn't need to tote. He takes something that isn't worth anything —or something that isn't particularly worth anything— and he makes it worth something. He takes mustard that is just like anybody else's mustard, and he goes about saying,

shouting, singing, chalking on walls, writing inside people's
books, putting it everywhere, 'Smith's Mustard Is the Best.'
And behold it *is* the Best!"

"True," said my uncle, chubbily and with a dreamy
sense of mysticism; "true!"

The intelligent buyer, pondering the unities that bind Daniel
Defoe's physick to Uncle Teddy's Tono-Bungay and last year's
Regimen, will find offshoots and echoes in all directions. One
can almost hear George reflecting in this passage (and Defoe
wouldn't have disagreed, although he would have said it
differently):

> Business propaganda must be obtrusive and blatant. It is its
> aim to attract the attention of slow people, to rouse latent
> wishes, to entice men to substitute innovation for inert
> clinging to traditional routine. In order to succeed, advertis-
> ing must be adjusted to the mentality of the people courted.
> It must suit their tastes and speak their idiom. Advertising
> is shrill, noisy, coarse, puffing, because the public does not
> react to dignified allusions.

But that appeared only a couple of years ago, in the revised
edition of *Human Action: A Treatise on Economics,* by Ludwig
von Mises.

And certainly the virus of excitement that infects Uncle
Teddy and Ewart is at work in the passage below (and was at
work with Defoe's doctor):

> There are two of us in my little office and in the last ten days
> we've both had the sneezes and the sniffles. . . . So in the last
> ten days one of us has plunked down 98¢ for a 36-tablet
> bottle of Anahist and the other has plunked down 98¢ for a
> similar bottle of Inhiston. Which fact tells a wonderful, in-
> spiring story of American private enterprise and competition
> in a cold capsule. . . . For what we've seen in the last month
> is the creation of a new, sensational multi-million-dollar
> industry. . . . What we're seeing and hearing now is Amer-

ican advertising, promotion, ballyhoo, hoopla at its loudest. . . . What we're watching is the always fascinating, always provocative development of intense competition. . . . Invention, mass manufacture, mass distribution—then slam, bang, hoopla, and the millions roll in. . . . As long as our businessmen come up with this sort of thing, American enterprise is O.K. . . . (Oh, yes, did the drugs cure our colds? We're not sure because they seemed to last just about the usual length of time. . . .)

But that was written only a few years ago by Sylvia Porter in the *New York Post*.

The description of the advertising job given by Rosser Reeves, chairman of the Ted Bates advertising agency (Anacin, Carter's Little Pills, etc.), has become a much-quoted classic:

A client comes into my office and throws two newly-minted half dollars onto my desk and says, "Mine is the one on the left. You prove it's better."

But it does put one in mind of Smith's Mustard.

3

<<<<<<<<<<<<<<<<<<<<<<<<<<<<<<<<>>>>>>>>>>>>>>>>>>>>>>>>>>

The Spirit of John Jones

THE time has come to move in closer on the sellers. It is all very well to exhibit them in those small set pieces where buyers can study some of their paces and so come to recognize them better. But this is not really fair to the seller himself, who is much more of a figure than these exhibits make him out to be. An ordinary buyer might think the seller is really no more than the genial fellow of Goldsmith's or Mandeville's tale, for example, given to being two-faced and hypocritical and, of course, a bit of a cheat ("with affection beaming in one eye," as Mrs. Todgers observed, "and calculation out of the other"); nor more than dreamy Uncle Teddy and artistic Ewart, cheating the customers right and left without meaning anyone too much harm, except for maybe a little kidney damage. But the intelligent buyer knows better.

Among other things, he is aware that the modern seller probably does mean the buyer at least economic harm. It is possible that he has encountered the estimate of several years ago by Mr. Franklin Huddle, a conservation specialist in the

Defense Research and Engineering Division of the U. S. Department of Defense, to the effect that the annual bill for unnecessary deterioration in consumer goods was running between 10 and 20 billion dollars a year. "There is a sort of double standard of morality in the United States," he said. "The producer of capital goods tends to give products longevity while consumer goods must last only long enough to satisfy the minimum expectations of the purchaser."[1] The same point was made indirectly, but a good deal more colorfully, in a memorable statement by Mr. R. H. Nelson, manager of the Boeing Company's Pilotless Aircraft Division:

> When we first started to work on missiles, we thought they would be a breeze compared to airplanes. We said, in effect, "here's a product that's expendable, that lasts only a few minutes, so we can forget the rigid quality control of the aircraft business and make missiles quick and cheesy, cheap and dirty, like a mass-produced consumer product."

The intelligent buyer may not be (although he ought to be) a reader of that highly informative trade paper, *Home Furnishings Daily*; but if his intelligence is active he will have at least an emotional familiarity with what goes on behind such a news item as this characteristic one from a recent issue:

> Retailers should try to fight the fallacy in the public mind that carpets should last a lifetime, the Wisconsin Floor Coverings Association was told here. Mrs. Lee Kolker, director of styling for C. H. Masland & Sons, pointed out that automobile builders have gotten themselves into the ideal situation, where they sell a product which will be next to worthless in five years and which will give trouble in the meantime.

---

[1] Mr. Huddle was explicit on a further count, too: "Who would want an automobile that would run a reliable 100,000 miles without a major repair? Who would want a lifetime storage battery, a lifetime muffler and exhaust pipe, rot-resistant lumber, double-lived shoe soles, woolen clothing, nylon hose, clothesline? We could make all of these, but we don't."

The intelligent buyer certainly must know that the advertising business in Japan, where American selling style is much admired, is probably the fastest growing anywhere—which lends pungency to the recent Reuters dispatch from Tokyo, noted in *Understanding Media*, by the Canadian writer Marshall McLuhan:

> Latest fashion among Japanese businessmen is the study of classical military strategy and tactics in order to apply them to business operations. . . . It has been reported that one of the largest advertising companies in Japan has even made these books compulsory reading for all its employees.

The buyer may also have read the nice (the word is used in its original sense) expression of the seller's attitude in *Fortune* some years ago; William H. Whyte, Jr., writing in that magazine, quoted a veteran salesman's explanation to an apprentice why the latter was not doing so well. "You're not going to sell a damn thing," said the veteran, "until you realize one simple fact: the man on the other side of the counter is THE ENEMY!"

Other students of the buyer-seller relationship dispute this dictum, not as being too harsh but as missing the point. The view in this camp is that the average seller is too contemptuous of the buyer to hate him as an enemy. It is a most interesting point; the seller's contempt has been noted earlier, but is it so great as to override the perhaps purer feeling of hatred, or enmity?

Partly the problem here is in determining what reflects hatred (or enmity) and what reflects contempt. The *Washington Post* only two years ago reported a speech by one Dr. Cecil H. Bliss before the District of Columbia Dental Society Postgraduate Clinic. This is what is, or used to be, known as a professional gathering. Dr. Bliss's words were as follows:

> Want to improve your fees? It's not hard if you work at it. . . . You'll discover that people will pay more to hear a good case presentation than anything else. . . . Explain decay.

Make it . . . romantic. . . . Then . . . tell the patient the difference between the gold [inlay] and the cost of a real good alloy. . . . Don't discuss the value of the gold . . . since it amounts to only about 85¢. . . . Tell her about the ultimate enjoyment, peace and happiness she'll have [with a gold inlay]. . . . If you work on the basis of $30 an hour, slowly raise it to $32.

A most interesting point; on balance, it would seem that there is really no hatred here; the feelings do not seem to be quite pure enough; much contempt but no real hatred.

But then let us turn to the comments of Mr. Elisha Gray II, the chairman of the board of the Whirlpool Corporation, as quoted five years ago in *Home Furnishings Daily:*

An engineer's principal purpose as an engineer is to create obsolescence. Any attempts by various people to toady up to the public by saying they are against planned obsolescence is so much commercial demagogy. To pose as a protector of the public has become a fashionable pastime.

What can one suppose was in Mr. Gray II's mind when he said this? Certainly it seems likely that "the public," which means us buyers, holds no very high position in this seller's scale of things. Mr. Gray II does not command the syntax of Sir Thomas Browne, and is speaking only indirectly of what Sir Thomas spoke about most directly, but one cannot escape the feeling that Sir Thomas' well-known defining of the public would not fit amiss here: "The multitude: that numerous piece of monstrosity, which, taken asunder, seem men, and the reasonable creatures of God; but, confused together, make but one great beast. . . ." Still, what is the intelligent buyer to conclude; does Mr. Gray II hate *him?*

Mr. Gray II is most likely upset here about some of his competitors, who have apparently strayed or tried to stray from the official seller's line of getting people to buy more than they need to by providing them with products that break down more than they need to. And the contempt for the public is beginning to ring and jangle, like a high-tension wire. But hate? No.

Indeed, it is difficult to find real evidence of that stronger emotion. Buyers have been known to hate sellers who have reduced them to penury with usurious credit charges, done them in with improperly labeled drugs, subjected them to lethal shock hazards in toasters and television sets, and such things, to which court proceedings and sometimes the newspapers bear more or less steady witness. But the seller really does not seem to hate the buyer, even though he may consider him an enemy; the consideration, in short, is cool. It would be no great undertaking to compile dozens of statements like Mr. Elisha Gray II's (the sentiment is quite popular among sellers, as the intelligent buyer doubtless knows already), and the coolness would be in all of them.

This is the difference between the modern seller and his ancestors. Affection no longer beams in the one eye, and the calculation in the other has become cooler and more difficult to appease. Regrettably, nostalgic stories of the old-fashioned seller linger on to confuse the modern buyer, who too often isn't aware that a divide has been crossed. One is put in mind of A. E. Housman's quatrain:

> The Grizzly Bear is huge and wild;
> He has devoured the infant child.
> The infant child is not aware
> He has been eaten by the bear.

Shortly we shall examine several examples of the seller-bear and the buyer-child, in the very moment of the devouring. But first a very brief historical review is called for.

It is not necessary to go back beyond the last century. The modern seller came to birth about the middle of it, although he had been a-borning in one country or another since the beginning of the Industrial Revolution in England one hundred years before. On the far side of this divide the commerce of the world, through all the stages of man's history, had been largely local. It is true enough that in the time of Ahab and Jezebel bazaar owners in Samaria had branches in Damascus; it is true that the Romans had trading stations as far away as India; and it is true that in the seventeenth and early eighteenth centuries there was enough trade between countries to help pay for the wars of mercantilism and to sustain a system of wholesale markets. But the rule remained that, except for luxuries and delicacies particularly, few products were heavily traded over considerable distances before the end of the eighteenth century.

Retail selling is considered by some to be man's oldest business, and the eighteenth century was probably the high point of the small private shop; but the shops hardly existed for anyone other than the well-to-do. Right on into the nineteenth century there was simply no such thing, for example, as a furniture store for people of lower income. Manufacturing was small-scale; nothing one could call a distribution system in anything approximating present-day terms existed; the department store had not been thought up; advertising techniques, mainly confined to posters and notices, were simple. The commercial spirit, in short, had not yet come to focus; or, at least, transportation, running behind it, kept it fragmented.

But through the first half of the nineteenth century the Industrial Revolution was moving to a climax. Steadily improving transport opened up large and distant markets to new manufacturing, already expanding from new inventions, and around new products new patterns of distribution and sale took shape. Almost from year to year the buyer-seller relationship grew in importance and complexity; and as it grew the modern seller emerged, with—in the precise words of Miss Porter from the last chapter—a slam, bang, hoopla, and the millions rolling in.

Nineteenth-century mechanics and inventors turned into businessmen, businessmen turned into industrialists, products that had been made by hand or not at all came out in endless copies, and it slowly became clear that endless buyers had to be found to keep the money rolling in—or, if not found, created.

It was along in here that Adam Smith's dictum of some years before on the role of consumption as the sole end and purpose of production got turned around. In that part of his dictum which usually doesn't get quoted he had gone on to say:

> The maxim is so perfectly self-evident, that it would be absurd to attempt to prove it. But in the mercantile system, the interest of the consumer is almost constantly sacrificed to that of the producer; and it seems to consider production, and not consumption, as the ultimate end and object of all industry and commerce.

But what happened under the mercantile system was as nothing to what happened as the standardized products of the Industrial Revolution rolled out and the money rolled in. A thousand laws and stratagems to strengthen the producer's hand came into being. And more and more the emphasis on production extended to the distributive machinery, where the seller's hand took over. The standard price followed the standard product; the department store was thought up; credit grew to draw more sales. And the buyers, very often, paid more and more for less and less. Right at the middle of the century, John Stuart Mill saw what was happening and told about it in his *Principles of Political Economy*, published in 1848:

> . . . But retail price, the price paid by the actual consumer, seems to feel very slowly and imperfectly the effect of competition; and when competition does exist, it often, instead of lowering prices, merely divides the gains of the high price among a greater number of dealers. Hence it is that, of the price paid by the consumer, so large a proportion is absorbed by the gains of retailers; and any one who inquires into the amount which reaches the hands of those who made the things he buys, will often be astonished at its smallness.

"True," Uncle Teddy would have murmured, had he been around at the time. "True!" But by Uncle Teddy's time, it was not just the retailers who were keeping their hands on such large proportions of the prices. For as the grandfathers and fathers of the Uncle Teddys moved into where the action and the money were during the last half of the nineteenth century, the techniques of modern advertising and the invention of values began to take form. They have been with us ever since, growing stronger and bigger and more inventive every year.

For the first time in man's history, not just consumption and production but selling itself has been the preoccupation, the end and purpose of a significant sector of the population, and one that grows steadily. In this sector the taking of something that isn't worth anything—or isn't particularly worth anything, or is just like something else—and advertising a distinction into it, has come to be looked upon as a wholly reasonable way for a grown man to spend his life.

It is true enough that there is some ancient precedent for the social sanction of this kind of activity. The intelligent buyer will recall the passage in the third book of Homer's *Odyssey,* where Nestor is talking with Telemachus. The old man turns to the young one and says: "The time has come for a few questions." "Are you," Nestor then inquires, "a trader or a sea robber?" The question is casual, as one might ask of another whether he is a doctor or a lawyer. The fact is that the chief merchants of the sea at that time, the Phoenicians, were also the chief pirates. And as the *Encyclopedia of the Social Sciences* observes in its section on commerce:

> From the earliest to comparatively modern times the people through whose hands international trade has passed have been partly merchants and partly robbers.

Such elegant observers as William Hazlitt could still murmur, even as the Industrial Revolution was hitting its full stride, to this effect:

> Persons who have been used to a petty, huckstering way of life, cannot enlarge their apprehensions to a notion of anything better.

"Even today," Nietzsche wrote near the end of the last century, "mercantile morality is really nothing but a refinement of piratical morality." And when the huckstering had taken over and become the order of the commercial day, Finley Peter Dunne's Mr. Dooley could render a characteristic opinion:

Glory be, whin business gets above sellin' tinpinny nails in a brown paper cornucopy, 'tis hard to tell it fr'm murther.

The growing commercialization of modern life—it has not been just in this country but the growth has been greatest in this country—brought forth, in fact, a whole flood of complaint, worry, and protest. Not much of it availed; the growth continued; but some of the protest has passed into the nation's permanent literature, there to become a part of the record for intelligent buyers to consult from time to time.

An appropriate time for the buyer to read or reread Edward Bellamy's classic, *Looking Backward*, might be on an evening after he has been sitting down with some magazines and newspapers, like the seller in Chapter One, stealing glimpses at his television screen. It would be interesting if the magazines included the *New England Journal of Medicine*, which carried not long ago a note about "the manufacturer of a proprietary liniment" who had suggested to "two young investigators associated with a Boston medical school" that they "use the product on a series of arthritic patients." However, it is possible that not all of my readers may have read this excellent publication, so I will presume to recall the *Journal*'s mention of the two conditions imposed: "The results would have to be favorable and they would have to be published before a certain date." In the context of the example of the commercial spirit in present-day Boston, Bellamy's story of young Julian West, who fell into a deep trance in Boston in 1887 and came to in the year 2000 to discover a wonderfully rationalized world, could have a special savor.

But Dr. Ernest Dichter, a motivational researcher who claims to have made thousands of studies and surveys, on which hundreds of advertising campaigns have been based, will serve nicely, too, as an appetizer to the meat of Bellamy. It was Dr. Dichter who suggested, in a book he wrote only two years ago (*Handbook of Consumer Motivations*), that "the citrus industry might consider the development of a yearly model, as in the automobile industry. Each year's crop could be presented as the current, improved model."

If the buyer missed this example of the seller at work or if it does not appeal to him, then it might be useful for him to turn to one of those trade journals mentioned in Chapter One. Here's *Home Furnishings Daily*, with a report on what Mort Farr, a former chairman of the National Appliance and Radio-TV Dealers Association Board, said:

> He cited how an optometrist works. After he fits the glasses, he tells the customer that it is $10, and if the customer doesn't blink, he follows with "for the frames and $10 for the lenses," or $20, or $10 each. We should learn from them how to inform our customers of service prices.

Such cullings from the rich veins of modern commercialism help to set off Bellamy, but in all probability a few glimpses at the TV set will sufficiently lay the groundwork for most intelligent buyers. They will remember how Julian West, after many adventures among the happy citizens of the year 2000, fell asleep and awakened once more, this time back in the world of 1887 in Boston again, back among the sights he had left:

> . . . There had been no personal advertising in the Boston of the twentieth century, because there was no need of any, but here the walls of the buildings, the windows, the broadsides of the newspapers in every hand, the very pavements, everything in fact in sight, save the sky, were covered with the appeals of individuals who sought, under innumerable pretexts, to attract the contributions of others to their support. However the wording might vary, the tenor of all these appeals was the same:

"Help John Jones. Never mind the rest. They are frauds. I, John Jones, am the right one. Buy of me. Employ me. Visit me. Hear me, John Jones. Look at me. Make no mistake, John Jones is the man and nobody else. Let the rest starve, but for God's sake remember John Jones. . . ."

I reached Washington Street at the busiest point, and there I stood and laughed aloud, to the scandal of the passersby. For my life I could not have helped it, with such a mad humor was I moved at sight of the interminable rows of stores on either side, up and down the street so far as I could see,—scores of them, to make the spectacle more utterly preposterous, within a stone's throw devoted to selling the same sort of goods. Stores! stores! stores! miles of stores! ten thousand stores to distribute the goods needed by this one city, which in my dream had been supplied with all things from a single warehouse, as they were ordered through one great store in every quarter, where the buyer, without waste of time or labor, found under one roof the world's assortment in whatever line he desired. There the labor of distribution had been so slight as to add but a scarcely perceptible fraction to the cost of commodities to the user. The cost of production was virtually all he paid. But here the mere distribution of the goods, their handling alone, added a fourth, a third, a half or more, to the cost. All these ten thousand plants must be paid for, their rent, their staffs of superintendence, their platoons of salesmen, their ten thousand sets of accountants, jobbers, and business dependents, with all they spent in advertising themselves and fighting one another, and the consumers must do the paying. What a famous process for beggaring a nation!

Were these serious men I saw about me, or children, who did their business on such a plan? . . . I went within and noted the hawk-eyed floor-walker watching for business, overlooking the clerks, keeping them up to their task of inducing the customers to buy, buy, buy, for money if they had it, for credit if they had it not, to buy what they wanted

not, more than they wanted, what they could not afford. . . .
The more wasteful the people were, the more articles they
did not want which they could be induced to buy, the better
for these sellers. To encourage prodigality was the express
aim of the thousand stores of Boston.

This is a pretty stirring indictment of the seller as viewed
by the journalist from Chicopee Falls, Massachusetts. The intelligent buyer can learn much from a thoughtful contemplation
of Bellamy's words, and assuredly their thesis cannot be con-
tested. The seller was rampant when Bellamy wrote and is still;
the costs of distribution were well on their way up the spiral
they have been climbing ever since; and the encouragement
of prodigality among buyers has become almost a fixed article
of faith among sellers, of whom Mr. Elisha Gray II, quoted
earlier in this chapter, is only one of many (we will have
occasion to cite more in later pages). Finally, the spirit of
John Jones remains the spirit of our times and his very words
are still to be heard in the land. A textile advertiser was
quoted in *The New York Times* recently, on one of the
days during which this chapter was being written; and this is
how he described the job of advertising:

Find your character, create your character, concentrate on
your character. Tell whatever story you want to tell, but talk
about youself.

It is possible that, for more conservative readers, the words
of the historian, the late Charles A. Beard, may be more illuminating than the words of Bellamy the journalist. Professor
Beard's words also serve to extend the picture forty years beyond Bellamy's time, for he put forth these views in 1927, in
the second volume of his treatise on *The Rise of American
Civilization*:

As the stream of commodities flowing from the factories
broke every barrier, the business of selling goods employed
an ever larger army of commercial officers and privates,

swelling the ranks of the middle classes with recruits of the mercantile color. Huge areas of American social power were now occupied by huckstering shock troops who, with a technique and a verbiage all their own, concentrated on ogling, stimulating, and inveigling the public into purchases. By raising the business of advertising to the intensity of a crusading religion, embattled vendors gained an almost sovereign sway over newspapers and journals, as they pushed goods, desirable and noxious alike, upon a docile herd that took its codes from big type and colored plates.

Under this economic drive the psychology of the salesman —as distinguished from that of the warrior, organizing capitalist, and creative inventor—became the dominant spirit of an immense array of persons who, in the view of "thoughtful editors," constituted the "sound heart of the nation." In this intellectual climate, trades which the landed gentry had formerly scorned as vulgar were crowned with respectability: real estate agents became realtors, undertakers assumed the role of morticians, and clerks expanded into salesladies. When the second census of the twentieth century was compiled there were seen to be at least four million people engaged in trade, including retailers, sales agents, and collateral forces under this general head.

One of the four million was George Babbitt; and the intelligent buyer should look in on him from time to time by way of fleshing out such professorial observations as those of Beard. George Babbitt may seem a little old-fashioned now; it's forty years since Sinclair Lewis put him together. But the intelligent buyer should not discount him, for, despite the fact that his style is rather more simple than that of some of his present-generation counterparts, he still means the buyer harm; no real affection beams from Babbitt's eye, although there is a certain plain nastiness about him that is not necessarily an element of the modern seller of the cool type. As Jane Austen wrote in *Emma*, "Business, you know, may bring money, but friendship hardly ever does"; and the sentiment somehow seems to bring George Babbitt to mind:

Babbitt's virtues as a real-estate broker—as the servant of society in the department of finding homes for families and shops for distributors of food—were steadiness and diligence. He was conventionally honest, he kept his records of buyers and sellers complete, he had experience with leases and titles and an excellent memory for prices. His shoulders were broad enough, his voice deep enough, his relish of hearty humor strong enough, to establish him as one of the ruling caste of Good Fellows. Yet his eventual importance to mankind was perhaps lessened by his large and complacent ignorance of all architecture save the types of houses turned out by speculative builders; all landscape gardening save the use of curving roads, grass, and six ordinary shrubs; and all the commonest axioms of economics. He serenely believed that the one purpose of the real-estate business was to make money for George F. Babbitt. True, it was a good advertisement at Boosters' Club lunches, and all the varieties of Annual Banquets to which Good Fellows were invited, to speak sonorously of Unselfish Public Service, the Broker's Obligation to Keep Inviolate the Trust of His Clients, and a thing called Ethics, whose nature was confusing but if you had it you were a High-class Realtor and if you hadn't you were a shyster, a piker, and a fly-by-night. These virtues awakened Confidence, and enabled you to handle Bigger Propositions. But they didn't imply that you were to be impractical and refuse to take twice the value of a house if a buyer was such an idiot that he didn't jew you down on the asking-price.

From the substance of the record so far as we have gone, it is possible to formulate a small analysis. The aim of selling is to make something out of nothing, or, at least, more out of less. In a successful sale the buyer seldom gets more than his money's worth and often gets less, but the seller—who has to make his living at selling, as the buyer does not have to make his at buying—always gets more than his product's worth; ergo, from the buyer-seller relationship the seller typically achieves something which, at least in the seller's terms and often in his own, the buyer does not; the seller succeeds, the buyer fails; the seller is a success, the buyer is a failure; successes look down on failures, and nice guys finish last.

At all events, there is really no reason for the buyer to look further for signs of hate or enmity on the part of the seller. As for that seller quoted by the *Fortune* writer, perhaps he was not a very good seller to begin with. The fact is that sellers generally do not view the buyers as enemies or hate them. Why should they? For people who have endured the numerous refinements of piratical morality that sellers have visited on buyers over the years, contempt would seem to be an entirely adequate feeling, and indeed the only possible one, unless pity might occasionally intrude.

4

‹‹‹‹‹‹‹‹‹‹‹‹‹‹‹‹‹‹‹‹‹‹‹‹‹‹‹‹›››››››››››››››››››››››››

The Irrational Price
and Related
Considerations

IT is time to draw another deduction from the record that has been compiled during the ascendency of the seller. This will not be expressed as a Great Truth, but simply as a conclusion to which much evidence has led. It may be stated as follows: the price of an advertised product tends to reflect a reality the seller invents. This is one of those concepts that may be clarified by a consideration first of what it isn't. We have all been taught very simple things about price in school; sellers tend to shy away from the subject on the grounds that the less said about it, the better it will be for them; and price means many things, anyway. The meditation that follows, extracted from the brain of Charles-Hubert in Jean Dutourd's novel *The Best Butter*, is a perfectly reasonable meditation on one kind of price—

> . . . Charles-Hubert had for several weeks been turning over in his mind a new philosophy which excluded good humor. Good humor, at least, as far as the customers were concerned. His smiles, his puns and his joviality were what re-

mained of the old Charles-Hubert. The new one to whom
events were giving birth was not to be slow to appear. From
1925 to 1940 trade had obeyed a certain number of psychological laws which he has assimilated, such as, "The customer
is always right," "Service with a smile," et cetera. By 1941
these laws had fallen into desuetude. The customer now
needed the tradesman in order to live. The law of supply
and demand, which was the framework, the mainstay, of
Charles-Hubert's thought, prompted him to a line of reasoning which the reader will consider oversimplified but which

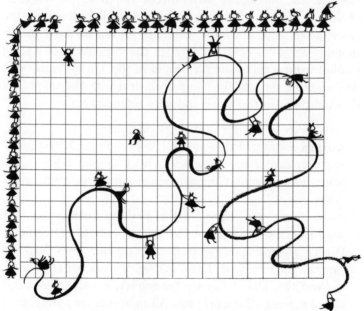

seemed to him a marvel of complexity. This bold analysis,
this unerring plan of attack, may be summarized as follows:
the demand is greater than the supply, consequently the
tradesman is in a favorable position. He should profit by it.
What does the customer do? A) he offers increasingly large
sums of money; B) he makes up to the tradesman. Conclusion: no need to worry oneself. Treat him like a dog and
he will still come back; he doesn't want to die of hunger.

Following which, there's no limit to the prices one can charge. "I sell him a quarter of black-market butter for thirty-five francs. If he protests, I say, 'Very well, let's forget it.' And he goes without his butter. As one can't live without butter, the tradesman wins out in the long run."

—but this is not the kind of price that the intelligent buyer in these times and in this country will learn from. Charles-Hubert's morality, while piratical, is rational, that is to say, old-fashioned. To examine the extension of this morality into practice, the intelligent buyer needs no more than a scene of simple, old-fashioned, piratical haggling. Bertolt Brecht provides such a scene in *Mother Courage*, his drama about the immorality of war as observed through the vicissitudes of a tough peasant woman following the armies in the Thirty Years' War. At one point she and the camp cook deal with the supply and demand thesis in this small and salty interchange:

COOK. Sixty hellers for that paltry poultry?
MOTHER COURAGE. Paltry poultry? Why, he's the fattest fowl you ever saw! I see no reason why I shouldn't get sixty hellers for him—this Commander can eat till the cows come home.
COOK. They're ten hellers a dozen on every street corner.
MOTHER COURAGE. A capon like this on every street corner! With a siege going on and people all skin and bones? Maybe you can get a field rat! I said maybe. Because we're all out of *them* too. Didn't you see the soldiers running five deep after one hungry little field rat? All right then, in a siege, my price for a giant capon is fifty hellers.
COOK. But we're not "in a siege," we're doing the besieging, it's the other side that's "in a siege" . . .
MOTHER COURAGE. A fat lot of difference that makes, we don't have a thing to eat either. They took everything in the town with them before all this started, and now they've nothing to do but eat and drink. It's us I'm worried about. Look at the farmers round here, they haven't a thing.

COOK. Sure they have. They hide it.

MOTHER COURAGE. They have not! They're ruined. They're so hungry I've seen 'em digging up roots to eat. I could boil your leather belt and make their mouths water with it. That's how things are round here. And I'm supposed to let a capon go for forty hellers.

COOK. Thirty. Not forty, I said thirty hellers.

This is a potentially subversive passage; all sympathies are with Mother Courage in her fight for survival; we must be strict, however: she is the seller here, and the intelligent buyer must not let his sympathies get in the way of his understanding.

Still, what the intelligent buyer needs most to understand he does not really find here; this is also too rational. His needs to know about price in these times lie in the area of the irrational, where a seller will make up a price to distinguish his product from other similar or identical products, or where he will simply make up a price for reasons which, being totally irrational, cannot be stated at all. Here is a classic example of apparent price irrationality, although of very recent vintage; it appeared in *Advertising Age* a few years ago and it should be read with due respect:

Mr. Laux related the problem encountered in marketing S. C. Johnson & Son's Car-Nu. The price of 69¢, the agency told Johnson, was too low; the average auto owner was afraid such a low-price product would damage the finish. [Foote, Cone & Belding's] recommendation: Add an innocuous new ingredient, enlarge the can a bit and put it on the market for $1.69. "It worked," he said.

What makes this a classic is the uncluttered aspect of the maneuver as reported; one is struck less by the apparent fraud than by the obvious ingenuity. There is also here reassurance that the old, piratical morality has not run too thin; the ballooning of the price from 69¢ to $1.69—an increase of nearly 150 per cent for "a bit" of enlarging and an "innocuous" ingredient—has a proper kind of piratical audacity to it.

We must be clear, however; there is no fraud too *small* for the modern seller to exploit, either. Just a few months ago, in the pages of *Advertising Age* again, the nation's largest single advertiser, Procter & Gamble (its advertising budget has been running over 200 million dollars a year), was reported to be benefiting happily from the incidental effects of a small windfall arising from a confusion over two of its products:

> P & G researchers came up with the discovery that . . . house-wives . . . were using Spic 'n Span in their wash. Never slow to latch onto a good thing, P & G marketers figured that it made more sense for housewives to use 5¢ worth of Spic 'n Span to wash their clothes than 3.5¢ worth of Tide.

Another interesting example of this genre—although not really a classic one because it is a little too diffuse—appeared in a small marketing note in *Daily News Record*. It read:

> Sheets—Retail activity fair, and a number of stores in this normally quiet pre-holiday period have increased prices to provide a basis for January White Sales . . .

The intelligent buyer will be aware that examples of this sort abound, and there seems no need to burden him with more, at least in the present context. He must bear in mind, however, that this kind of piracy, or selling, is not to be confused with the cruder and even more popular technique of selling *practically* the same product at different prices. An interesting example of this was provided recently in *Women's Wear Daily*:

> A store . . . decided to sell a particular blouse in three differ-ent departments, but in three different ways. [It was sold at the first] counter for $3.95. The same blouse . . . in another location within the store . . . packaged in a stock box . . . sold for $4.95.
> The same identical blouse was also merchandized in an-other spot with a better quality of buttons and with an em-

broidered crest on the pocket. It was packaged in a "custom" box . . . and the same crest on the blouse appeared on the box. This time, the blouse retailed for $9.50.

[All three were successful] as each sold to its particular brand of clientele.

Certainly we should all be attentive to a seller who can charge a dollar extra for a box that might conceivably cost a couple of pennies, and $5.55 extra for a crest, some buttons, and a box that might total 50¢ extra. On the other hand, this seller is giving the buyer *something*, however negligible, however disproportionate, for the money he is extracting from him. The intelligent buyer must always be at pains to distinguish the seller who wholly invents a value from the seller who only inflates it. There is no gain for the buyer in concentrating on such a distinction—it is very difficult for the buyer ever to achieve an actual gain in the buyer-seller relationship—but the effort will help him to keep his wits about him (always a useful thing), and also to appreciate the artistry that goes into much selling.

With respect to the latter, one of the most beautifully turned price-and-profit exercises of modern times was undertaken by Milo Minderbinder in Joseph Heller's *Catch-22*, an exceptional report on modern life in many respects, including this one not least of all. This is how Milo explained his activities to his friend Yossarian; he explained things very patiently so that Yossarian could understand, and the buyer, no matter how intelligent, should take full advantage of Milo's patience so that he may understand this high adventure in the seller's world, too:

. . . It was common knowledge that Milo bought his eggs in Malta for seven cents apiece and sold them to the mess halls in his syndicate for five cents apiece. . . .

Yossarian was riding beside him in the co-pilot's seat. "I don't understand why you buy eggs for seven cents apiece in Malta and sell them for five cents."

"I do it to make a profit."

"But how do you make a profit? You lose two cents an egg."

"But I make a profit of three and a quarter cents an egg by selling them for four and a quarter cents an egg to the people in Malta I buy them from for seven cents an egg. Of course, I don't make the profit. The syndicate makes the profit. And everybody has a share."

Yossarian felt he was beginning to understand. "And the people you sell the eggs to at four and a quarter cents apiece make a profit of two and three quarter cents apiece when they sell them back to you at seven cents apiece. Is that right? Why don't you sell the eggs directly to you and eliminate the people you buy them from?"

"Because I'm the people I buy them from," Milo explained. "I make a profit of three and a quarter cents apiece when I sell them to me and a profit of two and three quarter cents apiece when I buy them back from me. That's a total profit of six cents an egg. I lose only two cents an egg when I sell them to the mess halls at five cents apiece, and that's how I can make a profit buying eggs for seven cents apiece and selling them for five cents apiece. I pay only one cent apiece at the hen when I buy them in Sicily."

"In Malta," Yossarian corrected. "You buy your eggs in Malta, not Sicily."

Milo chortled proudly. "I don't buy eggs in Malta," he confessed, with an air of slight and clandestine amusement that was the only departure from industrious sobriety Yossarian had ever seen him make. "I buy them in Sicily for one cent apiece and transfer them to Malta secretly at four and a half cents apiece in order to get the price of eggs up to seven cents apiece when people come to Malta looking for them."

"Why do people come to Malta for eggs when they're so expensive there?"

"Because they've always done it that way."

"Why don't they look for eggs in Sicily?"

"Because they've never done it that way."[1]

"Now I really don't understand. Why don't you sell your mess halls the eggs for seven cents apiece instead of for five cents apiece?"

"Because my mess halls would have no need for me then. Anyone can buy seven-cents-apiece eggs for seven cents apiece."

"Why don't they bypass you and buy the eggs directly from you in Malta at four and a quarter cents apiece?"

"Because I wouldn't sell it to them."

"Why wouldn't you sell it to them?"

"Because then there wouldn't be as much room for a profit. At least this way I can make a bit for myself as a middleman."

"Then you do make a profit for yourself," Yossarian declared.

"Of course I do. But it all goes to the syndicate. And everybody has a share. Don't you understand? It's exactly what happens with those plum tomatoes I sell to Colonel Cathcart."

"*Buy*," Yossarian corrected him. "You don't *sell* plum tomatoes to Colonel Cathcart and Colonel Korn. You *buy* plum tomatoes from them."

"No, *sell*," Milo corrected Yossarian. "I distribute my plum tomatoes in markets all over Pianosa under an assumed name so that Colonel Cathcart and Colonel Korn can buy them up from me under their assumed names at four cents apiece and sell them back to me the next day for the syndicate at five cents apiece. They make a profit of

---

[1] Milo Minderbinder's reasoning is by no means an evasion. Compare John Stuart Mill's explanation of price variability in *Principles of Political Economy*: ". . . I believe it will often be found, in Continental Europe, that prices and charges, of some or of all sorts, are much higher in some places than in others not far distant, without its being possible to assign any other cause than that it has always been so: the customers are used to it, and acquiesce in it."

one cent apiece, I make a profit of three and a half cents apiece, and everybody comes out ahead."

Milo is a genius, obviously, and geniuses are not met with every day, among sellers or anyone else. Nonetheless, beyond the more familiar tricks and deceptions that are the seller's stock-in-trade, the artist's hand must be looked for, too. The buying-selling relationship is a contest (albeit a sinful one) and assuredly a seller not too far steeped in sin from time to time is moved to meet the challenge with an eye to the involvements of good form and nice balance along with the maximization of gain.

Certainly Herman Melville's story "The Lightning-Rod Man" shows the contest, if at a pure and elementary stage; a kind of basic form and balance emerge from Melville's description of his salesman at work at the height of a thunder storm. It is a long way from the form and balance of Milo Minderbinder with his eggs and tomatoes, and further still from the symmetry of a modern corporate squeeze play with multimillion-dollar advertising appropriations to lure the buyer on, small loans at high interest to help him take the bait, and repossession of the product at the end. We shall be studying this ritualized artistry in more detail further on. But it will do no harm for the reader to give a moment to the lightning-rod man as he practiced his turn a century ago:

"Tall men in a thunder-storm I avoid. Are you so grossly ignorant as not to know that the height of a six-footer is sufficient to discharge an electric cloud upon him? Are not lonely Kentuckians, ploughing, smit in the unfinished furrow? Nay, if the six-footer stand by running water, the cloud will sometimes *select* him as its conductor to that running water. Hark! Sure, yon black pinnacle is split. Yes, a man is a good conductor. The lightning goes through and through a man, but only peels a tree. But sir, you have kept me so long answering your questions, that I have not yet come to business. Will you order one of my rods? Look at this specimen one. See: it is of the best of copper. Copper's the best conductor. Your house is low; but being upon the mountains, that lowness does not one whit depress it. You mountaineers are most exposed. In mountainous countries the lightning-rod man should have most business. Look at the specimen, sir. One rod will answer for a house so small as this. Look over these recommendations. Only one rod, sir; cost, only twenty dollars. Hark! There go all the granite Taconics and Hoosics dashed together like pebbles. By the sound, that must have struck something. An elevation of five feet above the house, will protect twenty feet radius all about the rod. Only twenty dollars, sir—a dollar a foot. Hark!—Dreadful!—Will you order? Will you buy? Shall I put down your name? Think of being a heap of charred offal, like a haltered horse burnt in his stall; and all in one flash!"

The artist's approach to selling, of course, also brings to mind Uncle Teddy's friend Ewart, who was an artist in fact, a sculptor, as well as an artist at selling. And on the very point we are mainly considering in this chapter—some of the ways in which a seller's fantasy functions as a product's price —Ewart had a very artistic notion in one of his talks with Uncle Teddy. Since a thousand sellers, or perhaps a hundred thousand, or possibly a million, or maybe all sellers to some degree, have made use of this notion, it will serve the intelligent buyer well to let Ewart and Uncle Teddy speak out the notion here in their own words. Ewart starts the exchange:

"It's just like an artist; he takes a lump of white marble on the verge of a lime-kiln, he chips it about, he makes—he makes a monument to himself—and others—a monument the world will not willingly let die. Talking of mustard, sir, I was at Clapham Junction the other day, and all the banks are overgrown with horseradish that's got loose from a garden somewhere. You know what horseradish is—grows like wildfire—spreads—spreads. I stood at the end of the platform looking at the stuff and thinking about it. 'Like fame,' I thought, 'rank and wild where it isn't wanted. Why don't the really good things in life grow like horseradish?' I thought. My mind went off in a peculiar way it does from that to the idea that mustard costs a penny a tin—I bought some the other day for a ham I had. It came into my head that it would be ripping good business to use horseradish to adulterate mustard. I had a sort of idea that I could plunge into business on that, get rich and come back to my own proper monumental art again. And then I said, 'But *why* adulterate? I don't like the idea of adulteration.'"

"Shabby," said my uncle, nodding his head. "Bound to get found out!"

"And totally unnecessary, too! Why not do up a mixture —three-quarters pounded horseradish and a quarter mustard—give it a fancy name—and sell it at twice the mustard price? See? I very nearly started the business straight away, only something happened. My train came along."

"Jolly good ideer," said my uncle. He looked at me. "That really *is* an ideer, George," he said.

"Take shavin's, again! You know that poem of Long-fellow's sir, that sounds exactly like the first declension. What is it—'Man's a maker, men say!'"

My uncle nodded and gurgled some quotation that died away.

"Jolly good poem, George," he said in an aside to me.

"Well, it's about a carpenter and a poetic Victorian child, you know, and some shavin's. The child made no end out of the shavin's. So might you. Powder 'em. They might be anything. Soak 'em in jipper,—Xylo-tobacco! Powder 'em and get a little tar and turpentinous smell in,—wood-packing for hot baths—a Certain Cure for the scourge of Influenza! There's all these patent grain foods,—what Americans call cereals. I believe I'm right, sir, in saying they're sawdust."

"No!" said my uncle, removing his cigar; "as far as I can

find out it's really grain—spoilt grain . . . I've been going
into that."

"Well, there you are!" said Ewart. "Say it's spoilt grain.
It carries out my case just as well. Your modern commerce
is no more buying and selling than—sculpture. It's mercy—
it's salvation. It's rescue work! It takes all sorts of fallen
commodities by the hand and raises them. Cana isn't in it.
You turn water—into Tono-Bungay."

An interesting thing about Uncle Teddy and Ewart is that
they were really sellers of the old-fashioned type working in
the milieu of the modern world. The *feel* of a passage like
this is plainly not too remote from the feel of the passage out
of Oliver Goldsmith's *Citizen of the World*, which we examined in Chapter Two. And yet, along with the cheerfulness
that hangs on with Uncle Teddy and Ewart, there are the
coolness and the contempt, too. Although it was possible to
assume that the buyer in Goldsmith's story might have done
better if he had tried harder, it is not possible to assume that
a buyer would have been able to do much of anything about
the adulterated mustard that he might have found in the
stores—except to hope that a much overburdened Food and
Drug Administration would have done something for him—
if Ewart's train hadn't come along. The authentic props of
modern selling are all here; selling itself is the preoccupation,
and the slam, bang, and hoopla are clearly implied.

As opposed to this, there is a fascinating study of a modern
seller working amidst the trappings of an old-fashioned life
in Flaubert's *Madame Bovary*, a book that appeared just as
the world of the modern seller was beginning to open up and
only half a dozen years after John Stuart Mill was noting
down some of its pricing characteristics. In Flaubert's marvelous story of Emma Bovary, much flows from the relation
between Emma and Lheureux, the draper. The props of
Lheureux's trade are simple props: no slam, bang, and hoopla.
The dealing is on the smallest possible scale, just Lheureux

and Emma and her husband Charles; and the materials dealt with are the ordinary materials of Mandeville's mercer. But Lheureux, in his contempt for the buyer, and in the extent to which he concentrated within himself the psychology of modern commercialism, was the very model of a modern seller. Monsieur Lheureux may be seen at work brilliantly when, after enmeshing poor Emma with bills and debts, he takes advantage of an illness of Emma's to drive things further in with Charles, whose gloomy thoughts begin this passage:

To begin with, he did not know how he could pay Monsieur Homais for all the physic supplied by him, and although, as a medical man, he was not obliged to pay for it, he nevertheless felt some shame at this obligation. Then the expenses of the household, now that the servant was mistress, became terrible. Bills rained in upon the house; the tradesmen grumbled; Monsieur Lheureux especially harassed him. In fact, at the height of Emma's illness, the latter, taking advantage of the circumstances to make his bill larger, had hurriedly brought the cloak, the travelling bag, two trunks instead of one, and a number of other things. It was very well for Charles to say he did not want them. The tradesman answered arrogantly that these articles had been ordered, and that he would not take them back; besides, it would vex madame in her convalescence; the doctor had better think it over; in short, he was resolved to sue him rather than give up his rights and take back his goods. Charles subsequently ordered them to be sent back to the shop. Félicité forgot; he had other things to attend to; then thought no more about them. Monsieur Lheureux returned to the charge, and, by turns threatening and whining, so managed that Bovary ended by signing a bill at six months. But hardly had he signed this bill than a bold idea occurred to him, namely, to borrow a thousand francs from Lheureux. So, with an embarrassed air, he asked if it were possible to get them, adding that it would be for a year, at any interest he wished. Lheureux ran off to his shop, brought back the money, and dictated another bill, by which Bovary undertook to pay to his order on the 1st of September next the sum of one thousand and seventy francs, which, with the hundred and eighty already agreed to, made just twelve hundred and fifty, thus lending at six per cent. In addition to one-fourth for commission; and the things bringing him in a good third at the least, this ought in twelve months to give him a profit of a hundred and thirty francs. He hoped that the business would not stop there; that the bills would not be paid; that they would be renewed; and that his poor little money, having thriven at the doctor's as at a hospital, would come back to him one day considerably more plump, and fat enough to burst his bag.

The foolish woman, the confused husband, and the wily creditor constituted a triangle that may not have been new even 110 years ago. For all that, the actions, and, even more, the quality of the actions of Lheureux are laid over with the new commercialism that Flaubert's letters to his friends were lambasting in the 1850's, even as he was creating Lheureux. Like any present-day credit merchant, installment-contract seller, or small-loan operator, Lheureux knew that the unpaid bill was worth more than the paid and that he would get more from financing than from selling. It has been the working of this precise knowledge, over the last half century particularly, that has shaped one of the most ominous aspects of the buyer-seller relationship today; the enormous indebtedness of the country's buyers to the country's sellers.

In this area above all the buyer must keep his wits about him; and in this area above all the intelligent buyer should never let himself forget, as George Herbert tersely commented 350 years ago, that "the buyer needs a hundred eyes, the seller not one." If price itself is a reflection of the seller's private reality, then the price arrived at through credit charges is all too often

the gross distortion of an unbelievable enlargement of that reflection. As of this writing around 85 billion dollars in short-term
consumer debt (that is, debt run up for the acquisition of automobiles, appliances, and other consumer goods and services, as
opposed to long-term mortgage debt for homes) is outstanding
in the United States; and nobody knows the real, honest-to-
God significance of such a fantastic figure to the economy. The
phenomenon is too recent. The short-term consumer debt load
is 50 per cent more than it was only five years ago, and more
than double what it was ten years ago. Twenty years ago, when
the post-war era began, the debt figure that is now 85 billion
dollars was a mere 6.6 billion; those were still the days when
people mainly paid as they went.

Most of the new load of debt has been and is being run up at
true annual interest rates of 18 per cent, 30 per cent, 40 per
cent, and even more, and sometimes much more. More than a
third of it—or some 30 billion dollars' worth—has been run up in
the sale of automobiles, which are the leading artifact of our
particular civilization. Their sex and status symbolism, so be-
guiling to the motivation researchers and so bemusing to their
critics, has come to overshadow their more straightforward symbolism as the millstone of the economy. It is more fun to listen
to a Freudian trying to avoid being obvious in the transparent
underbrush of Cadillac fenders and Mercury chrome, but it
is more useful to listen to that excellent economist Alvin H.
Hansen worriedly pondering the automobile in his book *The
American Economy*:

> We are increasingly in danger of making our economic sys-
> tem a mere treadmill. We have reached a point in our
> development where mere emphasis on larger and larger
> output of mechanical gadgets becomes rather meaningless,
> if, indeed, not a detriment to truly satisfactory living. We
> spend billions and billions of dollars on automobiles, of
> which perhaps half is frittered away on mere size, gadgets,
> and chrome—all of which add little to the social utility

of comfortable transportation. And expenditures on automobiles, not including operation or the vast sums spent on roads, are twice as great as the aggregrate expenditure on schools, including school construction and other capital outlays for education.

It is very true, and he doesn't even mention the enormous amounts of the buyer's substance that are drained off through the workings of the very complicated machinery of auto financing.

What goes on in many automobile sales will tax the credulity of the most intelligent buyer as it taxes the defenses of the most vigilant. It is so important to the economy to move these artifacts that practically anything goes; still, from time to time one investigating group or another will take a look into the snakepit of auto financing. And recently there have been some looks which establish perfectly clearly that the cash buyer, once upon a time viewed by sellers as a noble creature, is becoming a modern pariah. It will be instructive to listen to the questioning of the president of the Northern California Motor Car Dealers Association as set forth in *Consumer Reports* about a year ago, and to the illuminating answers given to the questions:

QUESTION. May I ask you one question . . . ? Do you want to sell cars for cash?
ANSWER. I do not want to sell them for cash if I can avoid it.
QUESTION. You would not want to sell the cars you do for a cash price then?
ANSWER. No, sir.
QUESTION. Does this mean that you are not really in the business of selling automobiles?
ANSWER. It does not mean that at all.
QUESTION. But you don't want to sell automobiles for cash?
ANSWER. It means that I want to sell cars for the most

profit that I can per car. Finance reserve [dealer's share of the carrying charges] and insurance commissions are part of the profit derived from selling a car on time. . . .

Looking further, a California legislative committee examined some of the procedures used by the auto salesman who does not want cash. The buying public, the committee wrote, suffers from a fatal misconception of the objectives of the typical automobile salesman, and then added:

> Automobile salesmen do not serve the same function as do salesmen of retail goods generally. They do not actually sell cars. They have no authority to close deals. They are front men for management, and their function is to negotiate the terms of a deal with a prospective buyer and then to seek ratification by management. . . .

Among the techniques the salesmen use in seeking to negotiate terms, the "hot box" was the one with which the committee was most fascinated. A hot box is a bugged waiting booth, and this is how it works:

> [The salesman] excuses himself for a few minutes, leaving his customers alone in the booth to talk among themselves, and goes into a back office to listen to them. He hears a conversation that concludes with the wife's agreeing: "If we can pay $85 a month, it's OK with me. That way we can make these payments all right and still get by with the furniture loan also." The salesman soon returns to his customers, armed with the knowledge of their private thoughts, and asks whether they could afford "about $85 a month?" He has figured out that a 30-month contract at $85 a month is a little better even than the 24-month contract at $100 a month he was trying to write. . . .

In a column discussing examples of the seller's art of this sort, *Automotive News* carried the following illuminating dialogue between one of its editors and a Mr. Richard Williams, identified as a "sales specialist":

"Don't factory travelers know what is going on?" asked the editor.

"The factory men must know," replied Mr. Williams. "The only answer seems to be that the factories tolerate crooks if crooks move cars."

In the East, Williams said he found specialists in dealing with the poor but car-needy—people who couldn't possibly afford to buy a new car.

"They bully and browbeat them on the price, and then they really shoot the shaft to them on terms," said Williams. Naturally, these people can't keep up the payments, but the dealer makes out all right financially by repossession.

Looking out upon the welter of borrowed money, exorbitant interest charges, deceptive payment schedules, missed payments, bankruptcies, and repossessions that now supplies the context for a substantial part of all buying, the intelligent buyer can, as always, learn much from the sellers' own dialogue with themselves. Perhaps the very first thing the buyer should understand is that it is not all beer and skittles for the seller; he has his problems, and they can be quite ponderable, as the *Financial Post* recently made clear in reporting these words from a spokesman for the National Association of Retail Clothiers and Furnishers:

> . . . If a store offering credit at 1½ per cent a month had to tell customers this means 18 per cent per year . . . [it] would "create an undesirable psychological effect on the American consumer's buying habits. . . ."

What the spokesman fears is that some American consumers, if they knew the extent to which sellers were rooking them, might buy less or differently. But there is, unfortunately, not a great deal of evidence to support such fears. The seller has many more tricks and stratagems than most buyers can ever get past. The trade magazine *Mart* a few years ago gave the philosophical approach and illustrated it with one specific gimmick, all in ten lines:

> . . . Many of the sins committed in our industry are based on the premise that the consumer is stupid—if not stupid, at least a step behind the manufacturer, distributor, or dealer in his thinking. The philosophy has been, "By the time the consumer catches on to this gimmick, we'll have something new to pull on him. . . ."
> We have heard dealers boast: "The customer will fight for an extra $10 off on a unit. I'll give her the ten bucks off and more than make it up on my financing. They don't have any idea what they're paying in credit charges."

Mart's dealers are perfectly correct, too. It is doubtful that one buyer in a dozen is actually aware that such small-loan companies as Household Finance Corporation are allowed by law to charge true annual interest rates of more than 30 per cent, although, of course, they never advertise that rate. As far back as fifteen years ago, before installment buying had come anywhere close to its present enormous scale, a New York State legislative committee disclosed that persons buying automobiles on the installment plan in New York had been paying interest charges of 31.5 per cent to 52.1 per cent. There have been dozens of other studies of this sort and the findings have always been much the same. Quite as ominous as the numerous figures thus unearthed is the lack of any figures at all in large areas. A columnist in *Home Furnishings Daily* put the matter thus:

> I have long suspected that many hard goods retailers are, in effect, in the banking business. Their net at the end of the year does not reflect profit made in the selling of furniture or appliances, but rather profit from carrying charges paid by customers. The term carrying charge formerly meant that the customer paid a certain amount . . . "a small amount" is the way the ads put it . . . to cover the costs of the retailer

in financing the sale. But now it seems that these charges are going up, and the "small amounts" actually constitute the greater part of the retailer's profit. This is one of these subjects which is always discussed behind closed doors.

The prevalence of this milking of the buyer by the seller led Senator Paul Douglas of Illinois in 1960 to attempt the enormity of trying to get a bill through Congress, a very short bill calling simply for an honest declaration of charges in consumer credit contracts and providing that the charges be stated in terms of true annual interest so that buyers would be able to compare costs. The intelligent buyer should make careful note of what followed: aroused sellers descended on Washington, contributed most of the 900 pages of testimony that promptly piled up, and succeeded (or, at least, as of this writing five years later have succeeded) in stopping the bill dead in its tracks. The principal seller objection is that credit is a confusing business, truth is heady stuff, and buyers wouldn't really know what to make of it if truth and credit were blended. It may be so; on this front, as on so many others dominated by the sellers, there has been little chance for the buyers to find out.

Occasionally an effort on behalf of the buyer wells up from somewhere, but the resources of the sellers usually prove equal to the affront. One little flurry took place a year or so ago, when the Senate Banking Committee sent the Douglas bill back to a subcommittee for revisions. (The opportunities for revision are not numerous with this bill, since its text says very little more than that sellers should tell the truth; but then a very small revision could go a long way with that.) Some consumer groups had been pushing for action, and were even getting support from a major newspaper, the *St. Louis Post-Dispatch*; so the vote was taken on sending the bill back, and among those who voted to do this were Senator Wallace F. Bennett, a Republican from Utah, and Senator Edward V. Long, a Democrat from Missouri. Senator Long was president of two Missouri finance companies and a bank as well; Senator Bennett was one of the largest credit merchandisers in Utah. The Cooperative News Service issued a news release on this collection of possibly related facts, but it made headlines nowhere.

Our old friend Dr. Ernest Dichter, whose bold call for annual model changes in the citrus fruit industry was noted some pages back, has naturally addressed himself to the credit business, on behalf of the small-loan companies. Dr. Dichter has many fascinating perceptions to pass on, among them that the average borrower feels "paternal authority" in a bank but something "shameful" when he goes to a small-loan company. Dr. Dichter doesn't mention that small-loan companies may charge three times or more the interest rate charged by most banks, which would seem to be leaving out something not irrelevant, but his progress from point to point is otherwise entirely clear.

He says that "we have entered the era of consumerism. Our tremendous production facilities necessitate the creation of an equally potent consumer market. In a sense, our economic system has to produce consumers, whereas previously we only produced goods." Dr. Dichter is afraid that too many people have been brainwashed with ideas about "thrift" and "the morality of borrowing" that "have ceased to conform to today's realities." The soaring conclusion of Dr. Dichter's essay on small loans (it appears in a section of his *Handbook* entitled "Things of a Higher Order") runs as follows:

> It is quite possible that the old morality concerning money and borrowing is not applicable to the new situation of the midcentury United States, that it is the wrong kind of morality for the present generation.

A morality applicable to the new situation and the present generation emerged in passing from an article that David Riesman wrote for the *Bulletin of the Atomic Scientists* several years ago:

A reporter in Anaheim, California—a town dependent on
new and war-supported industry (and Disneyland)—in-
quired as to what residents might do in the case of a
depression. The latter were all . . . mortgaged 30 or more
months ahead for cars, furniture, etc., as well as for their
homes. One man replied: "No one is worried, because
there's a theory in town that if anything slips up, the Government will declare a moratorium on all debts. . . . These
kids really think it's true . . . because otherwise this whole
place might become a shambles overnight."

The morality that emerges from this is not a kind, one sup-
poses, to give any pangs to Dr. Dichter, who finds that borrowing "is no longer the anxiety-ridden act it used to be" and
that "the modern morality . . . knows no halts and consolida-
tion." Moreover, says the doctor, "borrowing should be a
masculine rather than a feminine thing. Clients must be represented as strong and enterprising men rather than weak
characters who need help." This rigamarole is presumably
read reverently by many sellers, who employ Dr. Dichter expensively to speak to them along such lines as these, and so
I suppose it is my duty to advise the intelligent buyer to read
Dr. Dichter, too. But there are limits, and the intelligent
buyer will have to make any such decision for himself.

Three alternative readings will do the buyer far more good
in the end. One is a small item from an issue of *Home Furnishings Daily*, and the reading time couldn't be more than
about fifteen seconds, although a somewhat longer reflection
time should follow:

When a customer sees good carpeting and learns he can
have it, wall-to-wall, for only a modest sum per month, he is
intrigued. Credit is wonderful.

Of course . . . there are a lot of bankruptcies by credit
splurging, but that's another story.

The second reading is in Arthur Miller's play *Death of a*

Salesman. The figure of Willy Loman looms up whenever the talk turns to false values, morality and immorality, or commercialism at all in American life. It therefore looms up properly in this discussion, but it is not as a salesman that Willy Loman has most relevance to our immediate concerns. In two brief and poignant moments Willy speaks out of that hopeless entrapment which a buyer almost has to feel from time to time in an economic system that must produce consumers like things.

As a buyer, Willy has been taken on all fronts. He is the buyer who wouldn't believe you if you told him the truth about interest charges and he is also the buyer with whom Car-Nu at $1.69 worked. He would have been happy at the fake markdowns Linda would have gotten at the January White Sales and he would have been eaten alive by Lheureux. And these two little dialogues with Linda, although they are not very long, will go on and on and on in the intelligent buyer's mind:

WILLY. (*Blaming her.*) What do we owe?

LINDA. Well . . . on the first there's sixteen dollars on the refrigerator . . .

WILLY. Why sixteen?

LINDA. (*Apologizing.*) Well, the fan belt broke, so it was a dollar eighty.

WILLY. But it's brand-new.

LINDA. Well, the man said that's the way it is; till they work themselves in, y'know.

WILLY. I hope we didn't get stuck on that machine.

LINDA. They got the biggest ads of any of them.

WILLY. I know, it's a fine machine. What else?

LINDA. Well . . . there's nine-sixty for the washing machine; then the roof, you got twenty-one dollars remaining . . .

WILLY. It don't leak, does it?

LINDA. No, they did a wonderful job. Then you owe Frank for the carburetor.

WILLY. I'm not going to pay that man! That goddam Chevrolet, they ought to prohibit the manufacture of that car!

LINDA. (*Not sad.*) Well you owe him three and a half. And odds and ends, comes to around a hundred and twenty dollars by the fifteenth. (*Hugs him.*)

WILLY. A hundred and twenty dollars! My God, if business don't pick up I don't know what I'm gonna do.

· · · ·

LINDA. . . . We're a little short again.

WILLY. (*Irked.*) Why are we short?

LINDA. (*Apologizing.*) Well, you had the motor job on the car . . .

WILLY. That goddam Studebaker . . .

LINDA. Well, you got one more payment on the refrigerator . . .

WILLY. But it just broke again . . .

LINDA. (*Laughing him out of it.*) Well, it's old, dear . . .

WILLY. I told you we should've bought a well-advertised machine. Charley bought a General Electric and it's twenty years old and it's still good, that son of a bitch!

LINDA. But, Willy . . .

WILLY. Whoever heard of a Hastings refrigerator? Once in my life I would like to own something outright before it's broken! I'm always in a race with the junkyard! I just finished paying for the car and it's on its last legs. The refrigerator consumes belts like a goddam maniac. They time those things. . . . They time them so when you finally paid for them, they're used up.

The third of the readings promised comes from Chapter Seven of *The Grapes of Wrath,* as perceptive a script of the economic tension of a buyer-seller relationship as is to be found in any literature known to me. There should be no tendency on the part of the intelligent buyer to assume that John Steinbeck's vivid picture of life on a used-car lot in Oklahoma in the 1930's is either regional or outdated. Life is like this, except that the prices are a lot higher and the body-work may be a little worse, on used-car lots on Long Island right now:

A lot and a house large enough for a desk and chair and a blue book. Sheaf of contracts, dog-eared, held with paper clips, and a neat pile of unused contracts. Pen—keep it full, keep it working. . . .

Over-there, them two people—no, with the kids. Get 'em in a car. Start 'em at two hundred and work down. They look good for one and a quarter. Get 'em rolling. Get 'em out in a jalopy. Sock it to 'em! They took our time.

Owners with rolled-up sleeves. Salesmen, neat, deadly, small intent eyes watching for weaknesses.

Watch the woman's face. If the woman likes it we can screw the old man. Start 'em on that Cad'. . . . 'F you start on the Buick, they'll go for a Ford. Roll up your sleeves an' get to work. . . .

Like to get in to see that one? Sure, no trouble. . . .

Get 'em under obligation. Make 'em take up your time. Don't let 'em forget they're takin' your time. People are nice, mostly. They hate to put you out. Make 'em put you out, an' then sock it to 'em. . . .

Flags, red and white, white and blue—all along the curb. Used Cars. Good Used Cars.

Today's bargain—up on the platform. Never sell it. Makes folks come in, though. If we sold that bargain at that price we'd hardly make a dime. Tell 'em it's jus' sold. . . .

All right, Joe. You soften 'em up an' shoot 'em in here. I'll close 'em, I'll deal 'em or I'll kill 'em. Don't send in no bums. I want deals.

Yes, sir, step in. You got a buy there. Yes, sir! At eighty bucks you got a buy.

I can't go no higher than fifty. The fella outside says fifty.

Fifty, Fifty? He's nuts. Paid seventy-eight fifty for that little number. Joe, you crazy fool, you tryin' to bust us? Have to can that guy. I might take sixty. Now look here, mister, I ain't got all day. I'm a businessman, but I ain't out to stick nobody. Got anything to trade?

Got a pair of mules, I'll trade.

Mules! Hey, Joey, hear this? This guy wants to trade mules. Didn't nobody tell you this is the machine age? They don't use mules for nothing but glue no more.

Fine big mules—five and seven years old. Maybe we better look around.

Look around! You come in when we're busy, an' take up our time an' then walk out! Joe, did you know you was talkin' to pikers?

I ain't a piker. I got to get a car. We're goin' to California. I got to get a car.

Well, I'm a sucker. Joe says I'm a sucker. Says if I don't quit givin' my shirt away I'll starve to death. Tell you what I'll do—I can get five bucks apiece for them mules for dog feed.

I wouldn't want them to go for dog feed.

Well, maybe I can get ten or seven maybe. Tell you what we'll do. We'll take your mules for twenty. Wagon goes with 'em, don't it? An' you put up fifty, an' you can sign a contract to send the rest at ten dollars a month.

But you said eighty.

Didn't you never hear about carrying charges and insurance? That just boosts her a little. You'll get her all paid up in four-five months. Sign your name right here. We'll take care of ever'thing.

Well, I don't know—

Now, look here. I'm givin' you my shirt, an' you took all this time. I mighta made three sales while I been talkin' to you. I'm disgusted. Yeah, sign right there. All right, sir. Joe, fill up the tank for this gentleman. . . .

5

<<<<<<<<<<<<<<<<<<<<<<<<<<<<<<>>>>>>>>>>>>>>>>>>>>>>>>>>>>

Sin, Complexity, and the Failure of Faith

THIS record is drawing on, there are many promises to keep, and the intelligent buyer would now probably be grateful for something of a summative character. But there is nothing meaningfully summative, so far as the buyer is concerned, of the buyer-seller relationship. It is always changing, usually for the worse from the buyer's perspective; and what is needed is the buyer's alertness (which continuing reminders serve) rather than his complacence (which fattens on summations).

"A peg will stick between the joints of stones, and between buying and selling sin is ground out." Didn't ben Sirach sum it up, at least in the general sense? He did, but the general sense no longer

("But old clothes are beastly," continued the untiring whisper in Aldous Huxley's Brave New World. *"We always throw away old clothes. Ending is better than mending, ending is better than mending, ending is better than mending, ending. . . .")*

serves. Much as the greatest damage to a boxer is done in the in-fighting that often eludes even the referee's attention, so the buyer, all aware of the sin, falls to the specific tricks and frauds that he has not bothered to learn. Once the knowledge of sin may have been sufficient, or reasonably sufficient, to the needs of the buyer. But one of the present troubles is that, under the long burden, the definition of sin itself has become blurred. The flat lie blurred long ago into the half-truth that blurred into the legal trade puffery that blurred into the forgivable exaggeration that turns out to be the old flat lie, except that it is all right now because modern advertising is modern advertising and modern selling is modern selling and goods must be moved at all costs.

("Our real problems are also concealed from us by our current remarkable prosperity," said Robert M. Hutchins, "which results . . . in part from our new way of getting rich, which is to buy things from one another that we do not want at prices we cannot pay on terms we cannot meet because of advertising we do not believe.")

("Surely," Wesley Clair Mitchell said in 1912 in his famous essay The Backward Art of Spending Money, *"no one can be expected to possess the expert knowledge of the qualities and prices of such varied wares. . . . The single family can no more secure the advantage of such division of labor in caring for its wants as consumers than the frontier family could develop division of labor in production.")*

Beyond this, and quite beyond the boundaries of sin, complexities have entered in that no one really knows how to deal with anymore.

What is the buyer to do, or the seller for that matter, about understanding and explaining the buying or selling of a product as complicated as an automobile, fashioned of unknown materials by unfamiliar processes in distant plants operated by faceless people? The answer is that even an honest seller is at a loss to convey and the most intelligent buyer at a loss to comprehend what a given automobile really is, how it truly compares with others, and whether it is actually a good buy at all. And the problem may be equally complex with a detergent, or a drug, which are also now made of very novel materials and may well have been inadequately tested for effects they may have on the person or the environment; or with a fabric or a washing machine or a can of paint, which may now be made wholly differently than a fabric or a washing machine or a can of paint was made even twenty-five years ago. We no longer have many really simple products: fresh fluid milk is a manufactured article; ham is adulterated with water; meat is tenderized with enzymes; bread is processed and chemicalized; fruits and vegetables are injected with dyes and coated with waxes; poultry is dosed with hormonal drugs.

The average buyer neither knows nor can learn from direct immediate handling much of anything about most of the products he now lives with. The most important clues to an automobile's performance lie not where they may be read in the product but in somebody's files in Detroit. And in the slack-filled box is the synthesized something-new of the unknown formulation.

The buyer, in short, is confronted not only by the seller's old sin, which is bad enough, but by the product's new complexity, which may sometimes be even worse. Buying therefore must be done increasingly on faith at a time when the

(". . . It is the general opinion of the [clothing] manufacturing industry," said Elmer L. Ward, Sr., president of Palm Beach Company, Inc., as quoted in The New York Times, *"that no fiber producer —not one—has ever sufficiently tested a new fiber before it is marketed.")*

("Furnish a model for your target group completely," said designer Gene E. Dreyfus, "or not at all. A partially furnished room leaves too much to the imagination and this is the segment of the buyer's mind you must control. . . .")

(". . . To develop new business . . . give out . . . some . . . type of

card that makes the cus-
tomer feel he will be
given special treatment
in your store," wrote a
columnist in Home Fur-
nishings Daily. "Instruct
the sales people to act
impressed when the cus-
tomer flashes this. . . .")

("Without some dissim-
ulation," the Earl of
Chesterfield wrote, "no
business can be carried
on at all.")

("Every design is a com-
promise," wrote Ernest
R. Cunningham in De-
sign News. "Is it wrong,
therefore, for a designer
to be cognizant of the
results and to make the
compromises accordingly?
Certainly not. It is filling
in an essential dimension
—time—when designs
are tailored to perform
for a specified period.")

("Arthur C. Fatt, then
executive vice-president
of Grey Advertising
Agency, Inc. . . . con-
tended that national ad-
vertisers were losing touch
with the masses in one
industry after another,"
wrote the New York Her-

people in whom, and the objects in
which, the buyer can reasonably place
his faith have been decreasing in number
and reliability. The resulting crisis—for
the buyer-seller relationship has by now
come to that—involves the buyer in relation to the whole range of selling functions, from the promotion of consumer
debt at usurious interest rates stated
misleadingly if at all, to meretricious and
false advertising claims, to the inadequacies of advertising even at its best,
to rigged prices, to packaging which is
deceptive on a hundred different counts,
to all the multitudinous tricks of cheapened product design, to the seller's broad
and overriding contempt.)

The crisis is the more upsetting, to
sellers and buyers alike, because both
have generally been so poorly prepared
for it. It is the sad truth that most sellers
and even a good many buyers have not
read the illuminating writings cited in
these pages (and it is a further sad truth,
alas, that many of them will not read
even *these* pages). Moreover, they have
been given, in school and through much
trade association promotion and many
inspirational articles (one glowing example of which we will discuss in some
detail further on), grossly oversimplified
models of the buyer-seller relationship.

In these neatly sculptured models all
sellers are notably honest, all buyers
notably rational and well-informed, all
products clearly defined and presented,

and the whole relationship perforce is notably static. Fraud and deception are not allowed in this marketplace, except in teensy-weensy amounts to justify excoriation. The buyer, possessed of precise and clear standards of evaluation, weighs matters with sharp discernment. Through his free and informed choice he guides production, and the seller's activities are thereby continuously shaped and reshaped by an infinitude of small nudges as each buyer exercises his sovereignty in each and every transaction. If any hitch develops at any point, the neat and simple economic model has a place for neat and appropriate social and political forces to bring things back to order. The buying and selling process is assumed to be embedded in a kind of moral and legal jelly which cushions shocks and is nourishing to trust and confidence.

The trouble is that when faith is shaken all the assumptions are shaken, too. And when the assumptions are shaken it turns out they weren't very valid to begin with; like the product in which the built-in obsolescence was built in too hard, they fall apart before they can be used. The marketplace is vastly more dynamic than the neat models make it out to be.

The buyer, of course, fits into the simplifications no better than the seller does. If the seller is not remotely the guileless do-gooder he likes to bill him-

ald Tribune. "Mr. Fatt makes it clear that he is not saying that national brands are overpriced for the values they offer, but rather that the price lines at which too many national brands are being sold are considerably above present-day mass buying levels.")

("There is a decided tendency in business to use the words 'legal' and 'honest' interchangeably," wrote E. B. Weiss in Advertising Age. "When the businessman says that most businessmen are honest, what he really means is that most businessmen operate within the law.")

("In the Overdeveloped Society, the standard of living dominates the styles of life; its inhabitants are possessed . . . by its industrial and commercial apparatus," wrote C. Wright Mills in Esquire. ". . . Society has become a great salesroom —and a network of rackets: the gimmick of success becomes the yearly

change of model . . .")

"*Walter Landor [a package designer]*" wrote the San Francisco Examiner, "*suggested that women shoppers . . . enjoy the experience of being seduced by packages . . . in the concealing intimacy of the supermarket aisle the same consumer who cried 'shame' in public will reach for the biggest-looking package on the shelf—even when she knows its contents are no greater.*")

("*The courts are no longer content to insist simply upon the most literal truthfulness. . . .*" said Judge Irving Kaufman of the U.S. Court of Appeals, "*for we have increasingly come to recognize that advertisements as a whole may be completely misleading although every sentence separately considered is literally true.*")

self as being, the buyer is by no means the rational entity nor the sovereign that the advertiser likes to tell him, and particularly her, that he and she are. Among other things the intelligent buyer must know about the seller is that the latter's frequently flattering descriptions of buyers are hollow mockeries of empty jests and can cause dangerous addiction if listened to incautiously.

The buyer is, to his disadvantage and as we all know, a creature of impulse, and sellers particularly know this and exploit it, since impulsive buyers spend more and think less. Even more to the point, the buyer is literally and daily shaped to one degree or another by the seller's advertising and its generally low and biased standards. Advertising provides the overwhelming bulk of all the product information that most buyers ever get, and this, of course, is a scandal.

Advertising is, to be sure, a tradesman's skill that can be turned to one thing as well as another. But it is hardly possible any more, after the waves of advertising that have rolled over us for all these years, to affirm that it *is* turned to one thing as well as another. It seems inescapable that advertising works better the lower the values and the meaner the ends. The intelligent buyer has many quarrels with advertising, having to do with its offenses to private taste and public decency and its outrages against simple sense. He has another quarrel, which should bother him more than it seems to, and that is that the force of advertising has been powered to an objective so minor, so relatively base—namely, the promotion and counter-promotion and counter-counter-promotion of brand names for products not meaningfully differentiated. This use of advertising, in a world in which wars go on and poverty exists and real needs are to be met, is also a scandal. And even for this meager use, since advertising lacks any institutionalized disciplines and standards, it is quite unreliable; its product information, for example, being never other than favorable, is never complete.

(*"How many of us here," said H. Lloyd Taylor, DuPont advertising executive, as quoted by* Advertising Age, *"can say he's never been a party to deceptive advertising?"*)

It is with the seller as advertiser (or advertising agent) that we will engage ourselves in the pages ahead. This will take us into a strange countryside, full of shifting grounds, dark woods, and economy-size sophists living in shiny palaces beside the small huts of their creations. To maintain that alertness stressed at the beginning of this chapter, and to minimize the complacence there warned against, the buyer needs a guide or at least a guiding principle. Let us proceed with Plato, or at least with the worried words he wrote in the *Protagoras:* "And we must take care that the sophist, praising his wares, does not mislead us as the merchants and shopkeepers do about the food they sell us. For they do not know which food is

(*"Wherefore do ye spend money for that which is not bread? and your labor for that which satisfieth not?"—Isaiah,* 55:2)

good for us and which is bad, but say that everything they sell is good. And the people who buy from them do not know either."

Things have got a great deal worse for the buyer since Plato's day, but it is along exactly such lines as these that they have got worse.

Part Two

‹‹‹‹‹‹‹‹‹‹‹‹‹‹‹‹‹‹‹‹‹‹‹‹‹›››››››››››››››››››››››››

When Words

Lose Their Meaning

6

‹‹‹‹‹‹‹‹‹‹‹‹‹‹‹‹‹‹‹‹‹‹‹‹‹‹‹›››››››››››››››››››››››››››

"The Sort of Extravagance
a Wealthy Society
Can Indulge In"

THE advertising business is a relatively small business in terms of the people who earn their livings directly from
it. Approximately 100,000 work on the advertising staffs of the
manufacturers who advertise. Another 100,000 or so constitute
the advertising staffs of retailers who advertise. Another 75,000,
more or less, make up the staffs of salesmen who sell space
and time for the advertising media, direct-mail firms, and so
forth. And probably no more than that number constitute the
staffs of the country's advertising agencies. These are the advertising specialists, who actually think up and prepare virtually
all of the national advertising that we see and hear daily,
and some of the local advertising as well; these are "the ad-
men," who devote to things the intensity of feeling that the
churchman devotes to souls and the educator gives to minds;
and in the process of making their devotions they have given
modern selling the rather mindless and the wholly physical
insistence that characterizes so much of it.

The advertising industry points out that hundreds of thou-

sands of other people—ranging from linotype operators to billboard lithographers, sign painters, models, skywriters, and so
on—one way or another earn their livings from advertising, too.
And many critics of advertising have muttered somewhat about
the numbers of people thus involved in what Stuart Chase,
forty years ago in *The Tragedy of Waste*, viewed as nonpro-
ductive employment. As he wrote, "if they lived in Denmark—
where advertising is restricted—they would have to turn to
some productive occupation."

> In other words [Chase wrote in 1925], the industry reaches
> down into the ranks of the gainfully employed, picks up a
> half million odd workers, and says to them "Now shout!
> and furnish the paper, ink and paint for shouting!" Mean-
> while the purchasing power of the country does not mate-
> rially vary. There are just so many dollars to be spent.
> Advertising creates no new dollars. In fact by removing
> workers from productive employment, it tends to depress
> output, and thus even lessen the number of real dollars.
> What it does do is this. It *transfers* purchasing power from
> A to B. It makes people stop buying Mogg's soap, and
> start buying Bogg's soap. Every drug store carries some 60
> kinds of soap and 35 kinds of tooth paste. It makes people
> stop buying shaving soap in mugs, and starts them buying
> it in tinfoil sticks. It can make A rich and ruin B. With
> a fixed and relentless number of dollars to play with, it
> can shift these dollars all over the map. But as Veblen
> points out, the game is played in a closed market. You
> cannot lift yourself by your bootstraps. Further, "in such
> a closed market, the volume of purchasing power will be
> narrowed by approximately the aggregate cost of salesman-
> ship." And Veblen quoted patly enough a remark at a
> recent (1923) conference of one of the big New York
> agencies: "Blank has the market, it is our problem to
> dislodge him.[1]

[1] See pages 104-106 below for Veblen's own discussion of the closed
market, salesmanship, and "saleable appearances."

On the subject of employment itself, the late Henry Pratt Fairchild took a more tolerant view. He wrote, more than fifteen years ago in *The Prodigal Century*, that this is "the sort of extravagance a wealthy society can indulge in, if it sees fit, without courting absolute disaster." And he went on to say:

> If society does not want to employ the labor of these people, and the materials that they use up, in some really useful activity it is better that they work at advertising than that they starve in idleness or be supported on a dole.

One might describe this as the humane defense of advertising, so to speak.

Like selling in general, the advertising sector of selling has lost steadily in prestige as a field of employment, even as the amount of advertising turned out has increased. In a survey made by *Sales Management* four years ago on more than a hundred college campuses, nearly a thousand male students were asked what kind of work they wanted to get into after graduation. "Selling," as the magazine reported unhappily, came out a poor fourth. But "advertising" came out an even poorer eighth, even though "public relations" and "promotion" were lumped in with it. The finding tended to confirm the feeling frequently expressed in school papers, articles and books on American values, etc., to the effect that the commercial spirit is not viewed by the questing young as much of a guide to where the important action is.

But eighth place, down with "psychology" and "journalism," is still rather startlingly low for a business which, however it has failed to make people take it altogether seriously, is supposed to offer attractive salaries and talks endlessly and almost poignantly to itself, at its conventions and in its trade journals, about how "vital" and "exciting" it is. The talk seems not to have been heard outside, and the salaries presumably are not attractive enough to counteract the widespread impression that the copywriter or account executive, working worriedly and hard at jobs that never seem to be worth all the effort, has become something of a symbol of the all-American square. There is little evidence that the air of meaningful potential that attracts the young job-seeker attaches to these well-starched figures or to their daily turns for indigestion tablets, cigarettes, or even Cadillac cars.

As Jules Henry has noted in his examination of American cultural values, *Culture Against Man,* "advertising is self-selective, so that youngsters with a traditional ethical sense avoid it. . . . Thus the dishonesties and distortions of advertising are bound to be self-renewing. . . . Spontaneous moral regeneration is . . . impossible for advertising because it does not know what the problem is. . . ."

Beyond this, it is true enough that the advertising commitment has tended to trail clouds of disreputability ever since perhaps the first mass use of it during the year of the plague in London, the year in which Defoe's "physick" peddler got his comeuppance from a buyer whose name should not have been lost to history (see page 22). Quacks and peddlers overran the city with advertisements and posters exploiting the population's fears all during that year, and one of the tragicomic aspects of the time was the fate of the quacks. Many of them, seeking to get the last penny possible, stayed on when they could have left, and died of the plague themselves, along with their customers. Others, apparently mesmerized by their own claims for their nostrums, died taking them. One way or another, London was notably free of quacks for a couple of years after the plague subsided. But Defoe's estimate of this situation was that the surviving quacks had simply fled into the country to unload their plague-waters, never-failing preservatives, and infallible pills on the outlying villages. So— exactly 300 years ago last year—mass advertising may have begun (Defoe really did let his pen run on), or, as one might say, "there'll always be an adman."

The story of the growth of advertising since then has been told in a variety of books, none better than E. S. Turner's

British-American study, *The Shocking History of Advertising*, to the whole of which the intelligent buyer is referred. Mr. Turner is a notably painstaking and fair reviewer of the subject. He is persuaded that "advertising, after all, is the mirror of man" and since he finds that "man has never been in serious danger of becoming bogged down in grace," he can report on the doings of the advertising fraternity over three centuries without dismay and equally without trying to pretty up the picture. His picture is downright ugly at times, as in his detailing of some of the promotional excrescences of the 1920's, when expensive campaigns for peripheral luxuries were mounted with war profits thus kept away from the tax collector—and when President Calvin Coolidge was paying tribute to advertising's role in "the regeneration and redemption of mankind." But, for most of the way, what emerges from Mr. Turner's history is closer to that simple disreputability noted earlier. And this has been surprisingly the same from year to year and from century to century. The techniques of the fake testimonial, the unsupported claim, the shrill repetition of nonsense or worse, and the child's reasoning with which any present-day buyer, intelligent or otherwise, is familiar from his own experience with advertising, were all used by the pill peddlers of the seventeenth century, the prostitutes and pimps of the eighteenth, the household-goods suppliers and snake-oil vendors of the nineteenth, and the intestinal specialists who made our own 1930's raucous. There is, of course, more to the use of advertising than is to be found in this strain; but this strain is a very large one, and it is always there. Currently it continues as the cigarette advertisers, for example, arrogantly and profitably mock medicine's and the government's painstakingly achieved findings that cigarettes are important causes of lung cancer, respiratory ailments, and heart disease (see Chapter Thirteen for a fuller discussion of cigarette advertising).

It is just possible that a college student, pondering his future, might be influenced by something like that. Or perhaps, weary with texts and fed up with the TV cigarette commercial following the news report about the health hazards of cigarette smoking, our student happens upon one of the trade papers mentioned earlier—*Tobacco*, say, whose capacities for enchantment were typified not long ago in the following poignant editorial note:

> The disturbing factor about the New York City school anti-smoking educational drive is that other cities might follow. It might deter all children from ever becoming smokers. . . .

Perhaps the student is a journalism major, with a feeling that somewhere in this life he might find challenge and reward and the sense of doing something useful. As a journalism major, perhaps he has been doing some auxiliary reading in the *Wall Street Journal* and happened to see this little item:

> While over 1,200 students watched, 20 teachers paraded down the aisle of the Abraham Lincoln High School in San Jose, Calif., a few months ago. The teachers were pedaling tricycles, pushing scooters and towing their 61-year-old principal in a child's wagon. They were trying to whip up student enthusiasm for a magazine subscription drive sponsored by the school and Curtis Publishing Co.

Or perhaps he is a business major and, with one eye on life's mission, happened to cast the other on *Barron's,* where he noticed the story quoting the president of one of the TV networks on some of its programming plans:

> We're programming for the younger, larger families—the ones with more teeth to brush, more bodies to bathe and more hair to shampoo.

At about the same time, if he had happened to see the *Philadelphia Evening Bulletin*, he could have further honed his sense of mission with this more detailed meditation on the young contained in an advertisement:

More and more, bubble baths are playing a vital role in the rearing of youngsters. Far from being simply fun, or a passing fancy, the bubble bath has become firmly established in family living. Very important, then, to every mother who wants the best for her child, is choosing the *proper* bubble-bath products.

Or let us assume that our student is uncertain about the future and is weighing both advertising and medicine. He has from time to time dipped into the *Journal of the American Medical Association*, and perhaps in one of these he read the report of a speech by Dr. E. Vincent Askey, president of the Association at the time, attacking advertising's distortion of the image of science. The world's eminent researchers, Dr. Askey complained, were not *wholly* caught up with toothpaste flavors or *wholly* preoccupied with the "vital task of making tablets dissolve faster in a tumbler of water." Interested by this, the student might have gone on to read in a subsequent issue a more precise discussion of the standards of advertising as applied to the materials of medicine:

> The incorporation of drugs into cosmetics [wrote Dr. Stephen Rothman] often is done for promotional purposes rather than for the benefit of drug action. . . . Drugs give an opportunity to construct attractive slogans. . . . Incorporation of a drug or a chemical does not only serve the purpose of effective advertising but it is also an excellent pretext to boost the price of a preparation, and to sell a jar of cosmetics for several dollars when it has a few pennies' worth of material in it.

Supposing that our student is one of the relatively rare ones actually studying for an advertising career, let us suppose also that his interest led him to follow the reports in *The New York Times* last year on the Regimen case, in which for the first time an advertising agency was prosecuted (and subsequently convicted) for its part in a fraud. The Regimen racket, described in the *Times* as "one of the most brazen mass-media frauds ever perpetrated on the public," involved sales described by an Assistant United States Attorney as "staggering," profits described as "substantial," medical tests described as the work of doctors "bribed" to "invent" favorable results, and other niceties not commonly dealt with in courses in advertising.

The fraud also produced some fascinating aspects of the advertising man in a situation of stress, where, as we all know, one's inner qualities come to the fore. The student, and with him the intelligent buyer, could therefore have learned much from the profile of the advertising man that took shape in the *Times* reports as the trial progressed. After the prosecuting attorney had set forth his case that the defendants "went ahead from 1956 to 1963 with reckless disregard to repeated warnings that the drug was worthless," one of the advertising agency representatives quickly scurried, with a surer sense of self-preservation than of dignity, to a familiar corner:

> Kastor, Hilton was only an advertising agency that prepared copy; the fact is, that's all it did. We did no more and we did no less than an advertising agency is required to do.

On another day another agency employee, described by the *Times* as "a slender and elegant young man . . . clearly uncomfortable as a prosecution witness," was asked if he had known that the Regimen campaign was dishonest. "Following a prod" from earlier testimony, as the *Times* put it, the agency man finally conceded that he had known. The student and the intelligent buyer could have learned of the fraudulence of Regimen's claims from *Consumer Reports* a long time ago, in February, 1958, to be precise, or not long after the false advertising began. But they may learn the lesson more memorably, perhaps, and more usefully to their general understanding of why advertising trails its cloud of disreputability from those words of 1965.

If, sorely puzzled, our student seeks guidance from seers close at hand, advertising as an occupation is not going to be helped. Educators by the dozens have found occasion to indict it as a corrosive influence on the best values in American life. If our student had been an Amherst student, for example, this is what he would have found in President Calvin H. Plimpton's fourth annual report last year:

Life today is wildly different from anything that has gone on before. One can read about the traffic jams in ancient Rome, but the quantitative and qualitative changes in traffic today bear no resemblance to the past. A loss of electricity, or water, or a major strike can paralyze a city. No longer can we escape to a Walden and appear self-sufficient. The repetitiveness of advertising is bludgeoning all our perceptive faculties into a state of concussion, complete with a retrograde amnesia. The prophecy ascribed to Confucius, that "When words lose their meaning, the people will lose their liberty," is being realized. There are thousands of middle men, middle machines, and middle words between us and reality. These complexities are nigh overwhelming and threaten a loss of identity for the individual and a loss of his significance.

Raked by such indictments over the years, and perhaps embarrassed a little by the degree to which his business sanctions frauds and inanity, the advertising man has become a moodier, more complicated reacter than he used to be in the simpler days of Calvin Coolidge and George Babbitt, or than he was through the unabashed vulgarity of the 1930's, when the first real organized efforts took form to create for buyers more reliable information than the advertisers were providing. The simplicistic reaction of many advertisers to the criticism that their excesses had brought down on them was perfectly expressed in a list of suggested answers to critics of advertising, submitted by members of the Sales Executives Club of New York in 1941. One of the suggestions was:

Let every phrase possibly imply that our cause is American and that detractors are un-American, and more likely to be tools or dupes of foreign isms.

And at just about the same time a New York advertising man, speaking before the Advertising Club of Springfield, Massachusetts (not too far from Chicopee Falls), put the point into broader context. The *Christian Science Monitor* reported him as saying:

> In these strange days a man who criticizes a government policy is very likely to be called a Fifth Columnist. If he criticizes an act of a labor union, he is a labor-baiter. If he criticizes the practice of the advertising profession, he is suspected of being a Red.

War, hot and cold, the nuclear bomb, and a certain amount of growing up have taken place since then. And the advertiser, certainly less sure than he was before the world changed, has even found some identity with his critics. The change on this front finds an almost startlingly clear illustration in two speeches made just twenty years apart by two executives of the Bristol-Myers Company, one of the most active of advertisers now as then. The first of these speeches was given by Mr. William H. Bristol, Jr., in 1940, and in the course of it he had this to say:

> I don't know how many of you are aware of the consumer movement so-called. There are 27 publications and organizations, such as Consumers' Research, Consumers Union, feeding old John Henry Public a lot of unsubstantiated and unsubstantiable so-called facts. It's grand reading, good fiction, and unfortunately it is growing and undermining our industry. Courses are given in schools and universities along the same line. It's a constant gunfire on our business, on our jobs. I don't think we can fight it single-handed, but I do think that we can do our share.

And exactly twenty years following that, in 1960, in a speech to the Sales Executives Club of New York, the very place in which criticism of advertising had once been equated with un-Americanism, the late Mr. Lee Bristol of the Bristol-Myers Company spoke as follows:

> The great American ailment is manifest on all sides by a deepening shade in our ethics (both business and social), a sloppiness in our services, a mediocricty in our manufacture, and a growing distrust and even anger in the public's mind.

Mr. Bristol was not only an executive of one of the largest advertisers in the country, but also was active in the industry's trade associations and was, at the time he spoke, chairman of the Advertising Council—an industry-supported, commercial charity agency through which advertisers promote socially approved causes (Smokey Bear is one of the Advertising Council's notable creations). He thus would seem to have been the very model of a modern American advertising man, particularly since practically all of his company's products (Sal Hepatica, Ipana, Ban, Bufferin, etc.) fall into the drug and cosmetic category, where much of the most unabashed advertising has characteristically been done. It is, indeed, American drug and cosmetic advertising preeminently which has created the international image of the American adman; and it was certainly the thought of such advertising as much as any that led Lord Reith some years ago, in an impassioned argument in the House of Lords, to classify advertising sponsorship of British TV programs with bubonic plague and the black death.

With Mr. Bristol in mind—the Mr. Bristol of 1960, that is, not the Mr. Bristol of 1940—the intelligent buyer might find it instructive to read a recent portrait of the businessman as advertiser by Roy Lewis and Rosemary Stewart in their most interesting book entitled *The Boss*, another British-American study and a fit companion to Turner's history. The portrait looks out upon the current scene from a brief chapter entitled "The Commercial Spirit," and it looks out from a British perspective, but the prespective turns out to be a familiar one:

> . . . The medieval distrust of business finds an echo in the lower status, so surprising to the American business man, given in Europe to business men who deal with the consumer. The reason is, it may be suggested, the closer contact with mass-advertising. The selling of machinery, transport or other producer's equipment needs the aid of advertising; but it is comparatively honest, informative, straightforward trade advertising—a class of business which, significantly, hardly interests the big agencies. The world of half-lies, fractional truths, and ceaseless fuss about trivia in which the advertiser lives is that of consumer advertising, and it is futile to suppose that either the business or the public's mind can be unaffected by it. In proportion as the businessman lays claim to some education and philosophy his attitude to his advertising tends to become one of mingled shame and defiance; of distaste for his product or contempt for his clientele. If he has none of these feelings he is either a cynic or quite simply a plain, pure, bloodlessly professional entrepreneur, to whom the selling of a product, good or bad, by any means, is merely an exercise in the maximization of net profit.

Mr. Bristol most assuredly would not have accepted certain warts in that portrait, but, if he meant what he said in his speech to the sales executives, he would have agreed with much of the portrait. Mr. Lewis and Miss Stewart are perceptive critics of advertising and Mr. Bristol was, as he had been for a long time, one of its leading practitioners; but their views do overlap. In this area of the overlap, I would suggest that the intelligent buyer spend some time comparing, testing, checking out; the modern advertiser may not be found here whole, but his footprints are to be seen.

This may not remain true. Advertising, which is most at

home and most effective with non-urgent needs and relatively unimportant desires, is currently at its most comfortable in economic terms. These are times of much money (relatively speaking and at least in this country), of depression or disillusion with the state of the world, and of a breakdown in inner security that has deepened slowly since the time of Galileo. These are therefore times when non-urgent needs may seem urgent, peripheral desires may seem central, and the easiest of values may come to seem the only ones. These are therefore times when advertising thrives, and an advertiser's criticisms of advertising may be no more than one of the luxuries that the times foster.

One should not forget, and most certainly the intelligent buyer should not forget, what happened during the war years that preceded the present boom. As many economists have pointed out, the function of advertising thins out as real demand arises. No one has said it better than John Kenneth Galbraith said it in his pungent book of eight years ago, *The Affluent Society*:

> The fact that wants can be synthesized by advertising, catalysed by salesmanship, and shaped by discreet manipulations of the persuaders shows that they are not very urgent. A man who is hungry need never be told of his need for food. If he is inspired by his appetite, he is immune to the influence of Messrs. Batten, Barton, Durstine, and Osborn. The latter are effective only with those who are so far removed from physical want that they do not already know what they want. In this state alone are men open to persuasion.

During the war there were prime demands for things that did not need to be advertised and other demands that could not be met because there was no supply. This created the kind of crazy, mixed-up reality with which the unrealities of advertising are least at home. And so the advertising business spent much time and money dinning in trademarks and slogans that it was afraid buyers might forget in the lack of the products. In the long history of mass advertising from the year of the plague on, there can be few more ridiculous giveaways of advertising's sometime pretentions to being taken seriously than this advertisement which appeared in 1944:

> A wonderful surge of courage brings your head up fiercely in the face of threats. A flash of your eyes measures the enemy. Sacrifice? Your answer is a short laugh. Sacrifice is a way to help. And you—magnificent lady—you'll help. You'll toil. You'll fight like a tigress. We know. We've seen it in the lift of your chin.

The point of this ad was to tell the lady she'd have to manage without a brand of bed sheets because production was going to the armed forces. There were hundreds of others almost as silly during the war years. And, it need hardly be said, the advertising business was very sensitive about criticism during those years.

Finally, one should not forget, and most certainly the intelligent buyer should not forget, what happened before the war, from the late 1920's—when advertising was riding high on the pablum of loose money· that always nourishes it—to the early 1930's, when advertising responded to depression and real need by turning away and committing its energies and what money it then had to the private preservation of its users and their peripheral products. The defense of the advertising business then was, of course, that "we did no more and we did no less than an advertising agency is required to do." But it was then, just then, that advertising entered its crisis of confidence, and that the criticisms of advertising for its failures and affronts became serious and meaningful.

7

‹‹‹‹‹‹‹‹‹‹‹‹‹‹‹‹‹‹‹‹‹‹‹‹‹‹‹‹‹‹›››››››››››››››››››››››››

First an Ordeal,
Then a Whisper

None of the criticism directed at advertising, to be sure, has had much effect on advertising. Advertising and the criticisms of it have grown right along together. And advertising's growth has probably been greater in the past century than that of any other business not actually born within the century. A hundred years ago, at the conclusion of the Civil War, the advertising business was a thing of shreds and patches, hardly a business at all. About 50 million dollars went into it in 1865.[1] The media included newspapers and magazines, none of which had much circulation, and the sides of barns as well. The foremost critics of advertising then were probably the users, both actual and potential. The personal salesman was still the main tool of selling, and the idea of letting a faceless block of type do one's selling offended many manufacturers, particularly those

[1] These and similar figures to follow reflect the published statistical work of various industry sources, of which the McCann-Erickson media research department under the direction of Robert J. Coen seems to be most widely accepted. All figures as used here have been rounded out.

in whom the "instinct of workmanship," as Thorstein Veblen would call it some years later, was strong enough to live through the compromises imposed by the new mass production techniques. The way advertising was used by the worst producers amply confirmed the distaste of the others. Trademarks were hardly known—there weren't more than about a hundred at the time.

All of this changed over the next few decades; things happened on all fronts. The congressional grant of relatively inexpensive mailing privileges to publications helped circulations. The development of the photoengraving process basically transformed printed media, particularly in conjunction with vastly faster printing presses. Under the pressure of free and compulsory education the literacy rate improved almost daily. Up to about the 1890's mass production was moving steadily up a high road, and the media which could have served it were still moving along a low road. Then, and within a very few years, some of the publications increased their readership ten and twenty times. With products pouring out on the one side and readers piling up on the other, advertising efforts bloomed like sunflowers. This may be viewed as the approximate point at which the age of the poster, the peddler, and the announcement yielded to the age of the mass medium, the slogan, and the creation of costly want. The total advertising expenditure, which came to about 200 million dollars in 1880, reached 360 million dollars in 1890 and 540 million dollars—or ten times its post-Civil War level—in 1900.

The principal critics of advertising during this period, interestingly enough, were the media which were transformed by it. There is no sign that magazine or newspaper publishers then foresaw advertising's coming economic dominance of their media. It was quite the other way around. With many publishers, as with many manufacturers, the instinct of workmanship and the resistance to compromise died hard. Frank Rowsome, Jr., whose book *They Laughed When I Sat Down* is an illustrated history of magazine advertising (and a very

entertaining one as well as a good history), told of some of the
ordeals of the advertiser:

> Of the quality magazines which were predominant up until
> the end of the century, only one, the *Century*, openly in-
> vited advertising. The others simply tolerated it. A publica-
> tion seldom actively sought ads. Instead, a prospective
> advertiser or his agent would appear at the magazine or
> newspaper offices, hat in hand, and would request permis-
> sion to announce his wares. If there was space open in a
> forthcoming edition, and if the advertiser was prepared to
> pay in full in advance—a widespread requirement that re-
> flected the general view that puffing was a shady pursuit—
> the ad might be allowed in. But *Harper's*, which took an
> especially stuffy attitude toward advertisers, once rejected
> $18,000 for twelve ads from a sewing-machine manufacturer,
> on the grounds that it preferred to advertise its own books
> on the page he coveted.

These ordeals, as I am sure we have all heard, were overcome. They were overcome so very well that, for the next fifteen
years on from 1900, while the Western world was living out
the last reach of its old securities, commercialization took charge
of life in America. What Thorstein Veblen said of "the machine process" in *The Theory of Business Enterprise*, published
at the beginning of this period (1904)—

> The machine process gives no insight into questions of good
> and evil, merit and demerit, except in point of material
> causation, nor into the foundations or the constraining force
> of law and order, except such mechanically enforced law and
> order as may be stated in terms of pressure, temperature,
> velocity, tensile strength, etc. The machine technology
> takes no cognizance of conventionally established rules of
> precedence; it knows neither manners nor breeding and can
> make no use of any of the attributes of worth. Its scheme of
> knowledge and of inference is based on the laws of material

causation, not on those of immemorial custom, authenticity,
or authoritative enactment. Its metaphysical basis is the law
of cause and effect, which in the thinking of its adepts has
displaced even the law of sufficient reason.

—what Veblen said in 1904 about the machine process of
manufacturing had become true, only a decade later, with the
development of a reasonable facsimile of the machine process
in advertising. As Veblen wrote, the worst of the patent medicine abominations were being cleaned up, in part by the media
themselves, which by now, far from looking down their noses at
the advertisers, were courting them. The Pure Food and Drug
Law went into force in 1906, laying down some broad and basic
ground rules. This was one of the first major laws to protect a
buyer, and it succeeded in sloughing off the unmitigated junk,
the unkempt nuisances, and the most disorderly frauds that
advertising had spawned and, to a degree, sponsored. (Some of
the leading advertising agencies of the time, including some of
the largest ones still active, not only promoted the nostrums but
owned parts of the companies making them.) Thus scrubbed,
at least in front, advertising was ready for the brighter day ahead.

In 1910 the total advertising expenditure passed one billion
dollars, twice what it had been only ten years before. One of the
heaviest-spending categories was, as always, food; and among
the foods the processed cereals were then unquestionably the
most active promoters. Nor were the deceits and tricks of cereal
advertising, making fortunes for Post and Kellogg, too much
different from the deceits and tricks of the advertising that had
made fortunes for the patent medicine enterpreneurs. Indeed,
the old patent medicine health claims promising vitality, health,
and regularity—and as groundless as ever—were used for
Shredded Wheat, Postum, Grape-Nuts, and other new products
of the sort. Again like the nostrums, the cereals were typically
priced at many times their cost to allow heavy advertising and
heavy-profit-taking simultaneously.

But the *style* was new; it had been learned that open indifference to the public interest could lead to criticisms which were, after all, a needless bother, since they could so easily be sidetracked with a little less openness and a little more care. The false claims of the cereal advertisements characteristically were skillfully written and simply laid out, and some of them achieved the ultimate absurdity of seeming to be actually understated.

The patent medicine advertisers, whose advertising had prostituted most of the press of the nation, had never bothered with any amenities. The scare headlines about "Lost Manhood," "Deterioration of the Blood," "All Female Weaknesses," and the like, had been set forth without stint over copy composed without restraint. Compare this excerpt from a cereal advertisement that appeared not much later:

> Of course, Puffed Grains are dainties. They are light and airy, thin and flaky, with a fascinating taste. They are the food confections. But they are also more than that.
>
> Puffed Wheat and Puffed Rice are whole-grain foods, with the grains puffed to eight times normal size.
>
> They are scientific foods, invented by Prof. A. P. Anderson—a famous dietitian.
>
> They are the only grain foods so prepared that every food cell is exploded. Digestion is made easy and complete, so that every atom feeds.
>
> It's a great mistake to serve such foods infrequently. . . .

It is an interesting piece of copy, with its temperate phrasing and its modest and mysterious claim that "every atom feeds." And the intimation that the cereals are somehow good for you is very skillfully conveyed. But about the best that cereals offer is quick energy at a low cost (their place in the diet is probably most justified as an accompaniment for milk). The very first report in the very first issue of *Consumer Reports* (May, 1936) was on cereals, and from this report the intelligent buyer of the time could learn what the advertising forgot to say: namely, that Puffed Wheat and Puffed Rice were by all odds the most expensive cereals to be found in the stores and hence they provided less energy for the price than did any other cereal.[2]

The advertising industry was further restructured in 1915 with the formation of the Federal Trade Commission. Initially this had nothing to do with the protection of buyers, at least directly, but was a means of keeping the advertisers from doing each other in with unfair methods of competition. Meantime the industry had completed the creation of a new public image by installing Truth as its patron saint, guiding star, and conscience calmer. The trade paper *Printers' Ink* had got some states to pass Truth in Advertising laws, which were relatively harmless but looked good as a point of reference. The Associated Advertising Clubs of the World came together in 1911 and adopted Truth in Advertising as the moral standard to which advertising men—some cynically, some devotedly, and all ineffectually—would dedicate themselves henceforth. In 1916 the clubs came together for another meeting at which the publisher of *The New York Times*, less enchanted than they, spoke to them:

> I doubt if there is any busines in the world in which there is so much waste of money, time and energy as in advertising and its correlative instrumentalities. . . . I affirm that more than 50 percent of money spent on advertising is squandered and a sheer waste of printer's ink . . . too frequently the dishonesty stamped on its face is about all the intelligent reader discerns.

But the total advertising expenditure had by then nearly tripled since 1900, and the first of the super-media was in business—the *Saturday Evening Post*, with a circulation up from 2,000 in 1897 to an unprecedented 2,000,000 in 1917 and with

[2] In 1936 Puffed Wheat and Puffed Rice cost, respectively, $3.85 and $3.75 for a month's servings of 1-ounce portions for a family of five. When Consumers Union checked up on cereals again in 1961, these two brands had moved up to $6.75 and $6.60 respectively; but some new brands had gone on to $9, $10, and $11.

an equally unprecedented advertising income of 25 million dollars. The *Post*'s sister publication, the *Ladies' Home Journal,* had achieved a similar distinction. Cyrus H. K. Curtis, the publisher of both magazines, made plain long ago to a gathering of potential advertisers (as quoted by Frank Rowsome) the precise nature of the distinction:

> The editor of the *Ladies' Home Journal* thinks that we publish it for the benefit of American women. That is an illusion, but a very proper one for him to have. The real reason, the publisher's reason, is to give you who manufacture things that American women want and buy a chance to tell them about your products.

Even before this, *Printers' Ink* had had the perception to see that advertising's exploding force had created "a time when almost any maker of a worthy product can lay down the lines of a demand that will not only grow with the years beyond anything that has ever been known before, but will become, in some degree, a monopoly." Monopoly at this time was officially a bad word, but such was the general belief in the power of advertising to lead on to a boundless future for everybody that nobody paid much attention to that.

The structure of modern advertising was, by the time of World War I or thereabouts, complete in all essential respects; the changes since then have been mainly changes in degree, with one important exception that we will deal with soon. But the functioning and relationship, one to another, of advertisers, media, customers, advertising techniques, accepted rationales, and even referees of a sort, were patterned and balanced half a century ago pretty much as they are now.

During World War I the advertising expenditure more than doubled, and by 1929 it was up to 3½ billion dollars, which was approximately sixty-five times what it had been sixty-five years before. The notion grew in the advertising fraternity, and particularly among trade association officials and public spokesmen, that advertising was not only profitable but a sure thing; you had only to advertise, your sales would increase, and the income would pay for everything, including the cost of more advertising to produce more income, etc.

Any justifiable cost ends up being covered, of course, if the company stays in business; but the feeling about advertising was approximately that the money had only to be spent to bring its return. This notion was akin to the child's notion that living in a hotel is free because you don't pay for anything, you only sign your name; that is to say, the notion is true some of the time but times do come when it is not true. Such a time came for the advertising business, along with the economy it served, with the 1930's. But during the 1920's a bland complacency lay over everything associated with advertising and selling; the middle class (i.e., the buyers) grew apace, the poor were ignored, the country's resources were exploited right and left, and everything was lovely and lucrative.

It was a time during which the advertisers proved rather curiously the accuracy of one of Alexis de Tocqueville's observations of eighty-five years earlier in *Democracy in America*:

> . . . If I seek amongst these characteristics that which predominates over and includes almost all the rest, I discover that in most of the operations of the mind, each American appeals to the individual exercise of his own understanding alone. . . . The practice which obtains amongst the Americans of fixing the standard of their judgment in themselves alone, leads them to other habits of mind. As they perceive that they succeed in resolving without assistance all the little difficulties which their practical life presents, they readily conclude that everything in the world may be explained, and that nothing in it transcends the limits of the understanding. Thus they fall to denying what they cannot comprehend. . . .

During the 1920's the general level of evaluation of advertising was about on a par with President Coolidge's sanctification of it right in the middle of the decade. But Stuart Chase, whom we have brought to bear on these proceedings once and will have occasion to call upon again, was writing his first books. And it is a marvelous irony that at this very time one of the sharpest observers of the American scene was writing out, to a small audience, some of the most telling analyses of the selling and advertising process ever set forth. The intelligent buyer should, indeed, listen at some length to Veblen as he wrote about what was going on (and has continued to go on) in his book *Absentee Ownership*, which appeared in 1923:

> Ever since this country began to make the turn from an agricultural to an "industrial" footing, the American manu-facturing industry has been producing for a closed market. The American tariff policy also took on an aggravated form about that time, and this has contributed greatly to restrict the available market to the purchasing power of the home population, at the same time that it has enabled American special interests to maintain a high level of prices for their output. The volume of this closed market has continually grown greater, with the growth of population and the use of larger resources; but the productive capacity of the manu-facturing industries has also continually increased at a more rapid rate, due to the same circumstances and to the ad-ditional factor of a continually increasing efficiency in the industrial arts. . . . On pain of bankruptcy, therefore, it has been incumbent on these business concerns to use modera-tion and limit their saleable output to the needs of the market ("the needs of the market," of course, means "what the market will carry off at profitable prices"), and at the same time to compete among themselves for profitable sales. Any business concern's need of sales is indefinitely extensible, while the total volume of sales at any given time is fixed within a narrow margin. Salesmanship is the art of taking over a disproportionate share of this run of sales, at a profitable price. . . . The whole duty of salesmanship is to sell dear and deliver a minimum. . . .

The traditional preconception which came down from the old order of industry, under the regime of husbandry, handicraft and neighborhood workmanship, ran imperatively to the effect that human work should be of some objective human use, and it has been a slow-dying prejudice. The bias of salesmanship on the other hand is, as it has always been, to get a margin of something for nothing, and the wider the margin the more perfect the salesman's work. . . .

The business reduces itself to a traffic in salesmanship, running wholly on the comparative merit of the rival commodities, or rather of the rival salesmen. One result has been a very substantial and progressive increase of sales-cost; very appreciably larger than an inspection of the books would show. The producers have been giving continually more attention to the saleability of their product, so that much of what appears on the books as production-cost should properly be charged to the production of saleable appearances. . . .

Any concern which neglects its opportunities and falls behind is in a way to fall out of the game. The net aggregate result is a competitive multiplication of the ways and means of salesmanship at a competitively increasing net aggregate cost. The selling-cost per unit of the goods sold rises accordingly, and the price to the consumer rises to meet the enhanced selling-cost. . . .

The experience of the last few years, since salesmanship has come unequivocally to take the first place in the business of manufacturing and merchandising, has also brought out a further peculiar circumstance which attaches to this enterprise of selling goods and services in a closed market. . . . Judicious and continued expenditure on publicity and the like expedients of salesmanship will result in what may fairly be called a quantity-production of customers for the purchase of the goods or services in question. . . .

(The production of customers by sales-publicity is evidently the same thing as a production of systematized illusions organized into serviceable "action patterns"— serviceable, that is, for the use of the seller on whose account and for whose profit the customer is being produced. It follows therefore that the technicians in charge of this work, as also the skilled personnel of the working-force, are by way of being experts and experimenters in applied psychology, with a workmanlike bent in the direction of what may be called creative psychiatry. Their day's work will necessarily run on the creative guidance of habit and bias, by recourse to shock effects, tropismatic reactions, animal orientation, forced movements, fixation of ideas, verbal intoxication. It is a trading on that range of human infirmities which blossom in devout observances and bear fruit in the psychopathic wards. . . .)

Current experience in publicity appears to show that among the human sensibilities upon which a sagacious salesmanship will spend its endeavors the most fruitful are Fear and Shame. Human credulity appears to be peculiarly tractable under the pressure of a well-conceived appeal to fear and shame, and to set into obstinate and extraordinary shapes (action patterns) on relatively slight habituation along these lines.

Hardly anybody agreed with Veblen, from Calvin Coolidge (who probably had never even heard of him) to most of his fellow economists (who, however, offered him the presidency of the American Economic Association, which he rejected) to Cyrus H. K. Curtis. He was gloomy, difficult, and bitter, none of which was allowable in the 1920's; moreover, he inclined to take a very long view of things and the short view was then in fashion. He told everybody that a crash and a depression lay ahead; nobody believed that either, and two months before they came to pass, in the summer of 1929, he died.

The intelligent buyer will, of course, have no difficulty thinking up dozens of illustrations of Veblen's "fear and shame" principle; but he may have forgotten one particularly interesting example of its use which appeared in Aldous Huxley's *Antic Hay*, a book published at exactly the same time as *Absentee Ownership*. In *Antic Hay*, Mr. Boldero, an advertising man, is discussing with Mr. Gumbril, a manufacturer, how to create an advertising campaign for the latter's Patent Small Clothes, which were a kind of air-filled trousers:

"Difficulties are made to be overcome [said Mr. Boldero]. We must find out methods for bringing the weight of public opinion to bear mockingly on those who do not wear our trousers. It is difficult at the moment to see how it can be done. But it will have to be done, it will have to be done," Mr. Boldero repeated emphatically. "We might even find a way of invoking patriotism to our aid. English trousers filled with English air, for English men. . . ."

Gumbril shook his head doubtfully.

"Well, it's one of the things we've got to think about in any case," said Mr. Boldero. "We can't afford to neglect such powerful social emotions as these. Sex, as we've seen, is almost entirely out of the question. We must run the rest, therefore, as hard as we can. For instance, there's the novelty business. People feel superior if they possess something new which their neighbors haven't got. The mere fact of newness is an intoxication. We must encourage that sense of superiority, brew up that intoxication. The most absurd and futile objects can be sold because they're new."

At least, that was the way it had been. The depression changed things a bit; it was harder to sell things to people without money. But the drive to sell salable appearances was never harder. Truth in Advertising was put aside, as it would be on numerous later occasions, while with "shock effects, tropismatic reactions, animal orientation, forced movements, fixation of ideas, and verbal intoxication" advertisers tried to drum up what business could be found. Many advertisers learned for the first time that advertising really wasn't a sure thing, that it was a cost of business like other costs, and, like them, it could be cut.

By 1935 the total advertising expenditure was down to 1½ billion dollars, less than half of what it had been in dollar volume at the time of the 1929 crash. And yet in precisely these years, in a way that not even Thorstein Veblen had foreseen, advertising entered its real future and found that it worked. It found radio, that is, the first of the electronic media —the major exception that I mentioned earlier, the missing link in the structure of advertising.

While advertisers and their agents squabbled for business through the 1930's, with the worst display of morality and simple manners since patent medicine days, it gradually dawned on some of the sharper operators and more thoughtful students of the business that advertising had at last got hold of a medium to match its characteristics. The great virtues of radio, right from the beginning, were that it had the potential to deliver a truly mass audience, in a sense which excluded even newspapers; and that it could deliver this audience in a mindless state, its receptivity uncluttered by any impedimenta such as reading matter or pictures unrelated to the product.

Another truth that made itself almost at once evident was that radio's distinction as the only medium invested with a public interest was not going to get in the way of its take from the advertisers. As early as 1932, when radio advertising was still in its infancy, Arthur Kallet and F. J. Schlink saw what was happening and reported it in their famous 100,000,000 *Guinea Pigs*:

Twenty or twenty-five years ago, almost any magazine or newspaper would accept almost any advertisement. Today the majority of magazines of national circulation and most newspapers will not accept some of the worst types of medicine advertising; but they still gladly accept advertising which is both fraudulent and dangerous, if not too obviously so. For the worst types of advertising, printed

publications have been to a large extent succeeded by the
radio, a medium where anything goes, and by personal
salesmanship.

Radio embodied a curious paradox: from the advertiser's
point of view it was the most public medium, while from the
buyer's point of view it was the most private. And the popular
rebuttal that advertisers made to numerous critics of their use
of radio—namely, that it was a free country and all the listener
had to do was turn the dial—was nonsense. The fact was
and is, and it is even truer for television, that it is a very
difficult thing to turn the dial. It is not hard to move your
eyes from one column or page to the next in a newspaper or
magazine. But the mesmerizing hold of the idiot box, either
the sound-idiot-box or the sight-and-sound-idiot-box, is beyond
the capacity of most people to break easily; perhaps the relationship is too personal to be lightly broken. (The intelligent
buyer will not like to think this of himself, and my suggestion
is that he contemplate the point in the context of its application to others.)

The great force of advertising as a technique begins, of course,
with money. Advertisers, and particularly advertising agents,
are fond of referring to their trade as though it embodied
highly specialized sets of procedures or rested on very unusual
powers. But it rests first of all on the very ordinary power of
money. It is true enough that a good or ingenious copywriter
can generally achieve a greater effect per advertising unit than
a dull or routine copywriter. But this is by no means always
true; and, besides, much of the time neither the advertiser,
the agent, the copywriter, nor anyone else can tell beforehand
whether a particular advertisement is going to work or, later,
why it did or didn't. But money in advertising almost always
works, unless it is so grossly mishandled as to tax credulity.
A big, expensive campaign, other things being equal, will
dominate a small, inexpensive campaign. The exceptions to this
rule, of which there are some isolated in the annals of adver-

tising, are approximately the number required to prove it.

Beyond money, the great force of advertising as a technique is its capacity for repetitiveness, for imprinting a person's mind with something—which helps to explain why a big campaign dominates a small one. Marshall McLuhan stated the point sharply in his recent book, *Understanding Media:*

> Ads seem to work on the very advanced principle that a small pellet or pattern in a noisy, redundant barrage of repetition will gradually assert itself. Ads push the principle of noise all the way to the plateau of persuasion. They are quite in accord with the procedures of brain-washing.

In *People of Plenty,* a perceptive study of (among other more important things) advertising as the institution of the abundant society, David Potter cites a couple of well-stated observations to the same end. He quotes an English critic who complained of American periodical writing that it "fixes the attention but does not engage the mind." And this, says Potter, "is a precise statement of the advertiser's formula." Potter also recalls a sentence Walter Lippmann wrote about politics, in *The Phantom Public,* a number of years ago: "The process . . . by which general opinions are brought to cooperation consists of an intensification of feeling and a degradation of significance." The remark applies, as Potter notes, "to all communication which involves masses of people"—and hence to advertising.

Now these colorful words and phrases—"money," "procedures of brain-washing," "fixes the attention but does not engage the mind," "intensification of feeling and degradation of significance"—add up to a definition of the electronic medium, i.e., radio in the simple form in which the medium made its appearance in the 1930's, and television since the start of the 1950's. At that point in time the total advertising expenditure, fattening on the flood of consumer goods released by the end of World War II, had moved up to about 5½ billion dollars, of which TV took a negligible amount. TV has now come to dominate the advertising scene, particularly the national advertising scene, and the measures of this dominance from point to point are startling.

Within only six years of its first use as an advertising medium, TV was carrying a greater dollar volume of national advertising than all the country's newspapers or all the country's magazines. In another six years it was carrying as much national advertising as all national newspapers and all magazines put together. According to the Arthritis and Rheumatism Foundation, TV had achieved another distinction by then; the great bulk of the millions of dollars spent annually on deceitful and fraudulent advertising of worthless nostrums for arthritis sufferers was going into TV.

In 1964, the dollar value of all TV advertising was approximately 2½ billion dollars (of which all but 375 million dollars was national); and this figure is a bigger figure than the total amount of money spent for *all* advertising, national and local together, throughout the country less than twenty-five years ago.

Early hopes that TV's vast public interest potential might somehow be utilized were fairly quickly deflated. Within a few years of the medium's start, public service in any sustained or meaningful sense had had its day, and soon it was down to the ragtag level, pushed forward occasionally as a child is pushed forward to recite when company comes. TV can do better than the child, of course, since it has more money and can still deploy taste and skill on behalf of meaningful communication when it tries very hard; but the assassination of a President is a high price to pay for the expression of a medium on its highest level. Commercial TV is the subject of these sentences; educational TV is a very different thing and my strictures do not apply to it.

After ceasing to matter in general as a public service medium, TV soon ceased to matter in general as an entertainment medium, except on a level seldom before associated with the word. But while these losses were being incurred, *Fortune* could write as follows:

P. & G. salesmen are informed when they sign on with the company that "nearly one billion Procter & Gamble messages are delivered to the housewives of America each week."

And Gerald Stahl, the president of an industrial design firm, could tell the Advertising Federation of America why things weren't better than they were:

> Our dynamic market is being blocked by a barrier of consumer indifference. . . . Consumers are blocking themselves off from: a TV commercial every 1.7 seconds—totaling 18½ million TV commercials this year. . . .

The discrepancy between Mr. Stahl's figures and the P. & G. statistic can doubtless be cleared up by anyone who's interested. And while he's at it, he can extend his clarification to take care of the statistic provided by David Ogilvy in his recently published *Confessions of an Advertising Man:*

> The average consumer, poor dear, is now subjected to 10,000 commercials a year. Make sure that she knows the name of the product being advertised in your commercial. Repeat it, *ad nauseam,* throughout.

The statistics vary, but they all lead to the point, which is that television has achieved its majority as the ideal advertising medium.

It remains true, of course, that the airwaves are owned by the consuming public and that the costs of television, whether indirectly assessed through advertising or directly through the cost of electricity and set acquisition and maintenance, are consumer costs. Advertisers are there incidently as nonpaying guests in the home and are not to be obnoxious, deceitful, stupid or inane. Program content is not the creature of the advertiser, dedicated by his dictates to the lowest common denominator of mass taste. All those things are true, of course; the only catch is that nobody pays attention to them any more. The *practical* truth is that commercial TV and advertising have eyes only for each other.

And the Federal Communications Commission, charged with some surveillance of television with respect to the public interest which it is supposed to serve, has not seen fit to get in the way of this liaison. What former Commissioner Newton Minow said about television in a public speech in 1961, when he called it a "vast wasteland," could only be repeated by Commissioner E. William Henry when he assumed another rostrum in 1965. And the twelve steps that Consumers Union's Editorial Director Mildred Edie Brady recommended to the Federal Communications Commission in 1960, whereby the FCC might bring television into some semblance of its official commitment to the public interest, have none of them been taken as of this writing.

In explanation of TV's commercially glittering achievements, the colorful words and phrases mentioned earlier may be less illuminating than a set of very simple words and phrases put forth by the Television Bureau of Advertising as one reason why advertisers should buy TV time rather than, say, newspaper space. This particular reason was number five in a list of eight compiled by the Bureau, and, in its entirety, it read as follows:

> In static media, the reader must act to receive your message. In dynamic media, the viewer must act to avoid your message. In print, you must overcome the disinterest of your public before you can even present your message. In television, the audience is already watching . . . whisper if you wish.

The Television Bureau of Advertising is right, too. Most of advertising's critics, disgusted by the stridency and repetitiousness of the TV commercials for salable appearances, have missed the real point about TV advertising. So have many advertisers and advertising agents. The sales cries that grate the viewer's teeth are quite unnecessary, for the viewer isn't going anywhere. In a great many cities he has only one station to watch and in many more only two. Even where there are more, the viewer no longer bothers to switch channels to avoid a commercial, since he will only get another; and the mesmerizing hold even of what now passes for program content is too strong for most people to break by turning the set off altogether. The advertiser can whisper if he wishes; increasingly he will, and to an increasingly silent audience.

One may bow one's head in another kind of silence thinking back more to than a quarter of a century ago, when television was young and innocent, and General David Sarnoff presented it to history at the New York World's Fair of 1939:

> It is with a feeling of humbleness that I come to this moment of announcing the birth in this country of a new art form so important in its implications that it is bound to affect all society. It is an art which shines like a torch of hope in a troubled world. It is a creative force which we must learn to utilize for the benefit of all mankind. In dedicating this RCA building as the birthplace of a new American art and industry we have in mind the conception of a great service which will benefit our social and economic lives and the national ideals of our people.

The words were brave and inspiring, and they looked into a future of nobility, and they were hopelessly wrong. For General Sarnoff forgot to take into consideration how television was going to be financed and to whose uses it was going to be put.

Now that we all know, it is still possible to marvel from time to time at the extent to which the considerations apply. One occasion for marveling was provided early this year when the Columbia Broadcasting System stopped live TV coverage of the first Senate Foreign Relations Committee hearings at which this country's conduct of its adventures in Vietnam was brought under some objective, official review. The head of the CBS News Service, Fred Friendly, who had worked hard to get the live coverage on the air, protested and resigned. The CBS administration defended its action with a variety of explanations, including a lack of interest which it imputed to the daytime

housewife audience—the women in their 44 kimonos. William
F. Fore, Director of the Broadcasting and Film Commission ot
the National Council of Churches, probably got closer to the
center of things in a small insight he contributed to *Christianity and Crisis* in April of this year.

> We believe the problem lies deeper. During that week [of
> the live coverage] CBS and NBC lost $1 million each, and
> their respective affiliates another $1 million, in advertising
> income. Obviously neither network could regularly afford
> losses of that magnitude, but in light of a profit in excess
> of 20 per cent for most TV stations over the past decade,
> the question might well be raised as to whether television in
> America is licensed primarily to serve public needs and
> interests or only those of the stockholders.

But, in fact, the question has already been answered.

8

<<<<<<<<<<<<<<<<<<<<<<<<<<<<<<<>>>>>>>>>>>>>>>>>>>>>>>>>>>>>

The Hum of Destruction

THE enormously rapid growth of television advertising must be seen in the context of the growth of advertising
in all forms since the end of the war; for TV's achievement has
been on a scale so big that it must be accounted one of the
marvels or one of the follies of the century. The 5½-billion-
dollar figure for all advertising in 1950 was already double the
figure for the last year of the war. Five years later the figure
had almost doubled again, to just under 10 billion dollars,
about 6 billion of which went into national advertising and
about 4 billion of which went into local or retail advertising.
Five years later, in 1960, the total expenditure had moved
up to over 11.5 billion dollars; in 1962 it was 12.5 billion; in
1964 it was just short of 14 billion; in 1965 it reached, or
initially reached, 15 billion (9 billion for national advertising
and about 6 billion for local), and 1966 reports are that the
figure continues up. This is roughly three hundred times the advertising total of a hundred years ago, and almost thirty times

the total of 1900. Most astonishing of all, it is five times the total as recently as the end of the war.

Advertising is so much with us that we all tend to take it for granted to some degree. But advertising, to reach this status, has grown at a rate far in excess of the population, the gross national product, or even sales and profits.[1] By way of putting things in some sort of scale, the figure is now more than the whole of the U.S. export trade to Canada, the United Kingdom, France, West Germany, Italy, Mexico, the Netherlands, and Japan, which were our principal customers as of 1963. The figure is about a hundred times the Peace Corps budget as of 1965. It is more than five times our economic aid to all the rest of the world and ten times the last reported budget for the Anti-

[1] For example, *Printers' Ink* reported that between 1962 and 1963 "sales volume of the cereal industry increased from $565 million to $600 million —a gain of 6.2 per cent. At the same time the advertising investment of the industry . . . increased 17.4 per cent—from $61.8 million to $72.6 million."

Poverty Program, which is aimed at people not aimed at by advertising. The world of the advertising agent does not directly take in many of those poor people whom Michael Harrington has called "the other America."

Advertising, the tool of selling, is wholly uninterested in any who cannot buy, and is less interested in those who buy little than in those who buy much. This is not to say, of course, that advertising does not reach low-income people with its limited product news and its goads to the good life. It reaches them, all right; given the ubiquity of advertising it could not fail. But the advertiser does not invent or devise or fashion his skills with the lower-income buyer in mind; that buyer must respond to what the techniques of advertising have fashioned for his economic betters; and the reality of American life for the advertiser and the advertising agent consequently is often as much an invention as the reality reflected in a product's price. Michael Harrington told an illuminating anecdote in *The Other America:*

When I first began research on the culture of poverty in the United States, I was writing a piece for *Commentary* magazine. The article was in galley proof when I got a call from one of the editors there. Someone, he said, had just run across an analysis in *Fortune* that gave a much more optimistic picture of the income pattern in the United States. How could this be, given the fact that I was arguing that there were 50,000,000 or more poor people in this land?

I read the article. *Fortune* was using the same basic research that I was quoting. The difference was in point of view. The *Fortune* writer focused on the development of the middle third in American society—the organized worker in well-paying industry, those who benefited from rising levels of education, and so on—and there was indeed a heartening rise in standard of living for these people. Yet, in the *Fortune* analysis the bottom group was there. It was simply that these people were not commented upon.

For the whole population the U.S. advertising expenditure now figures out to about $75 per year per person—man, woman, or child. The phenomenon is not worldwide. No other country in the world is up to more than about a third of that, with the exception of our next-door neighbor and commercial partner, Canada, where the per capita expenditure is about half of ours.

Nearly forty years ago Stuart Chase and F. J. Schlink viewed the advertising of that time in their book *Your Money's Worth,* which took its chapter headings from *Alice in Wonderland.* Chapter One was headed:

> "I can't believe that," said Alice. "Can't you?" the Queen said in a pitying tone. "Try again: draw a long breath, and shut your eyes."

It was with the impact of this book that the consumer testing movement started ("O Mouse, do you know the way out of this pool?"); and one of the curious economic pictures of the last forty years is presented when the curve of advertising's growth is superimposed on the curve of Consumers Union's growth. Up until a few years ago the two growth rates made almost identical designs. The advertising curve was in billions of dollars, to be sure, and the CU subscription curve was in hundreds of thousands, but the curves themselves were very much the same. What consumer testing did was to provide a necessary and usable correction to the distortions and inadequacies and biases of advertising, as well as a kind of home base where harried consumers could rest up from the battles of the marketplace and study up for more to come. But consumer testing did nothing to halt the steady spread of commercial propaganda for products, i.e., advertising. Nor was any attempt made beyond pointing out its excesses, which grew more familiar the more advertising grew; that is doubtless one of the reasons the curves were so alike.

The economics that have prevailed for a long time now are the irrational economics of efficient waste, and any number of economists and social critics have worried over them under

one name or another (although the economists have been as
ineffectual in furthering reason as the advertising fraternity
has been in furthering truth). Endless advertising, committed
to no social objective, lacking in social responsibility, acting
on the acquisitive nature of man (and acting to inflame it
when it weakens), is a perfectly reasonable tool for that kind
of economics. One must add for the benefit of those advertising men who have not yet learned the facts of life pertain-
ing to their business and are therefore even quicker to defend
it against fancied slights than against real ones, that advertising does not *have* to be used only as an aphrodisiac for
greed; it is simply that chiefly that is the way it *is* used.

The underlying issue was stated with succinct irony only
about eight months after the great crash of 1929 by Kenneth
Burke, writing in the *New Republic:*

> The more we learn to use what we do not need, the greater
> our consumption, the greater our production; and the
> greater our production, the greater our prosperity. . . .
>   If people can be educated to the full realization of their
> function as wasters, if they can be taught to throw things
> away before they are worn out, the demand for these dis-
> carded commodities will be enormously increased, and our
> rate of production can be doubled, tripled, quadrupled,
> what you will. If people can be taught to waste enough,
> they can be kept busy for at least 18 hours a day replacing
> the wasted commodities. By this system business need
> never face a saturation point. For though there is a limit
> to what a man can use, there is no limit whatever to what
> he can waste. The amount of production possible in a prop-
> erly wasteful society is thus seen to be enormous.

The production has come to be enormous, so has the waste,
and the properly wasteful society thus would seem to have
been achieved. Or perhaps it would be safer to say only that
it is very well started; predictions have been made that we

have seen really nothing as yet. *Advertising Age*, the leading industry trade paper and an admirably thorough and straight-forward journal, three years ago quoted Arno Johnson, senior economist of the J. Walter Thompson Company, the largest of all advertising agencies, to the effect that "an advertising investment of $25 billion will be required by 1972 if the U.S. economy makes its planned advance to an $800 billion gross national product." And Mr. Johnson was quoted further in a memorable statement that the intelligent buyer will do well to keep in mind as he contemplates life and the marketplace:

The whole structure of an expanded $800 billion production economy would topple if consumer markets were not expanded to utilize what can be produced.

The intelligent buyer will note that the expansion thus called for to keep our economy from toppling has nothing to do with needs or even with wants; if necessary, the expansion will have to be rammed right down our throats.

Occasionally the buyer lags and must be prodded. In 1962, a year in which the economy and the advertising expenditure fell off slightly in their steady rise, *Printers' Ink* wrote an alarmed editorial:

Our economy will grow only in one way. People must continuously buy more goods and consume them. The only way to persuade them to buy, and consume more, is to advertise—advertise, and sell, more and more and more.

Now is the time for marketing men to speak up. They must—absolutely must—take on much of the responsibility of persuading top management why, and how, they must act.

The Macfadden-Bartell Corporation pondered this cry and found it good, although lacking a little in urgency. In a Marketing Memo, the corporation quoted *Printers' Ink's* words and then spoke up, per instructions:

It is true that there are many questions arising in national and international areas. But none of them are currently decisive or vital. They are no excuse for a summer hiatus in business, and in planning for progress.

There *were* some questions in national and international areas that year. We put our first three astronauts into orbit and the Russians put up their third and fourth; the crisis in Cuba built up and was narrowly averted; there were riots at the University of Mississippi as the drive for civil rights mounted; Pope John opened the historic 21st Ecumenical Council. But, as it turned out, all of these things were kept in their places. There was no real summer hiatus in business that year. The advertising expenditure continued up through all divertisements.

That year was also the year in which the late President Kennedy issued the first Presidential message ever given over wholly to the problem of protecting consumer interests. It was an historic statement and it reads well in counterpoint to almost any expression of the doctrine of efficient waste:

> Consumer choice is influenced by mass advertising utilizing highly developed arts of persuasion. The consumer typically cannot know whether drug preparations meet minimum standards of safety, quality and efficiency. He usually does not know how much he pays for consumer credit; whether one prepared food has more nutritional value than another; whether the performance of a product will in fact meet his needs; or whether the "large economy size" is really a bargain.

And on that note President Kennedy set forth a variety of recommendations for strengthening existing government programs and adding new ones to help consumer rights and interests; moreover, President Johnson has continued and even strengthened his predecessor's program, at least in this domestic area, whatever his performance in other areas. But the buyer does not often get support from such a high level for what John Quincy Adams once called "equity in commercial transactions." The intelligent buyer must bear in mind also that there have been consumer programs and consumer counsels in government before; significantly, there has never been a Department of the Consumer.

The distinct and pressing problems of those bulwarks of the economy, the ones who do the buying, continue now as always to be dealt with piecemeal, spread out over more than thirty different government agencies devoted largely or partly to other concerns. The government's relation to the consumer's problem still must be viewed as somewhat tangential.

In his most recent consumer statement this year President Johnson called for action on deceptive packaging and deceptive financing charges. But possibly because he was preoccupied with the more interesting deceptions in Vietnam—where our bombs were outrunning our explanations of how we were supporting freedom of choice for a people whose country we were gutting on behalf of a military dictatorships wholly committed to the denial of free choice—President Johnson forgot to mention that legislation to correct packaging and credit abuses has been waiting in Congress for years. His failure to mention Senator Hart's Truth-in-Packaging bill or Senator Douglas's Truth-in-Lending bill probably doomed both, at least for the current session of Congress.

Meantime, in opposition to the government's tangential interest and the buyer's own modest defenses, the litany of the economics of efficient waste is intoned directly and in a never-ending din. The buyer who is overborrowed to meet his installment payments, or the buyer who just plain doesn't want to buy anything for a while, or the angry buyer who can't figure out which if any of the thirty-odd government agencies in Washington he should write to find out whether he has legitimate liability claims against his new washing machine which just broke down in its third week of use—all such buyers go right on being scolded by such as Victor Lebow, the marketing consultant, who wrote those ringing words so often quoted from the *Journal of Retailing*:

Our enormously productive economy demands that we

make consumption our way of life, that we convert the
buying and use of goods into rituals. . . . We need things
consumed, burned up, thrown out, replaced and discarded
at an ever increasing rate.

The trade journals are full of such calls to rituals of waste as
Mr. Lebow seeks to convene. The subject has been dealt with
for a long time because it has been building up for a long
time. It has even been given the accolade of a philosophical
statement suggesting that existing ethical systems are no longer
adequate to the advertiser's needs. This provocative doctrine,
assuredly worth the close attention of all intelligent buyers,
was stated by E. S. Stafford in *Design News:*

Astute marketing analyses and mature management de-
cisions on planned existence-spans of products may well
become one of the greatest economic boosts to the American economy since the origination of time-payments.
Such a philosophy demands a new look at old engineering
ethics. Respected engineers have long sought to build the
best, or the lightest, or the fastest, or at the lowest cost
—but few have been called upon to provide all of this with
a predetermined life span. It is very possible that a new
factor is entering the economic scene, through the skill
of the engineer. This new factor is Time, in a new costume,
requiring new techniques, new concepts—perhaps new
ethics. . . .

A simpler man, one Mr. Henry Bertram of California, made
the point more simply to the Retail Furniture Association of
his state, as quoted by *Home Furnishings Daily:*

"Let's put a date on our furniture. Stamp the year of a
sofa's manufacture on the platform. Burn it into the drawer
of a chest."

He argued that this technique would serve as a constant
reminder to the consumer that the merchandise was growing older.

And looking ahead to the present, specifically to 1965, a vice-president of the Westinghouse Company, speaking in 1958 to his company's stockholders, told them that 10,000 dissatisfied Americans were born daily, and then added:

What's more, they are going to be dissatisfied every day of their lives. Whatever they have they are going to want more . . . 190 million dissatisfied Americans by 1965.

More recently, the doctrine of efficient waste has cast another kind of shadow across the buyer. The testers of Consumers Union began to notice it in increasingly poor workmanship in the products that the organization's shoppers bought for testing. Slipshod assembly and premature breakdown have been found particularly among the so-called durables—the washing machines, refrigerators, ranges, and the like—in which production has been booming and buying has been proceeding with commendable wastefulness, urged on by gimmicky model changes and other tricks with which all buyers are familiar.

An analysis of the repair histories of 76,000 washing machines bought by Consumers Union members over a period of eight years (1955–62) showed that nearly 46,000 had required some kind of service. The Maytag record was best; 45 out of every 100 Maytags covered in the survey had to be serviced during the eight years. The Norge and Westinghouse were the most trouble-prone of eleven other brands; approximately 75 out of every 100 owners of these two brands answered yes to the question: "Has your machine required the service of a repairman since you have had it?" Troubles showed up to some degree on all twelve brands with the first year of service, and of course they got more costly from year to year. But even in the first two years more than 10 per cent of those machines that needed service ran up bills of more than $50.

The most expensive single product that most consumers buy is an automobile. It is a complicated product, and it breaks down, and with bad quality-control at the factory it breaks down even more. All but one of thirty-two automobiles that Consumers Union purchased for testing during 1963 came down with some kind of trouble—some minor, some major, but all of it requiring repairs—within the first 2,000 miles of driving. Of the first twenty-five cars bought for the 1965 testing, all, without exception, showed troubles of one kind or another. Not a single car came through the dealer trouble-free. And see page 188 for the industry's own sad confession.

What a ridiculous record! These were not unimportant products made by fly-by-night companies on the fringe of the American economy; these came from the largest corporations in the greatest of our consumer industries. And the contempt and indifference contained in such a record are, quite possibly, getting to be as difficult for the economy and the nation to afford as the products themselves are for the buyer. On any level, too much shoddy gets to market. Too many tricks and gadgets are used to seduce the buyer; too much bad workmanship turns the seduction into rape; the beautiful and useful are besmirched and what is moral is debauched.

But the correlation between a production schedule determined by a distributing machinery designed to blast out sales at all costs and a quality breakdown within the production is perfectly predictable. Or, as Raymond S. Reed wrote in his column in *Home Furnishings Daily:*

> It's axiomatic that when [sales] volume soars, inspection slackens . . . [and] the more defective and sloppy [production is] likely to be.

Or, as *Advertising Age* reported:

> European consumers think that American products have poor workmanship and little durability—on purpose—but excel in package and product design that gives them "dressed-up practicality." . . . The "insufficient durability" of United States products is not blamed on incompetence, but on the need to keep America's industrial wheels turning by frequent replacement of their output.

Or as E. J. Tangerman wrote, on somewhat similar lines, in *Product Engineering:*

In too many fields, the distinction between [U.S.] products and European and Asiatic ones is not the one we prate about—cost of labor. It's in quality of product. . . . Says Prof. [L. V.] Colwell [of the University of Michigan], after eight months of study in Europe: "It is obvious that the United States has lost its European market for machine tools except for some gear-cutting machines and a few special types of automation equipment. Even American gear-cutting machines are rapidly being displaced by those of German design . . . most of the credit goes to superior quality, since quality, not cost, determines the relative success of machine tools in the market."

The same hold for watches, instruments, precision measuring devices, machinery and most capital goods. It seems even to have its effect in cameras, automobiles, radios, record players and other consumer items, where the purchaser is conscious of quality in results.

Or, as *Electric Appliance Service News* said, quoting Earl T. Holst, president of the National Appliance and Radio-TV Dealers Association:

[Mr.] Holst . . . on a visit to the production line of a particular manufacturer pointed to a new product and said, "The first three of those that we received didn't work." He was told that the factory knew about this, but shipped them anyway, figuring it was cheaper to repair them in the field. . . .

Or, as Francis K. Burr said in a paper presented to the American Chemical Society:

Some of the criticism which has been leveled at the clothing industry for less than satisfactory performance on the part of some of their products is due not to a lack of know-how as much as it is due to the economic and competitive pressures which frequently convince a converter or garment manufacturer to settle for something less than the best that is available.

Or, as *Refrigerating Engineering* wrote back in 1958:

> The level of performance of many products gives serious evidence of having fallen off appreciably. "Within a few years," Robert S. Geran of Kelvinator told [an engineering conference], "the average American family will have to budget $500 a year for servicing operations upon the various appliances and devices used in its home!" . . .
>
> Ours has been called an economy of waste. It is all of that.

Or, as *The New York Times* wrote at the end of this past year, reporting a speech given to the Southern Furniture Manufacturers Association by J. Paul Sticht, vice-chairman of Federated Department Stores, Inc.:

> "Perhaps the most sobering facts I can give you about quality," Mr. Sticht told the producers, "are some illustrative figures on our rate of returns on furniture—customers who send the stuff back to us, in most cases because it is faulty. At Shillito's [Cincinnati], one piece out of seven is sent back—13.8 per cent—as compared with 9 per cent on gifts, an item on which people notoriously often change their minds. . . ."

What is the intelligent buyer, and indeed what is any one, to do about this? It is a very difficult question; it is a shame that it must be asked; and it is an equal shame that there is no ready answer for the buyer. An answer is all the harder to come by because sellers often confuse the issue by acting as though they cannot hear the question. The ineffable Dr. Dichter, whose voice has been raised on so many buying and selling topics, raised it to one of its very highest pitches a few years ago when he said: "You can't buy anything bad any more." He was talking on that occasion to a group of sellers, and his point was that, since technical improvements are "universal," there is no longer any basis for sellers to compete with respect to the quality and performance of their products; they should compete in selling techniques.

The intelligent buyer knows, or ought to know, what that means. It is the call to open wide the gates to Wonderland. But then the evidences of breakdown, of the sort detailed above, are part of Wonderland already, perhaps seen through a distorting mirror. For the time being, the intelligent buyer might prefer to put such reading as this aside and seek solace and refreshment in something a long way from the marketplace—say, in D. H. Lawrence's *Studies in Classic American Literature*. This is one of Lawrence's best books, and he has some uncommonly trenchant things to say in it. For example:

> The deliberate consciousness of America so fair and smooth-spoken and the under-consciousness so devilish. *Destroy! destroy! destroy!* hums the under-consciousness. *Love and produce! Love and produce!* cackles the upper consciousness. And the world hears only the Love-and-produce cackle. Refuses to hear the hum of destruction underneath. Until such time as it will *have* to hear.

In E. M. Forster's old story "The Machine Stops," the time when the world had to hear came rather late, when the great global machine that fulfilled all human needs from light and food to automatic beds and medical care broke down. Lights dimmed; the air became foul; the automatic beds stopped functioning. Then there was darkness and in the darkness those born and raised under the machine realized for the first time that it made a humming sound. Then the hum stopped. But Mr. Forster's story goes somewhat beyond ours.

9

◄◄◄◄◄◄◄◄◄◄◄◄◄◄◄◄◄◄◄◄◄◄◄ ►►►►►►►►►►►►►►►►►►►►►►►

The Beloved Buyer
and Other Illusions

Tʜᴇ time of which Lawrence and Forster spoke has
not come. The hum is audible but does not yet afflict the hearing, and in any case is mostly lost in the more raucous sounds
of the marketplace. Having stood so much selling pressure
we can doubtless stand more, and may even stand it better
(for awhile) for having stood so much. Moreover, in the
abundant world of midcentury America there are still plenty
of resources to be wasted, and there seems to be no body of
values extensive enough or strong enough to have any real
deterrent effect on the waste. On the contrary, as we have seen,
accepted doctrine continues to speak·for the general view that
he is derelict and even immoral who gears his buying to his
needs or desires rather than to what the seller tries to make of
them. If the buyer requires an inspirational goad, he is told
to buy as an act of faith; and if he questions this he is told to
buy anyway. He is, in short, expected to shape his life and his
family's life to the buying of the products which the sellers in
this or any other technological society can produce almost

limitlessly. What one seller can do in the area of consumer goods another can generally do as well, and so arise those non-distinguishable differences on which advertising grows fat.

Voices are raised against this heavily supported doctrine and its consequences. Social critics, economists, sociologists, and such moralists as myself worry the subject from time to time. And Mrs. Esther Peterson, who is the President's Special Assistant for Consumer Affairs and a very active and knowledgeable holder of the title, spoke very sharply to the subject even as this book was being written. She was arguing for an economy which would get its direction from consumers properly trained to exercise their rights and properly informed about the processes of consumption; only trained consumers, she felt, could insure that the national resources and productive facilities would be used in "a wise, efficient and tasteful manner." The alternative, she said, was the "consumption-directed" economy, and she drew a graphic picture of it:

In a consumption-directed economy anything would be permissible. Deceptive and false advertising would be per-

fectly okay as long as it made people buy. Planned obsolescence as a means of increasing consumption would be the
rule rather than the exception.

In this kind of a system, skill, craftsmanship and quality
are unimportant. All that is important is that there be
many things to buy and that they be bought. This system
frowns on frugality and financial planning and promotes
overextended credit buying.

But the consumption-directed economy, despite Mrs. Peterson's well-mannered subjunctives, is far closer to reality than
the consumer-directed economy for which she was speaking.
It is consumption itself—the indifferent buying, wearing out,
throwing away, and using up of goods—rather than the consumer which remains the central focus of production. The
seller, making money from his production, cannot understand
why everybody shouldn't buy more and more of it ("What's
good for General Motors is good for the country"). The advertising agent, making money from the seller's account, de-
voutly holds the same view. And both look sternly at the buyer,
up to his ears in debt, and beginning to drag his feet—a sort
of market version of Lucky in *Waiting for Godot*. David Potter
has remarked the origin of the situation very clearly, although
by no means all economists agree with him:

> In a society of scarcity, or even moderate abundance, the
> productive capacity has barely sufficed to supply the goods
> which people already desire and which they regard as
> essential to an adequate standard of living. Hence the
> social imperative has fallen upon increases in production.
> But in a society of abundance, the productive capacity can
> supply new kinds of goods faster than society in the mass
> learns to crave these goods or to regard them as necessities.
> If this new capacity is to be used, the imperative must fall
> upon consumption, and the society must be adjusted to a
> new set of drives and values in which consumption is
> paramount.

It may be arguable that the U.S. society is as abundant as all this, with the median income still under $6,200 a year; and it would seem that the imperative should be modified somewhat for at least some considerable part of Mr. Harrington's "other America." For the America to which Mr. Potter's words apply, however, the fit is good and helps to show the contours of the consumer's new problem with consumption—which is that, while he ought to have an important say in the shaping of the new drives and values, he doesn't have, and increasingly he has less. In the final exchange of goods and services the seller and the buyer are seldom endowed equally at any time with the knowledge and experience relevant to fair bargaining, and the situation by now is getting out of hand.

Modern industrial technology has in two short generations sent a mass migration from the countryside into the cities. The United States, which was largely a farm population at the turn of the century, is now nearing 90 per cent urban; and this rapid and profound change of a way of life wiped out a whole backlog of familiarity with goods based on custom and lore stored up within a family. Most of the products sold now were simply unknown not so long ago; there are also vastly more of them. And how much knowledge can a buyer store up from one purchase to the next as technology or the quest for sales shifts product designs from year to year? Moreover, notwithstanding Dr. Dichter's certification of all products as good, the fact is they haven't been doing so well. The experience of J. Gordon Lippincott, an industrial designer, as he told of it in a frequently quoted article a few years ago, is unfortunately not unique:

Manufacturers have downgraded quality and upgraded complexity. . . .
My mother had the same washing machine for twenty years. She has the same refrigerator now she had when I went to high school. My own family built a leisure home five years ago . . . we're on our second washing machine

and our second dryer. They require a maintenance man once a month. We threw out the disposal. In fact, we threw out three disposals. We're on our third vacuum cleaner.

We are living in an over-gismoed culture. People today are subject to two kinds of stress. First, there's thing stress. Life is futzed up by many things, closets full of things, garages full of things. You solve this finally by hiring people —maids, maintenance men—to do things about the things. Then you get involved with people stress. . . .

I am well aware that I have been over this ground before, but this is central ground and will stand a second visit. It is profoundly important that the intelligent buyer comprehend wholly that the man whose grandfather could tell much out of his own experience about the horse he sought to buy, and also probably knew its history and genealogy and the livery man and his wife as well, now buys his car most of the time without knowing much of anything about the technology involved in it. He may or may not get a good buy; he will find out later but not from the advertising or, typically, from the salesman. And he will buy often enough from a dealer who will promptly transfer the paper to a finance company.

"Technology," as Percival and Paul Goodman pointed out in their book *Communitas*, "is a sacred cow left strictly to (unknown) experts, as if the form of the industrial machine did not profoundly affect every person; and people are remarkably superstitious about it." And the Goodmans make the implications clear:

Certainly this abdication of practical competence is one important reason for the absurdity of the American Standard of Living. Where the user understands nothing and cannot evaluate his tools, you can sell him anything. It is the user, said Plato, who ought to be the judge of the chariot. Since he is not, he must abdicate to the values of engineers, who are craft-idiots, or—God save us!—to the values of salesmen. Insecure as to use and value, the buyer

clings to the autistic security of conformity and emulation,
and he can no longer dare to ask whether there is a relation between his Standard of Living and the satisfactoriness
of life. Yet in a reasonable mood, nobody, but nobody,
in America takes the American Standard seriously.

It may be the latter fact that has saved us so far. Meantime,
the buyer has just about lost his sovereignty, i.e., his power to
function as a rationally motivated, well-informed arbiter in
the marketplace. Yet it is from the assumption of consumer
sovereignty that the free-enterprise system gets the social justification for its division of rewards for effort. Withdraw consumer sovereignty, and the marketplace becomes a jungle and
free competition a kind of warfare (in which the buyer must
listen for the warning rustle of the seller's upraised hand). But
the sovereignty has been draining away slowly over the past
seventy-five years or so, almost unperceived in the accelerated
development of modern technology.

The forced draft of advertising during the same time, had
it generated really pertinent, reliable, objective information
about products, might have helped to make up for the lost
product familiarity so that the buyer could still have functioned
intelligently in making his choices. But not even an advertising
agent will defend the worst of advertising, except as a means
of making money. And even the best of it falls far short of
giving consumers that disinterested information which alone
can help them to sort truth out of the inevitable superlatives.

Advertisers are very fond of proclaiming that whenever a
buyer purchases their products he is registering a vote of confidence in them, although they are also very fond of pointing
out that emotional and irrational sales appeals are an essential
part of the magic web that advertising spins over you and me.
But a sale achieved irrationally adds up to an irrational vote,
which is to say no vote at all so far as the product is concerned.
And, again, even the best of advertising remains partisan, in-
complete (where does the buyer learn of the product's bad

1 3 6) *Part Two:* WHEN WORDS LOSE THEIR MEANING

points?), unrealistic (with what information can the consumer compare the product with its three or thirty competitors all making similar claims?), and trivial (on what other level can two identical half dollars be differentiated?).

To the extent that advertising fails to give useful information or spreads misinformation, and to the extent that it is used to move into homes bad or dangerous products or misfits, it serves to debase our tastes, dull our judgments, and waste our resources. It is one of the inescapable findings of the disinterested and comparative product testing done by Consumers Union for nearly thirty years that advertising, to a very serious extent, does fail to give useful information, does spread misinformation, and is used to move bad or dangerous products and misfits (in one recent three-year period more than seventy appliances were rated Not Acceptable because they presented a shock hazard; the great majority of them, a meaningful portion of the appliances of all kinds tested by CU during this period, carried nationally advertised brand names). But advertising, as we have already noted, provides most of the product information that most buyers ever get; and advertising messages hit the consumer, it has been estimated, approximately 1,600 times every day.

This is probably the most stupefying statistic I know. It means that 1,600 times a day the consumer is pointed at, talked at or shouted at, diverted or cozened or lured or seduced—on TV, in the newspapers and magazines, on billboards, from cards in buses and trains and cabs and subways, in his mailbox, in telephone solicitations, on matchbooks, from river barges and blimps in the sky, in radio commercials for the captive audiences of supermarkets, and from God knows where all.

How could the consumer possibly function rationally when he is told 1,600 times a day in an endless assault upon all his senses that all products are wonderful, all are best, and why doesn't he buy, buy, buy, *buy,* BUY?

The intelligent buyer must get it perfectly clear that, by and large, the seller cannot understand why anyone should be upset about all this. It seems perfectly natural to him, for as the consumer buys goods are moved, and what the hell else is there? And if the consumer is shaped by the seller's advertising and his standards, well—why not?

We are back to the seller's contempt again; indeed, it is not easy to escape it. But it is perhaps time to make clear that the seller's view of buyers is no single thing; it has some variety, though not much, and at least in its manner of expression it runs a range, and can at times take very devious forms, as we shall see in a moment. On the simplest level, when an advertising man is talking to a convention of advertising men, as Mr. Rodney Erickson of the Universal Broadcasting Company was talking when *Advertising Age* quoted him a couple of years ago, he can get very down-to-earth:

> Forget your personal dislikes and likes and address yourself to the real audience to whom you must sell—a guy in his underwear with a can of beer, a fat dame with a 44 kimono, and two snotty-nosed, screaming kids. If you forget that picture when talking to a mass audience you are in real trouble.

When an advertising man is talking to other advertising men, but in print, as the Young & Rubicam advertising agency was talking in a house ad not long ago, he dresses up the picture some; at least he takes off the 44 kimono. The Young & Rubicam ad showed half a dozen pretty ballet dancers in the supermarket, and the copy was clean, candid, and rather more ominous than the other:

> Whose tune do they dance to? The ritual dance of the American housewife is performed before crowded shelves— stretch, bend, point, reach—every movement has as its goal the choice of a product, but, whose tune does she dance to? It is usually a tune that is running through her own head.
>
> But the words and music were written by an agency that picked the right theme and knew how to make it memorable.

When a buyer presses a seller too far—that is to say, if he so much as makes a peep—the seller can get very indignant (the operative principle is *Cet animal est très méchant. Quand on l'attaque il se défend*—This creature is very wicked. He defends himself when attacked). Here is what a department-store salesman had to say on one sore point, as reported in the trade journal *Mart*:

> These [CU] reports can be a vicious monster. Maybe up to 10 per cent of the customers have some awareness of these; but, more important, this group is growing all the time. . . . They come in armed with this thing and it is obvious that they have more information than the salesman.

The perceptive authors of *The Boss* drew a most detailed picture of the buyer as seen in ideal form by the seller. The intelligent buyer can learn much from it; he will, of course, find nothing of personal application in this portrait, but he might want to study it for what it reveals of the character of the seller:

> Man or woman, he has an insatiable desire for things. But he does not want much that is custom-made and lasting. He wants things as advertised in stock sizes and the standard range of colours which minimizes cost of production. He is guided by advertising in all media; his taste and intellectual level is that of commercial TV, mass-production newspapers and pulp magazines. His education warms him to funny brand-names, which he asks for in the shops. He never buys raw materials unwrapped, unhygienic, without a cellophane[1] cover, but, like the child who liked his milk from a nice clean bottle, not a dirty cow, he wants his goods in plastic covers. He accepts the suggestion that these goods will make him happy, successful, beautiful, handsome, popular, healthy. These are the only virtues he seeks to acquire. He will judge food by its appearance, not its taste. He will be ceaselessly

---

[1] Properly, not to give offense, Cellophane.

and expensively occupied during his leisure; on Sunday
mornings, for example, either out in his car, or involved in
some hobby, like cine-photography, which consumes a lot
of costly materials; any culture he takes in he would prefer
punctuated by advertising plugs. Having a good time will
involve paying an entrance fee somewhere. Courting a girl
will involve expensive courses of self-improvement, lotions,
unguents, apparel, and so forth—as it will involve a girl in
even more; marital happiness will be ensured by a continual
exchange of large presents, which will no doubt reach their
apogee at Christmas—but other occasions, anniversaries,
etc., will be similarly commemorated. A baby will set off a
vast cycle of consumer capital investment, precisely plotted
by the market research department. Old things will be
ruthlessly discarded; the purchase of new things will be high
on the list of good causes. While sitting about and doing
nothing is not excluded, it must be done in a hotel, holiday
camp or cruise liner far from home. What has no future
from the commercial point of view is bird-watching or
country walks. The business man can only admire the decision made in *Brave New World* to set up a conditioned
reflex against love of country walks when it was found that
this left transport and organized sport under-utilized and
uneconomic.

A fully-fleshed portrait of the buyer as the seller sees him.
And yet, despite all such things, sellers can also be quite forward, even shameless in their idealization of the buyer, particularly when they are being criticized or think they are being
misunderstood. People who make their living at advertising
get terribly uneasy when this happens, and want friends and
supporters, particularly among the paying customers. Not
being too sure of their capacity to justify much of what they
do, advertising people generally don't know quite how to deal
with criticism, and their frequent equating of criticism with

attacks on the American way of life is really an expression of this; they do not know where to begin answering a criticism, and so they do not know where to stop.

When Arnold Toynbee says he "cannot think of any circumstances in which advertising would not be an evil" and that "the destiny of our Western civilization turns on the issue of our struggle with all that Madison Avenue stands for" —as David Ogilvy quotes him in his *Confessions of an Advertising Man*—the criticism is general enough to be absorbed and even put aside with a pat on its head, which is what it gets from Mr. Ogilvy. But when a criticism gets particular and names names or promises to lead to some kind of action, why, that is all different. Advertising managers or advertising agents of large and dignified companies have been known to inveigh against government interference or "those bureaucrats" or even "those reds" down in Washington on hearing that the FTC is proceeding against them for fraudulent copy claims or rigging TV commercials or engaging in any of a number of other such common deceits.

It's too late then to say, along with Uncle Teddy, "Shabby . . . Bound to get found out." And it no longer serves, as it did many years ago, to argue that such sin is confined to fly-by-night chiselers or that "insignificant minority" which has served advertisers so well, even though it appears always to be composed of others who appear always to be absent. At the time Paul Rand Dixon took over as chairman of the Federal Trade Commission four years ago, a rundown of only the recent actions to halt misleading advertising took in such companies as General Motors, Ford, Chrysler, Colgate-Palmolive, Eversharp, Aluminum Company of America, Sears Roebuck, Standard Brands, R. H. Macy & Company, Quaker Oats, and Lever Brothers.

The feelings aroused on those occasions when Consumers Union reported that a company's product didn't pan out too well in its tests, or panned out plain badly, used to run very deep. They still do often enough, although they are not expressed so strongly any more. More than once in the old days an aggrieved advertiser, struck dumb by a Not Acceptable rating, called to announce that we were a bunch of crackpots and/or Reds and he'd have us all in jail before dusk. He never did, and the fact is he hardly ever even tried. The data of objective, duplicable tests run on bona fide samples bought anonymously at retail are very stubborn things; they cannot be shouted down and they do not change under pressure.

Over the years most advertisers came to respect, however grudgingly, an undertaking that they found to be honest and competent, however ill-begotten from their point of view. And increasingly advertisers studied the test reports and made improvements in their products accordingly (one might say that Consumers Union also helps to move goods, up as well as out). As a skeptic by instinct and training, I suspect that advertisers also weigh 1,600 advertising impressions a day against twelve issues of *Consumer Reports* a year to the conclusion that this odd organization can be tolerated—much as a Mississippi county might not mind three Negroes on the voting registration roles.

But the cruelest blow to an advertiser is a congressional investigation in the hands of a dedicated public servant, of whom the late Senator Estes Kefauver and the very much alive Senators Philip Hart and Paul Douglas are good examples. The anguish of the drug industry as Senator Kefauver and his staff built up their evidence of price gouging and all-but-incredible advertising costs was piteous to behold. And the indignation of the food industry as Senator Hart has gone about his exposure of its intricate array of packaging deceits has been equally impressive. Investigations like these can lead to laws; the laws sometimes deprive the sellers of some profitable tricks; and—but really, the sellers cry, who owns this economy anyway, who's moving all those goods?

It is at such moments that the seller sets forth to make an ally of the buyer, or at least to confuse him with love and flattery into neutrality or doubt. The advertisers and advertising agents, say the advertisers and advertising agents, are decent chaps who are, if one could only see things in the round, saving the buyer from the fuzzy do-gooders, moralists, and other woolly-minded sorts, or worse. This approach can build up to a quite considerable operation; and it might help the intelligent buyer —who sometimes, for all his intelligence, *is* confused, and most particularly by a seller's protestations of affection—to examine an example of such an operation in some detail.

One cannot properly call this advertising, but it is an extension of advertising, as war is an extension of diplomacy. And a distinguishing mark of such an operation almost always is that it exhibits the advertisers and the media in that intimacy which we all know to be but which they are usually loath to reveal. It is true enough that an advertiser may choose to exercise no direct control over an advertising medium; and it is also true that individual media may fight such an exercise if it is attempted too crudely. In the clinches, though, some things, like money or simply that intimacy already mentioned, can turn out to be thicker than integrity. Consistent with the simple purpose of this book, which is to cast light on the buyer-seller relationship in as many ramifications as possible, let us now review the recent relationship of the chairman of General Foods, a seller, and Mary Jones, a buyer.

The beginning of this story was four years ago, when Senator Hart held his first hearings on his still pending Truth-in-Packaging Bill. These hearings involved the whole food industry, and nine times out of ten an industry under legislative inquiry will get itself lined up at once to fight the threat en masse. But deceptive packaging had led into so many alleyways that the food industry couldn't pull itself together in time. The package had become an important device for diverting customers from one brand to another; big boxes contrived to hold small amounts, containers carefully designed to look like a pound while cheating the consumer out of an ounce, and other such deceptions compounded endlessly had turned food marketing into a pretty rough business. Some of the packagers themselves were more than a little harried by this rat race, and not everybody in the food industry was too unhappy when Senator Hart cast his eye in this direction and set his staff to work.

A good many buyers testified at Senator Hart's hearings, and their testimony came as a dreadful surprise to the industry. As is the sellers' wont, they had become so caught up with the fascinations of their packaging tricks that they had quite put out of mind any thought of the effect of their practices on the customers. And then, as one witness after another appeared before Senator Hart's committee to call for some action on packaging malpractices in baby foods, cereals, cooking oils, canned goods, cake mixes, detergents, frozen foods, cookies, candy, crackers, scouring pads, paper napkins, soft drinks, fruit juices, bread, toothpaste, bacon and so forth, the point got across. *Advertising Age* expressed the seller's standing objection to all congressional inquiries, but conveyed a sympathy for what was coming out, too:

> There are a good many things about governmental probes that we don't like, and we have the continuing feeling that the investigators can do better with their time and energies in most instances, than by fooling around with relatively minor points in marketing or advertising.
>
> Yet we must confess that, as consumers, our sympathy lies with the statements of Senator Hart's subcommittee which concern deception, and particularly deceptive packaging. It would be nicer, we think, to live in a simple world in which "pound" packages contained 16 oz., and not 15 or 14½; in which "quart" bottles were actually quarts, not fifths, or even maybe 25 oz.; in which packages containing the same weight or volume didn't look as though one were twice as big as another . . . and so on.

Other trade papers also had some things to say. *Food and Drug Packaging*, for example, saw the "rumblings of consumer discontent," always a touchy thing. But the food industry could get along well enough with the comments in the trade press, which don't get out to the public much. It was what happened in the public press, usually quite indifferent to complicated subjects like the economic cheating of deceptive packaging, that shocked the industry. No one could say that the nation's news services were swept off their feet, but they did report the issue. Deceptive packages were even shown before a few television cameras to illustrate what it was that consumers were complaining about.

The intelligent buyer will hardly need to be reminded that many newspaper editorials called Senator Hart silly ("our housewives are too smart to be fooled") or sinister ("regulation will curb the freedom of enterprising packagers"). But the food industry, so long accustomed to an unquestioning press, was not looking for any dialogues.

The food industry is an 80-billion-dollar industry, with more than a hundred separate national trade asociations in the food processing business alone. The structure extends down into thousands of state and local groups; and it extends up to the Grocery Manufacturers of America at the top, and on beyond to the Chamber of Commerce of the United States and the National Association of Manufacturers. But communication throughout this commercial network is effective. Any one of the component organizations, or all of them together, can be deployed against such fearsome threats as, say, Senator Hart. Local bottler associations, for example, can take over the job of talking to congressmen in their home areas while Chambers of Commerce can stir up a letter-and-telegram campaign to Washington, D.C., where lobbyists can put the pressure directly on members of the House and Senate. For an industry like food, this is standard operating procedure.

So, by the time Senator Hart was getting ready for his second round of hearings in 1963, more than a year after the first, the food industry had converted the dreadful surprise of the first hearings into a state of alert. It was opposed to *any* packaging law. And it was even more opposed to any more nonsense about its misdemeanors. It fell to the president of the Grocery Manufacturers of America, Mr. Paul Willis, to make the industry's stand clear beyond mistake to the public media.

The manner in which Mr. Willis proceeded to do this may be sampled from his appearance before a national convention of the Television Bureau of Advertising, whose use of precise English we noted at the end of Chapter Seven. Mr. Willis is a precise user of English himself. He told the television people that he was asking them to help his food industry to improve on its public image by telling, as he put it, the "whole story." He felt that the criticisms of "professional consumer agitators" had been getting too much attention on TV. He told how food advertisers had taken up their problems with a number of magazines. "We wanted to discuss with them," Mr. Willis said in an amiable voice, "the facts of life covering advertising-media relationships." Mr. Willis then went on to say the following words, as quoted by *Sponsor*, a trade journal for radio and TV advertisers:

> We suggested to the publishers that the day was here when their editorial department and business department might better understand their interdependency relationships as they contribute to the operating results of their company; and as their operations may affect the advertiser—their bread and butter.
>
> While emphasizing that we would fight to the hilt to preserve their freedom to publish material of their own choice, at the same time, we invited their consideration of publishing some favorable articles about the food industry instead of only singling out isolated cases of criticism.
>
> Certainly there are many fine things to say about this industry of interest to their readers: and as the readers turn the pages and come across an interesting article, they will react more favorably to the advertisement, and be more inclined to purchase the product.

Mildred Edie Brady, who was one of the most careful researchers and most articulate writers anywhere on the subject of the buyer-seller relationship, watched what was going on and followed it through to its conclusion. Let her take the story from this point, as she related it in a memorable article in *Consumer Reports* last year:

> [Mr. Willis] told his audience that . . . the magazine people . . . had understood. They had begun to run articles to create "a favorable public attitude" toward food advertisers. He regretted, however, that he could not say "similar nice things about the relationship of our advertisers with television." Television stations received, he pointed out, "about 65% of their advertising revenue from GMA members." These advertisers, he said, "have seen some television newscasts where they seemingly took great delight in bellowing out stories that were critical of this industry." He referred to Senator Hart's hearings specifically in complaining of critics who "used isolated cases as examples of wrongdoings and smudged the entire food industry." And he closed his remarks with a question: "What can you do additionally that will influence your advertiser to spend more of his advertising dollar with you?"
>
> The broadcasters, it appeared, knew the answer. Except for a mention on NBC's *Huntley-Brinkley Report* and a discussion on the CBS program *Calendar*, television, so far as CU has been able to find, paid no attention to the 1963 packaging hearings. On radio, only the labor-sponsored commentator, Edward P. Morgan (ABC), gave news about them. And since then, several scheduled television appearances of Senator Hart have been cancelled. "Off the record, I was told advertisers had objected," he said.

So the food industry enters the 1965 legislative year with its trade groups coordinated and the news media under control. A new phase begins in the campaign against a deceptive packaging law. An article in a recent issue of *Look* may suggest what this new phase is.

Look was named by GMA's Paul Willis, along with

Reader's Digest, Life, Saturday Evening Post, Ladies' Home Journal, Good Housekeeping, and others, as being among the magazines whose editorial departments had agreed to cooperate with food advertisers. In the January 26, 1965, issue, *Look's* editorial pages displayed the by-line of an advertiser, Charles G. Mortimer, Chairman of General Foods Corp., as the author of an article, "Let's Keep Politics Out of the Pantry."

Mr. Mortimer's essay elaborates familiar themes. He salutes the American housewife, whom he calls Mary Jones. He finds her a shrewd and happy woman—shrewd because "when it comes to clever buying" she "can give lessons to a Yankee horse trader" and happy because "she takes it for granted that what she has bought is the purest, most nutritious, easiest-to-prepare food the world has ever seen." He pays handsome tribute to the laws safeguarding our food in making his point about how confident Mary Jones can be when she shops, evidently assuming her (and the reader's) unawareness of the fight the food industry waged against the passage of the very laws he praises. (Recorded against his own company, incidentally, are 28 violations in the last 25 years against one of those laws, the Federal Food, Drug and Cosmetic Act.)

What disturbs him deeply, Mr. Mortimer writes, is that "Mary Jones probably does *not* know" that her great good fortune as a food shopper results from "the machinery of free competition"—a free competition that is "the heart of our free-enterprise system." The sophisticated reader will find Mr. Mortimer's eulogies to competition even more intriguing than his fond protestations on behalf of existing governmental regulations over food. For he is, after all, the chairman of a food combine that is the nation's largest and a prime example of what the Federal Trade Commission has called "economic power and market concentration created by the great merger movement." General Foods was created in the 1920's by mergers; it grew into a huge empire by still other mergers (it markets 250 products); it is currently challenging an FTC order, issued under the anti-monopoly law, to dissolve a more recent merger; and the earnings from its many merger-acquired companies are such that it commands over $100,000,000 worth of market-manipulative advertising power a year.

Yet the chairman of the General Foods Corp. finds competition endangered by, you guessed it, Senator Hart. The sequence of his thought gets a bit fuzzy as he develops that idea. It seems to go like this: Competition is good. The food industry has made Mary Jones happy and that is a good thing. So the food industry is good. Therefore the food industry is competitive. Ergo anything that might upset Mary Jones is an attack on competition. And that is what "some Government officials . . . 'playing politics in the pantry' " are up to. They are causing "consumers to question the very system the Mary Joneses of this country find so satisfactory." Esther Peterson, the President's Special Assistant for Consumer Affairs, is the only government official named, aside from Senator Hart. When she urged housewives to send in complaints to her, she "created doubts in the minds of consumers where none had existed," thereby threatening the happy, but apparently fragile, confidence of Mary Jones. Senator Hart's threat is, of course, Truth-in-Packaging.

After the article appeared, Senator Hart wrote to *Look*'s publisher and editor-in-chief, Gardner Cowles, pointing out that the legislation had been inaccurately described, suggesting that there was another side to the packaging issue, and asking whether he (Senator Hart) might not be given the opportunity to clarify some of these matters for the readers of *Look*. Mr. Cowles replied, saying: "I will be interested to see how much attention the general public pays to this subject in the next several months." If interest should prove high, he might consider asking the Senator to do something on the subject, he indicated. He went on to say, however:

"It is my present guess that the public does not feel any strong need for reform in the area Mr. Mortimer was discussing; but I could be wrong."

Look added a final fillip to its latest venture into cooperative publishing by taking full-page ads in other magazines, including a number of the trade journals read by GMA members, to publicize its sponsorship of "this compelling article." And very likely *Look* will pull out the plums that go with being such a good boy. The comic opera aspects of Mr. Mortimer's overtures to Mary Jones and *Look's* unabashed exploitation of them, however, cannot lighten the somber implication of this story for our times.

Under such a story as that, Lawrence's hum of destruction sounds a little louder. It might even reach a seller's ear. Moreover, the proportions of propaganda, paid or free, to other commodities in a modern publication have been worked out rather carefully, with an eye not so much to the buyer's interest as to the seller's; and the seller may lose something in the end if he weights this proportion with *too* much contempt for the buyer. Marshall McLuhan gives one interesting explanation of why this might be so in *Understanding Media*:

> The ads are by far the best part of any magazine or newspaper. More pains and thought, more wit and art go into the making of an ad than into any prose feature of press or magazine. Ads are *news*. What is wrong with them is that they are always *good* news. In order to balance off the effect and to sell good news, it is necessary to have a lot of bad news. Moreover, the newspaper is a hot medium. It has to have bad news for the sake of intensity and reader participation.

If the seller is going to tamper with the components of his medium, he will be better advised to follow the lead of the ingenious Interstate Drug Exchange, Inc., a wholesale drug distributor. The Exchange, in a promotion leaflet, was describing some of the selling virtues of its soft gelatin capsules for standard medications. "Not the least benefit derived," the leaflet read, ungrammatically but clearly, "more 'sophisticated' patients are unable to recognize standard medication in this new dosage form." But the point of the soft gelatin capsule is that it deceives by concealing totally. For all the pains and thought, for all the wit and art, that go into the making of an ad, they are almost never enough to conceal totally when the ad takes the form of free propaganda as it did in Mr. Mortimer's ardent plea to Mary Jones.

10

<<<<<<<<<<<<<<<<<<<<<<<<<<<<<<<< >>>>>>>>>>>>>>>>>>>>>>>>>>>>>>

Truth in Advertising
and Still More
Illusions

Somewhere, in one city or another, at some convention, the call to Truth in Advertising is undoubtedly being
sounded again, possibly at this very moment. "This abstraction
called truth," as it was described in an Advertising Truth Book
issued by the Advertising Federation of America a few years
ago, is being searched out once more; eminent advertising men,
like the publisher of *The New York Times* fifty years ago, are
reproaching their colleagues; and the trade papers are duly reporting the new development for the younger advertising men
to read and nod and shake their heads over. The thought of
this well-routinized performance, the motions of which have
been so gravely gone through so often, is touched with humor
and sadness and obscenity.

The typical advertising man puts Truth on a pedestal; his
voice shifts into a slightly lower register when he speaks of it;
he becomes a little self-conscious, and in general is apt to act
somewhat like a schoolboy in the presence of mysteries with
which he is not yet familiar, a fair enough parallel for the

advertising man and Truth. Examples of this syndrome abound. Mr. Walter Weir, chairman of the executive committee of West, Weir & Bartel, a major advertising agency formerly known as Donahue & Coe, and the author of a recent book called *On the Writing of Advertising*, provides a representative set of sentences:

> The "appeal" employed in advertising is by itself insufficient; it must be clothed in and fortified by truth; it must, in short, be believed or nothing will result from its having been made. This seems so elemental I ask myself why I bother to voice it.

But this is not elemental; this is sub-elementary, and meaningless to boot. Mr. Weir proceeds from the apparent idea that truth is rather like some kind of protective plastic to be draped over the "appeal"; and he goes on to suggest that truth and believability are the same thing. An advertising man, above all, should know that this is not so. Truth is often unbelievable, and believability can be compounded of almost anything, depending on the skill of the copywriter and the ignorance of the reader.

Let us see what Mr. Rosser Reeves has to say on the subject. Mr. Reeves is chairman of the board of Ted Bates & Company, even more noted as a copywriter than Mr. Weir is, and one of the industry's most acclaimed masters of the hard sell. Mr. Reeves also wrote a book recently, called *Reality in Advertising*, and in it he set down the following (among many other things that will amuse, interest, and instruct the intelligent buyer):

> The public (which has absorbed an enormous amount of misinformation about the advertising business) believes that an advertising man can tell almost any lie and get away with it. The exact opposite is true. Such a course leads, at the least, to wasted money and, at the most, to commercial suicide.

I do not know that an advertising man can get away with "almost any lie." There may be some that would not work. But if a lie means a statement that imputes to a product a characteristic or level of performance that it does not have, then the public is, as it often is, quite right. One thinks of mouthwashes, into the advertising of many of which very much money has gone over the years and out of the advertising of which many lies to the buyer and much profit to the seller have come; and of hundreds of brands of soaps and cosmetics, ditto; and of those breakfast cereals of which we have already spoken, ditto; and of stereo phonographs which could not and did not deliver stereo sound, ditto; and of a great variety of proprietary drugs, ditto; and of numerous flimsy and poorly performing appliances, ditto; and of dozens of worthless reducing preparations, ditto; and so forth.

One of the broadest and most irresponsible affronts to Truth in Advertising has been the enormous campaign of mendacity and misinformation which the cigarette companies have mounted without letup, year in and year out. The exploits of the industry in subverting "this abstraction called truth," while fighting off the efforts of government and many parts of the medical profession to bring the industry's irresponsibility under some control, will be examined at length later on (see Chapter Thirteen). Meanwhile, it must be noted that if the public believes an advertising man can tell almost any lie and get away with it, the public has good and sufficient reason for its belief in the advertising of the cigarette industry alone, not counting all those others. Such naïve declarations as those of Mr. Weir and Mr. Reeves, set against the untruths and immoralities of half a century of highly profitable cigarette advertising, seem faint and distant and not so much untrue as unreal.

Against the background of decades of simply nonsensical cigarette advertising, and in the light of the more serious affront to health and morality of the past ten years or so, some advertising men themselves could no longer stomach the spectacle. Mr. Emerson Foote, one of the most eminent of advertising agents, resigned from the McCann-Erickson agency and joined the

National Inter-Agency Council on Smoking and Health to try
to do something about smoking. (He failed rather notably, as
Chapter Thirteen makes clear; but he did join the fight.) And
Mr. David Ogilvy, whose *Confessions of an Advertising Man*
we have already mentioned, spoke up on television to the following effect:

> I see the handsome athletic young man drawing in a mouth-
> ful of cigarette smoke and then inhaling it down into his
> lungs, and I'm appalled to think that I belong to the pro-
> fession which can perpetrate that kind of villainy. I see
> other cigarette commercials, which are written by what we
> call in our business "weasel merchants," which are essays
> in the art of casuistry. They are intellectually dishonest
> and the men who wrote them and who paid for them
> know it. . . .

But David Ogilvy, a more sophisticated man than Walter Weir
or Rosser Reeves seems to be, seems in turn to be a little too
sophisticated when he comes to confront the issue of truth in
his book. "Is advertising a pack of lies?" he asks himself and
his reader. "No longer," he says, thus rising above the appalled
state in which he viewed cigarette advertising on the television
program. Mr. Ogilvy also asks, "Is advertising a vulgar bore?"
He then quotes from a *New Statesman* article by C. A. R.
Crosland:

> [Advertising] is often vulgar, strident and offensive. And it
> induces a definite cynicism and corruption in both practi-
> tioners and audience owing to the constant intermingling of
> truth and lies.

"This," says Mr. Ogilvy, "is now the gravamen of the charge
against advertising among educated people." Whereupon Mr.
Ogilvy says not another word about the lies and confines the
remainder of his comments to "tasteless typography, banal
photographs, clumsy copy, and cheap jingles," which he finds to

be the province of television. And thus he concludes that it is television advertising "which has made Madison Avenue the arch-symbol of tasteless materialism."

But what happened to Mr. Crosland's lies, which are part of the gravamen? Mr. Ogilvy has perhaps forgotten on page 162 of his book one of the rules which he enunciated on page 130: "Compromise has no place in advertising. Whatever you do, go the whole hog." It is my opinion that Mr. Ogilvy, who is considered one of the industry's outstanding copywriters and agency executives and has been around for a long time, does not go "the whole hog" here not because he cannot follow the animal but precisely because he does belong to the profession.

Things come through more clearly elsewhere in the book, where he approvingly quotes Dorothy Sayers as saying:

Plain lies are dangerous. The only weapons left are the *suggestio falsi* and the *suppressio veri.*[1]

Lies, a blunt Anglo-Saxon four-letter word, thus yields to sounds more graceful, and Mr. Ogilvy, a book writer of charm and obviously a first-rate copywriter, comments winningly:

Surely it is asking too much to expect the advertiser to describe the shortcomings of his product? One must be forgiven for putting one's best foot forward.

One of the numerous objections to such a pliable philosophy as Mr. Ogilvy's is that an advertising man's foot too often ends up on the buyer's toes. An additional objection, as we learn from another television appearance of Mr. Ogilvy, is that he doesn't seem able to tell his feet apart, which may end by tripping the buyer if not Mr. Ogilvy. When he told the TV audience that he was trying to "state the case factually for my

[1] The late Max Radin, a well-known professor of law, took a sharper view of this loophole in his book *The Lawful Pursuit of Gain:* "There are those less obvious forms of falsehood which in casuistry and in law are called the *suppressio veri* and the *suggestio falsi,* concealing the truth and hinting a lie, methods which certain types of advertising have carried to a pitch of skill and success that leaves us breathless."

product," Mr. Albert G. Seidman, an attorney for the Federal Trade Commission, protested, "but you don't tell the faults about your product." "My products," said Mr. Ogilvy, going the whole hog, "have no faults."

It is plain to see that this year's call to Truth in Advertising will have obstacles to surmount, big and small, hard and soft, sharp and diffuse, and, in the end, too much for the crusade, as always. The record of Truth in Advertising is (in truth) a poor, sad thing and offers little hope to the buyer. Some very intelligent buyers may remember that the Truth-in-Advertising section of the Federal Trade Commission Act was put into the Act in 1938. It may be useful to remind the buyer, who may have forgotten, how this addition came to be made. The Federal Trade Commission had started an action against the Raladam Company, which made a reducing nostrum called Marmola—one of the prewar equivalents of Regimen. One of the reasons for the action was that a number of doctors had found that Marmola was widely injurious to health. The Raladam Company, never having heard of Mr. Reeves's thesis that lies in advertising do not work, had fought the case through the courts. Blake Clark, whose book *The Advertising Smoke Screen* was a relatively early attempt to bring light into the buying-selling relationship, reported the verdict in the case and some of the consequences:

> Raladam won the case before the Supreme Court on the grounds that, although Marmola may have hurt many a customer, it had never hurt a competitor, since claims made for all rival products were equally false! . . . The Wheeler-Lea Amendment was then passed, giving the FTC the power to act in the public interest as well as in the interests of business. Passage of this amendment had an immediate effect upon the nature of the claims made in advertising copy. . . . Before 1938, "Lawyer Ross Eases his Throat Instantly and Wins his Case," thanks to Bayer Aspirin. Now, Bayer advises him to see his doctor if his cold persists. . . .

The intelligent buyer may remember also that 1938 was the year in which the FTC set out after Fleishmann's Yeast, which had been making a joke of truth with its profitable plays on the fond and foolish fears of adolescents for more than a decade. But it was not until 1947, by which time Fleishmann's Yeast had exploited the young for twenty years, that the agency got the company to stop its false advertising.

Further changes have been made in the FTC's structure in recent years, and the agency now works somewhat faster. In 1960 it issued a complaint against Colgate-Palmolive (one of Rosser Reeves' accounts) for faking a Palmolive shaving cream commercial on TV. The FTC finally got this action through, too —the Supreme Court upheld it, early last year, approximately five years after the complaint was issued. At the time the complaint was filed, *Advertising Age* reported that Mr. Reeves's agency, which was having other trouble with the FTC over Colgate's Gardol toothpaste and Life cigarettes and with a broadcasting review board over Preparation H and with the Supreme Court over Carter's Little Pills, was "estimated to be reshooting or to have reshot more than 100" of its TV commercials. But an official of the agency said this number was exaggerated.

It would seem quite an achievement, however, to have been possibly false and misleading in seventy-five or even fifty commercials all at once, particularly in an agency whose chairman does not believe that this sort of thing works.

It is very likely that the advertising business aims too high and in the wrong direction when it aims for truth, particularly since it never seems to catch it. "The object of advertising is to sell goods," said Raymond Rubicam a quarter of a century ago. "It has no other justification worth mentioning." Raymond Rubicam is one of the most respected of advertising agents; he was one of the founders of Young & Rubicam, although he has not been active in it for some years; no less an authority than David Ogilvy ranks him as the greatest living copywriter. Accepting his definition, the intelligent buyer may hope that other and lesser advertising men will some day come to limit their frequently too sanguine claims for their trade.

It is not a profession, since it calls for no specialized training. It is not, most certainly, a scientific discipline. To whatever extent it is an art, it is an art of surfaces, and transient ones at that. It is not really a medium of news, except on those rare occasions when it is used straightforwardly to convey meaningful information, and even then, as Mr. McLuhan has pointed out, the news is never other than good. It is obviously not the sire of modern technology, and it is only one of the consequences. Finally, it is not a part of the institution of education, as advertising men like to think of it almost above all.

That famous advertising man, Dickon Clissold, stated the case for this concept about as well as it could be done, and it does not stand up. This is how he put it to his brother Billy in H. G. Wells's novel *The World of William Clissold:*

> "Advertising; what is it? Education. Modern education, nothing more or less. The airs schoolmasters and college dons give themselves are extraordinary. They think they're the only people who teach. *We* teach ten times as much. . . .
>
> "Schoolmasters! What do you mean by education? When you get down to hard tacks. Just old-fashioned, primitive advertisement done by word of mouth in a room! Why! a classroom schoolmaster teaching by shouts ought to be as out-of-date nowadays as a town-crier!
>
> "The only use I've got for schools now is to fit people to read advertisements. After that, *we* take on. Yes, we—the advertisers. You may laugh, Billy; it's true. All new ideas come as a shock at first. Don't just laugh at it like that. Don't sit like an oaf and grin. Tell me what's wrong with it. . . .
>
> "Why, Billy! Look at things plainly. With all reverence—"

He adapted his ruddy face roughly and quickly to express all reverence. It was just an habitual concession unnecessary in my case.

"What were the twelve Apostles? Drummers, just drummers. Travelling in salvation. Introducing a new line. Why did Paul raise his voice at Athens? Because he hadn't a megaphone. And the miracles they did? Sample bottles. To this day it's advertisement. What is a wayside crucifix?— an advertisement of faith. What is Christianity?—an advertisement campaign. Tell 'em. Tell 'em. Tell 'em all you can. It's the method of social existence."

He turned to biology, to the poetry of life.

"The very flowers by the wayside, Billy, are advertisements for bees!"

My grin armed the fighting spirit in him.

"Vulgar you think it is?"

"Frightfully."

"If there's anything vulgar about modern advertisement, Billy, it's because it's been so concerned about pills and soap and pickles. Just a passing phase. . . ."

But the phase continues, and when all is said, one must still speak of the single justification for advertising that is worth mentioning. No one can reasonably expect the whole truth from a man engaged in selling; by definition (to say nothing of Mr. Ogilvy's astonishment that anyone should expect him to tell the whole truth about his product), truth and the selling of goods just don't go together. Certainly the intelligent buyer doesn't often expect truth (except, and at best, in a very narrow sense) and he doesn't often get it from a 15-billion-dollar institution indifferent to all values save one and wholly dedicated to the movement of goods at a profit. But how has the single legitimate justification of the advertising business come to spawn so many illegitimate children?

When Raymond Rubicam was defining advertising's aim a quarter of a century ago, Neil Borden of the Harvard Business School—who is to the economics of advertising roughly what Raymond Rubicam is to the creativity—was reviewing the state of the advertising business as it was recouping from the depression of the thirties. This is what Professor Borden said in his study, entitled *The Economic Effects of Advertising,* published in 1942:

> Advertising is under fire. Its adverse critics come from many camps and their complaints tend to become increasingly vehement. Certain economists complain that its extensive use involves undue cost and is a bar to free competition, with a resultant adverse effect on the operation of the free price system. Home economics teachers charge it with being a poor guide to consumption. Students of ethics accuse it of showing frequent display of poor taste and misrepresentation. Business men themselves have not infrequently doubted its effectiveness for business purposes.

Looking into these criticisms, Professor Borden arrived at a number of conclusions, including these:

> The overall effects of advertising on total distribution costs cannot be traced. . . .

> It is impossible from cost data to trace a clear causal relationship between decreased production costs and advertising. . . .

> Businessmen in their efforts to maximize profits often are inclined to try to put off entering into active price competition. . . .

> The evidence shows that advertising has contributed to price rigidity. . . .

The intelligent buyer will, or should, note some things about this statement and the conclusions. The writing isn't very sharp; that is to say, no copywriter would write them this way. This is exposition rather than writing; the words say some relatively straightforward things and they say them in a relatively straightforward way. There are awkward phrases, such as "resultant adverse effect," which no copywriter ever would let by. On the other hand, the words and phrases deal with a situation which no copywriter ever would see or comprehend, let alone deal with.

It is a point possibly worth making that the creative people in advertising, such as Ogilvy, Reeves, Weir, and others, are the ones who generally write the books about the business and they are also the ones who usually are least attuned to the consequences of what they are doing. For Marshall McLuhan was perfectly correct in saying, some pages back, that "more pains and thought, more wit and art go into the making of an ad than into any prose feature of press or magazine." As an exercise in the simple mechanics of writing, the job of a copywriter can be an arduous and absorbing one; it also tends to overwhelm him with details and specifics. The workings of advertising as a social force to a person who is concerned with advertising mainly as a means of expression may come through very vaguely if at all when he writes his book.

On this general head, the intelligent buyer may be interested in the review of the Reeves and Weir books written for *Consumer Reports* by John Brooks, well known for his *New Yorker* reporting on Wall Street and business doings, and a good novelist besides. Mr. Brooks, having noted that Mr. Reeves "makes no bones about taking a pragmatic view of his business" and that Mr. Weir "is almost pathetically anxious to make advertising become more intellectual and respectable," goes on to report certain interesting similarities that he found in the thoughts and thought habits of the two well-known advertising men:

> Both profess love of and respect for words, yet both have a tendency to use words barbarically. . . . On the problem of deceptive advertising, both argue against it (defining deception somewhat differently) on the ground that it does not work; this, of course, makes it logical to suppose that if at any time they found deception working, they might then be in favor of it. And both seem to make an exceedingly modest appraisal of the intelligence of the consumer. . . .

Both writers, near the end of their books, go a long way toward undercutting their basic theses—Mr. Reeves by suddenly arguing that advertising can hardly be considered a menace by anyone because its influence is not all that great, and Mr. Weir by defending advertising on the old familiar ground that it caters to public taste and can give the people no better than they deserve. One ends up feeling that behind Mr. Reeves' aggressiveness lurks a certain defensiveness; behind Mr. Weir's defensiveness, a certain aggressiveness; and the meat of the matter has escaped them both.

It takes someone like Professor Borden, who probably could not care less about a copywriter's sanction, to get to the meat of the matter—to state the issues and explore them to some conclusions. And so his were statements of some importance from a man respected in the business when the business was about a tenth of its present size but already exhibiting its unsocial qualities. In the bulk of the study from which these excerpts came, Professor Borden was at pains—an economist's rather than a copywriter's pains—to justify advertising reasonably against its critics. But at about the same time, Albert L. Meyers, senior economist for the U. S. Department of Agriculture, an expositor rather than a writer, just like Professor Borden, was carving into the meat of the matter right to the bone. No one before or since has put the matter more sharply, although dozens of economists and writers have put it more fully, more elaborately, and more elegantly. This is what Albert Meyers said in 1941:

Under monopolistic competition the individual firms generally attempt to expand their sales by increased advertising and selling expenses rather than by lowering their prices. This is often the wisest policy from the viewpoint of the individual firm, but it has serious consequences for the economy as a whole. The firms which survive and expand do so not so much because superior efficiency allows them to undersell their competitors but rather because superior advertising and selling methods and greater appropriations enable them to gain and hold customers. From the point of view of the general public, selling expenses which serve merely to entice customers from one seller to another are an economic waste.

We have been living with that economic waste for a long time now, except that everything contributing to it has been scaled up many times since Dr. Meyers wrote. The intelligent buyer will have noticed the increase in scale, for he will have borne the brunt of the effects; and from his own loss of sovereignty in the marketplace, as set forth in the last chapter, he will know that the trouble with things runs far deeper than "tasteless typography, banal photographs, clumsy copy, and cheap jingles."

Advertising, a legitimate mover of goods, has not spawned its illegitimacies because of its vulgarities or even its lies. For it is a curious truth that we tolerate on the part of sellers what we would deny to beggars—displays in public, however uncouth, of the agonies associated with decayed teeth, indigestion, constipation, dripping noses, acid stomachs, blinding headaches, infected sinuses, ingrown toenails, and itching piles. And in the midst of contributing to the drives of the American Heart Association and the American Cancer Society we continue to blink blandly at the healthy young lovers strolling through springtimes of cigarette smoke on the TV screen and to study gravely the code-approved magazine advertisement showing the vigorously healthy outdoor sportsman enjoying, for example, "Camel's real taste."

But the intelligent buyer knows that this is only the visible part of the burden. He comes closer to its base when he struggles through a big supermarket where, on an average, 5,000 to 8,000 brands, sizes, and models of products are on display, many of them competing with each other within one seller's line. Here is the veritable debauchery of the gains that mass production and mass distribution made possible. The necessarily self-serving, widely misleading, and vastly mesmerizing output of product persuasion that works on the buyer before he gets to the store thus prepares him for the chaos of the meaningless product differentiation and the salable but indecipherable containers once he gets there. And yet, as we all know or ought to know, the proper functioning of our economic system depends on the wisdom of informed consumer choices in the marketplace. We are skating on thin ice, which is what Professor Borden was saying in part and Dr. Meyers was saying in full twenty-five years ago, when the ice was thicker.

The situation is not going to be cured, or even appreciably modified, by this year's Truth-in-Advertising campaign. It would not be cured, although it might be somewhat modified, even if buyers were to act in appreciable numbers on the advice given many years ago by Mr. H. A. Batten of N. W. Ayer & Sons, Inc., one of the country's most important advertising agencies. Mr. Batten was quoted as follows:

> "Even a brief excursion through the advertising pages," Mr. Batten said, "is, for the advertising man who respects his calling, a disheartening experience." And the only way to put an end to advertising which, he said, was "a stench in the nostrils of the civilized world" was for consumers to refuse to buy the advertised products.

Nor is the situation going to be cured or modified by hiring Dr. Dichter to probe a new substratum of consumer motivation, for example, or even by giving the Federal Trade Commission and the Food and Drug Administration more of the budgets they need than they usually get. No such action will equip the buyer to deal importantly better with the seller's endlessly growing power or to play the socially necessary role of umpire in a game that is getting to be almost unplayable for the lack of an umpire—a truly sovereign buyer.

There was a time, about one hundred fifty years ago, when groups gathered in small halls here and there across the country to discuss the lack of standards in quality, the lack of credit at non-usurious rates, the lack of meaningful labeling, the lack of resources to establish and enforce standards of quality and performance, and, finally, the lack of any disciplined effort to enhance our national standard of living. These gatherings were called Agricultural Societies. We were then, as we remained for another century, largely a country of farmers—pioneers whose knowledge of credit, soils, seeds, markets, husbandry, hybrid species, and so on, was woefully limited. Out of those gatherings developed the United States Department of Agriculture, whose far-flung activities eventually touched and influenced the life and living of nearly every farmer. But it was not until the Department of Agriculture was established as a branch of the federal government that we were able to make that remarkable collective effort in the production of farm goods that has been, and still is, the envy of the world.

The moral, I trust, is clear. But the achievement may be some way off. Meantime, we might try another approach. Suppose, through legislation and trade practice, we could adopt the principle that any and all sales claims or inducements to buy be constituted precise warranties to the buyer, firmly enforceable through the courts of the United States? This would have the effect of making a seller, in effect, put up or shut up, whether he were selling a mediocre Edsel car aborted from a misinterpretation of consumer motivation at a cost of a quarter of a billion dollars, or a table of fake wood veneer offered as something it isn't to an uneducated resident of East Harlem.

There are no reasonable grounds in a modern industrial system for the *caveat emptor* philosophy, which was beginning to lose its relation to reality by the end of the nineteenth century. Only a *caveat venditor* philosophy fits the reality of the second half of the twentieth century. For a buyer cannot be required to beware if he has no way (or at least no adequate way) of knowing what to beware of. It is the seller who has (or has access to) that knowledge now. *Caveat venditor*. Nor is this so radical an innovation as it might at first appear. We have already accepted as reasonable and necessary the seller's responsibility in the processing of foods and drugs when there is a hazard to life. We have gone further. We require in many cases a full disclosure of ingredients. And recent legislation under the federal Food, Drug, and Cosmetic Act has shifted the burden of proof of safety from the enforcing agency to the producer.

To be sure, the extension of *caveat venditor* to all goods and services, covering economic cheats as well as threats to life, covering all of those lies that Mr. Reeves says don't work and hence would not be missed by sellers, would take us a long step from where we are. Still, it would be a step along the way so gingerly entered upon—if the phrase is not too strong—at all those conventions where Truth in Advertising has been so loudly hailed. The fraternity of sellers may have these proposals for free. Perhaps they can use them to devise a Truth-in-Advertising campaign with a couple of teeth in it—a novel thought. The rational consumer just might follow.

Part Three

‹‹‹‹‹‹‹‹‹‹‹‹‹‹‹‹‹‹‹‹‹‹‹‹‹‹‹‹‹‹‹››››››››››››››››››››››››››››

Pride and Prejudice

11

‹‹‹‹‹‹‹‹‹‹‹‹‹‹‹‹‹‹‹‹‹‹‹‹‹‹‹›››››››››››››››››››››››››

The Good Life
and the Added Value

CAVEAT VENDITOR, in all likelihood, is not just around the corner; Truth in Advertising will no doubt continue toothless; and the rational consumer will have to wait in the wings (they are somewhere around the corner). The mixture, in short, will probably continue to be as it has been through all the period we have been surveying. And the advertising fraternity will continue, as before, to veer between the stance of a misunderstood innocent and the stance of a repentant sinner. In one position or the other, the advertising man has generally been found ever since the first popular revulsion to his methods brought into force the first laws against advertising's excesses.

Out of much practice in these roles and in making quick transitions from one to the other, many advertising men have developed remarkable capacities at a kind of emollient logic to serve their need. For example, they sometimes argue that the buyer has become so accustomed to exaggeration and deceit that he discounts all claims, hence honesty and candor would not be rewarded in the marketplace, and so it is asking too much to ask advertising to practice them. Or they will protest that advertising is a profession or even maybe a science or that it at least operates by rules and meaningful codes, but that it should not, God forbid, be regulated by the states or the government or anyone because its practitioners are artists and can't be regimented. On the one hand, an advertising man may contend that advertising is a means of informing the buyer so that he can exercise his freedom of choice; and, on the other hand, he will defend, for example, the widespread system of spiffs or push-money that succeeded in corrupting the retail store clerk (once viewed with some justification as impartial or even as the buyer's friend) into a pusher for whichever product the advertiser had given him the money to push. The adman will argue that this is necessary and useful to move goods, which is what provides the good life.

Advertising's contribution to the good life has worried, bedeviled, and aroused hopes and fears in advertising men from the beginning of the business. Their hope that there is such a contribution and their fear that the contribution isn't really very much constitute the basic conflict of the advertising man, and probably do most to explain the almost ceaseless self-justifications to be found in the odd literature of advertising. Thus Dr. Ernest Dichter, in commenting on what he felt to be the "Puritan concepts" of Vance Packard and other critics of advertising's performances:

> We have to learn to accept the morality of the good life. . . .
> Whether advertising is considered helpful or harmful . . .
> depends on whether you prefer constructive discontent or
> cowlike satisfaction.

That is an example of a self-justification that seeks less to justify than to divert, less to define than to confuse. It is helpful with a pronouncement of this sort to know what the speaker means by the disguises he uses for his circular thoughts, and, from previous exposure to Dr. Dichter in these pages, we should have some conception of his meanings and hence may move on.

At the opposite pole from Dr. Dichter, in style at least, is such a self-justification as this one from Mr. Dan Seymour, president of the J. Walter Thompson Company:

> We are the ones who start and who power the economic drive-shaft. To us it is basic that we are the main force in the world in changing people's ideas of what their standards of living should be.

Mr. Seymour as an economist may be quietly passed by; plainly his genius lies in other fields. But he speaks in a straight-forward, uncomplicated manner, quite in the style of a nine-teenth-century *obiter dictum*. It is a very proper way for the head of the world's largest advertising agency to speak, particu-larly at an advertising convention, where Mr. Seymour was on this occasion.

Another approach to self-justification comes from the semi-literary type of advertising man, with which the business is thickly populated. This approach generally leads to a kind of watered-down tone poem or to what Rosser Reeves called, in a recent interview with *Advertising Age*, the "artsy-craftsy" style. Mr. Reeves was talking about advertising technique and the kind of ads that he felt would not sell. But the term applies quite as aptly to such a self-justification as the following, a house ad for the Young & Rubicam advertising agency (long after Raymond Rubicam had left):

> There is no chestnut more overworked than the critical whinny: "Advertising sells people things they don't need." We, as one agency, plead guilty. Advertising *does* sell people things they don't need. Things like television sets, automobiles, catsup, mattresses, cosmetics, ranges, refrigera-tors, and so on and on. People really don't *need* these things. People don't really *need* art, music, literature, newspapers, historians, wheels, calendars, philosophy, or for that matter, critics of advertising, either. All people really *need* is a cave, a piece of meat and, possibly, a fire. The complex thing we

172) *Part Three:* PRIDE AND PREJUDICE

call civilization is made up of luxuries. An eminent philosopher of our time has written that great art is superior to lesser art in the degree that it is "life-enhancing." Perhaps something of the same thing can be claimed for the products that are sold through advertising. . . . Our unique and restless economy . . . is fundamentally devoted to the production and distribution of things people don't need. Among them are toothpaste, electricity, outboard motors, artificial satellites and education. Without advertising, that economy cannot exist.

This remarkable collection of words would seem to be about as pretty an example of self-justification as the mind of advertising man could devise. It is a very popular ad in the advertising business (among its admirers, interestingly enough, is Rosser Reeves), which is always happy when someone can find a way to link toothpaste with philosophy and the like. But it is not, despite its pretensions, the supreme statement along these lines. That honor assuredly must go to a speech made before the American Association of Advertising Agencies five years ago by Charles H. Brower, then president, now chairman of the board of Batten, Barton, Durstine & Osborne, Inc. As a semi-literary exercise in self-justification, it is without peer; and as the summation of the economic myths that appeal to advertising men, it is well-nigh complete. The intelligent buyer should sit down, put his feet up, and read the following excerpts from Mr. Brower's speech carefully, meantime stealing occasional glimpses at his television screen:

> What, for instance, made the Golden Age of England golden? Did Shakespeare, Marlowe, Spenser, Fletcher and the rest make that age? Or did the age make them? The answer seems clear? A new creative climate made both! . . .
>
> Why, may I ask—if we want it badly enough—is it not possible to create a climate of greatness in an advertising agency—or, better still, in the whole agency business? . . .
>
> Perhaps advertising should clean its house. But, friends,

let us first know the kind of house we propose cleaning. . . .

The house of advertising is a mighty fortress in our economy, and those who attempt to pull stones from its walls had best consider for a moment the consequences of what they are doing. . . . Pull down advertising and a frightening number of things will fall with it. For there has never in the whole history of the world been an economy like ours—so mightily effective, so delicately poised.

Essential to this economy are the eager seeking for the new and the restless impatience with the old that lead to the discarding of goods before they are actually worn out. A European of the middle class may wear one overcoat his entire life. Here we change styles, we invent new fabrics, we want different coats for different seasons. As far as plain everyday sense is concerned—no man's or woman's life would be the shorter if American manufacturers provided just one good old-fashioned bar of soap that would serve for toilet, bath, shampoo, dishes, floor scrubbing and even brushing the teeth. But advertising has taught us not to be happy that way. Unthinking intellectuals call this "selling people things they do not need." But those of us who know better know that our economy would limp to a shuddering halt if it were based on the sale of things that are "really needed."

Last year the top ten advertisers alone paid the federal government over two billion dollars in taxes. Is it too much to say that advertising stimulated at least half of this? Is it too much to say that without advertising and the desire it spreads, we could hardly meet our military budget alone?

We have a right to that fierce pride in our business that must begin any renaissance of creative greatness. We have a right to be proud of ourselves—and the things we have done for our country. And anyone in the land should be proud to know us.

This may be considered a Grade-A example of what Martin

Mayer, in his book, *Madison Avenue, U.S.A.*, refers to as the "nuisance" of "the advertising man's apparently insatiable need for self-justification." My own advice to Mr. Brower[1] would be to get his pride in check and read some Veblen, or even a little more of Martin Mayer. For Mr. Mayer, having remarked the advertising man's insatiable need, goes on to point out what the intelligent reader will already have noted; namely, that "none of the usual self-justifications . . . stand up very well under logical analysis."

An equitable man, Mr. Mayer finds a parallel to the nuisance of the advertising man's need in the nuisance of "the advertising critic's apparently unceasing attacks on the business." He urges that both, the advertising man and the critic, find surcease in his own theory of added value—which is that "advertising, in addition to its purely informing function, *adds a new value to the existing values of the product.*" The italics are Mr. Mayer's, and the concept is well liked along Madison Avenue.

As an example of this theory in practice, Mr. Mayer considers "the case of a soda pill, a placebo, which is advertised as a headache cure." Mr. Mayer concedes that the pill has "virtually no value"; on the other hand, he says, it will actually cure the headaches "of a number of the people who take it." Or, as Mr. Mayer concludes, "the suggestion power of the advertising has created a value for a worthless product."

This is a most interesting theory, and if Mr. Mayer's urging of it will have the effect of heading off some of the more desperate ventures in self-justification, that would be a contribution to the general good. But however the theory of added value works to soothe the advertising man, I do not think it will work to soothe the intelligent buyer. Moreover, it raises very thorny questions about the good life that Dr. Dichter assures us is at hand.

---

[1] One of his agency's bids for greatness was the shampoo TV commercial filmed before the product had been developed (see Chapter One). Another is the advertising for Lucky Strike and Tareyton cigarettes.

One can see that the suggestible person whose headache is cured by the worthless product might enjoy life better in consequence, embrace the good life, and even see advertising as a mighty fortress. But what can one do about all those others whose headaches are real, including those whose headaches may be signaling glaucoma, an abscess, or brain tumor, for instance, or any of the long list of other real diseases of which headache is the major symptom (it is, in fact, one of the most common disease symptoms of mankind)? These people clearly are a bother to the good life, for while the pill whose worthlessness is all unknown to them will have no effect on their headaches, the advertising may well beguile them into postponing treatment until it is too late. It may be that people with actual headaches will just have to be read out of the good life; their needs are too real.

But there is more to the plot than this. Suppose the worthless pill, called Mogg's Suggestabs, has a rival, equally worthless, equally well-advertised, known as Bogg's No-Ake. Each of these brands sells for 79¢ per dozen pills, which allows a markup of approximately 1000 per cent, a relatively moderate one. Now, if Mogg's Suggestabs is a step to the good life, if the mighty fortress might tremble from (for example) a note in *Consumer Reports* saying that Mogg's Suggestabs is worthless, if our unique and restless economy (so delicately poised) really needs us to buy this worthless product, then—if we are to accept the morality of advertising's good life—we should buy it.

But what about Bogg's No-Ake? What happens to the good life, the mighty fortress (*Consumer Reports* says Bogg's is no better than Mogg's), and our unique and restless economy (even more delicately poised from Bogg's point of view) if we ignore it? We don't need it, any more than we really need art, philosophy, education, toothpaste, or Mogg's Suggestabs. But is Bogg less important to the good life than Mogg? Musn't our eager seeking and our restless impatience reach to Bogg as well as Mogg?

It is at this point that Dr. Dichter, Mr. Seymour, the writer of the Young & Rubacam ad, Mr. Brower, and (let us say) part of Mr. Mayer come together: all would have to agree that it doesn't make any difference which we buy. Beyond this, we will act fully in accordance with the morality of the good life as laid down by Messrs. Dichter, Brower, etc., only if we buy them both, thus subsidizing the sales costs for two products and two advertising agencies instead of one. Among other things, this would provide more of the jobs that the *Printers' Ink* editor was so worried about losing early in Chapter One. But the intelligent buyer still may want to ask a question: Is there really a place in the good life for him?

Walter Lippmann addressed himself to the question of the buyer's place in the seller's scheme of things at a time when the good life as a euphemism for the seller's standard of living had less currency than it now has. Mr. Lippmann, writing in the wake of the muckrakers' disclosures of corruption and waste in American life and analyzing the great public response to them, had high hopes for the potential of organized consumer activities; he saw these as the emergent "real power" in the nation. One might say that that prospect still eludes, but Mr. Lippmann's incidental dissection of the consumer's entrapment in advertising's toils of fifty years ago was sharp and precise; it also reflected his sense for the underlying structure, and consequently these lines from *Drift and Mastery*, first published in 1914, delineate a situation all too familiar to the youngest readers of the new edition, published in 1961:

> The consumer is sometimes represented as the person whose desires govern industry. Actually, he is an ignorant person who buys in the dark. He takes what he can get at the price he can afford. He is told what he wants, and then he wants it. . . . Where there is a monopoly the consumer is, of course, helpless, and where there is competition he is almost entirely at the mercy of advertising.
>
> Advertising, in fact, is the effort of businessmen to

take charge of consumption as well as production. . . .
By advertising . . . I mean the deceptive clamor that dis-
figures the scenery, covers fences, plasters the city, and
blinks and winks at you through the night. When you
contemplate the eastern sky ablaze with chewing gum, the
northern with tooth-brushes and underwear, the western
with whiskey, and the southern with petticoats, the whole
heavens brilliant with monstrously flirtatious women, when
you glance at magazines in which a rivulet of text trickles
through meadows of automobiles, baking powders, corsets
and kodaks, you begin to accumulate a sense of the disas-
trous incompetence of the ultimate consumer. . . .

In our intricate civilization the purchaser can't pit himself against the producer, for he lacks knowledge and power
to make the bargain a fair one. . . . The simple act of
buying has become a vast, impersonal thing which the ordinary man is quite incapable of performing without all
sorts of organized aid.

It is indeed true; and in its particulars it is truer by many
billions of dollars (the advertising outlay was only a little over
one billion dollars when Mr. Lippmann wrote those words),
by tens of thousands of new products, and by thousands of new
kinds of products since 1914. There are innumerable testimo-
nies to this truth, many of which have been set forth or touched
on in the foregoing pages. The intelligent buyer must always
remember, however, that truth is often a very iffy thing to an
advertiser and that bilking the consumer may be viewed as
no more than a part of the truth of the good life. The advertiser does not usually use phrases like bilking the consumer;
he says, rather, that he is developing wants the consumer
doesn't know he has, and so forth. But the point is that a
seller who has really drunk deep of the good life brew may
come to view any and all advertising and selling activities as
part of the design of the greater good, as a justifiable means
to the all-embracing end.

The casting off of this spell must be largely a private undertaking, like growing up. The advertising man must make the discovery for himself—although perhaps he might hire Dr. Dichter to help him work up some new needs and desires— that the concept of the mighty fortress, however stirring, however self-justifying, however just plain comfy, is as inadequate to explain the actual functioning of advertising as Mogg's (or Bogg's) pill is inadequate to cope with a real headache. But if the advertising man can get this far, then I can help him from that point on.

My associate, Colston Warne, a professor of economics at Amherst College and the president of Consumers Union ever since its founding, has formulated something that I will call Warne's Myth Suppressor. It is a well-made, handy-sized, satisfying line of thought, and it ran as follows when he last offered it to an audience of advertising men:

> I do think that the advertising industry counts too heavily on our lack of sophistication when it offers as one of its justifications for its existence the statement that advertising is responsible for mass production. Mass demand cannot be said to have been the egg to the production chicken. The over-fed and too-long tolerated immodesty of advertising is most evident in this industry argument. Mass production did not flow from a copywriter's pen. It is, rather, a total cultural achievement. Its technology has come from our common heritage in the development of science. Its fortunate development here on our shores centrally stemmed from 1) a wealth of natural resources; 2) one of the widest free trade areas in the world; and 3) the development of the economics of scale in competitive production. The centralizing impact of advertising has today carried production concentration far beyond the point dictated by the requirements of this mass production and has had a blighting effect upon traditional competition.

I should explain that Warne's Myth Suppressor comes in two parts to provide deeper, more lasting therapy to the short-sightedness commonly associated with the myth syndrome. The taker should read the first part, as just given, and let it penetrate for a few minutes; then he should take the second part (all at once if possible), which goes as follows:

> The claim has been made that a waste of resources in the form of unstable goods, built-in obsolescence, meaningless product differentiation, a wasteful distributive system, speeded-up replacements, not to mention the costs directly linked to advertising appeals, are necessary extravagances to keep the economy afloat. If this be true, if it is indeed necessary that we must maintain a vast business-sponsored WPA, a gigantic make-work movement in order to keep our economic system functioning, then the time has come for us to face this most lamentable fact and to call it by its real name—a make-work program. I, for one, do not believe that American ingenuity has been so strained that only through this kind of mounting outlay of men and resources can we manage to keep ourselves functioning economically. But if we *do* have to shore ourselves up with a make-work program, then I would also have to say that there are other areas of activity (low-cost housing, for example) where it seems to me the task would be more productive and less wasteful.

It is quite possible that all of this, which may be of interest to the intelligent buyer, will be considered much too simple by most advertising men. Advertising men who try to justify advertising on economic grounds usually end up being less coherent but more complicated than the economists. Indeed, in general, the advertising man loves to be thought complicated almost as much as he loves to be thought a realist or an educator and is delighted when anyone tells him he works at a complicated trade.

For if you tell an advertising man that all he has to do is

to set down the facts he will view you with loathing. Tell him you can't understand how he can play like an organist on all those terribly involved motivations that make people buy, and he will adore you. On the record, he usually appears so reluctant to set down the facts that he will involve himself in complexities beyond counting to arrive at those presentations that will help him to avoid the simply factual or merely truthful.[1]

But a careful commentator on advertisers must be concerned, of course, not with what they think they're doing but with their actual doings. Let us now consider in some detail a few examples of their work.

[1] I do not mean to imply here or elsewhere that the seller functions solely out of a black intelligence and the will to evil; he will often achieve his effects with hardly any thought at all. Thus, for example, the price of this book was scheduled to be $4.95. This is a classic deceptive price, designed in this instance to make you feel in $4 terms while getting you to pay in $5 terms. Practically all books published today, and many other things, are priced thus misleadingly. I tried to avoid the deception with a recent revised edition of a novel of mine that came out originally ten years ago. The publisher chose to restore it to print, for reasons that were thoroughly lost in the subsequent comedy of errors and thoughtlessness. The catalogue that mentioned the book's appearance referred to it as "already published" a month before the presumed publication date; a kind of quarterly record of the firm's publishing activities ignored it entirely for nine months thereafter; not a single copy ever got into a bookstore; and not a line of promotion ever appeared for the edition. But the edition did represent one small success; I had protested the $5.95 price proposed for it (the book had appeared at an honest $4 originally) and finally had won the publisher's agreement to a $5.75 compromise. But this slightly more honest price completely disrupted everybody; nobody could believe it. And so the $5.95 price was printed on the jacket anyway and had to be removed, and the $5.95 price got into the trade listings and had to be corrected. Months later a friend of mine called the publisher's office to ask if a revised edition of my book were available, as he had heard, and was told that nothing was known of a *revised* edition, but that the book *was* available—at $5.95 a copy.

12

<<<<<<<<<<<<<<<<<<<<<<<<<<<<<<>>>>>>>>>>>>>>>>>>>>>>>>>>>>>

A Little Inaccuracy
Saves a World of
Explanation

O_{NE} cannot quite say of advertising that the more
it changes the more it is the same. The general tone is certainly
higher than it used to be; an out-and-out fraud has a harder time
than it once did; the cycles that operate in advertising as in
other institutions have brought some practitioners to a current
belief that reasonably *stated* claims (though the claims themselves may or may not be reasonable) can help sales, and so
long as the belief continues such statements will continue to
be heard along with the more familiar shouts and clamors. Despite the inadequacies of the intermittent attempts to achieve
Truth in Advertising, there is doubtless more of it than there
once was (if we remember that the whole truth is not under
discussion), since some of the discipline lacking within has been
imposed from without.

Legislation designed to protect buyers doesn't reach very far
and has a hard time getting passed against the sellers' lobbies
or maintained against the sellers' tricks and the buyers' all-too-
common indifference to their own interests. But at the begin-

FOR
DISPLAY
ONLY

ning of the century there was virtually no such protection, and not until advertising's excesses in the thirties forced some action did the protection become very meaningful. The general pattern has been to proceed from catastrophe to treatment; thus, for example, the anarchy of turn-of-the-century patent medicine advertising led to the first Pure Food and Drug Law, the anarchy of the thirties led to its improvement, and the tragedy of thalidomide led to its further improvement. Learning is expensive on this basis, but still some things are learned.

The trouble is that the problem grows faster than our learning; the steadily increasing complexity of products outreaches further each year the essential simplicities of the legislative efforts; and in the din that 15 billion dollars buys it becomes increasingly difficult to hear any voice other than those that give us our instructions from the television screens they now command, or to read any word that runs counter to the edicts and the orders in the advertising space of the newspapers and magazines, or even to avoid for a moment the spreading aura of the billboard picture. The vast, smothering size of the commercial blanket has come to threaten us almost most of all. In this connection the intelligent buyer may learn something from an interesting paragraph which appeared almost thirty-five years ago in the *Encyclopedia of the Social Sciences*:

The manufacturer of consumption goods produces for the market rather than for an identifiable individual consumer; he tries to produce what will make the most profit, either through large sales or through wide profit margin. The easiest way to make a profit is not to wait until some consumers evince a demand for a product but to devise something for which a demand can quickly be created by advertising its real or fancied excellence. Were consumers universal experts in choice, this might lead merely to rapid improvement and cheapening of goods. Actually, not only does the initiative rest with the manufacturer and his sales force but the survival of the manufacturer is conditioned by the ignorance and suggestibility of the isolated consumers. If attractive color rather than durability leads to salability, the producer will use the resources of science to discover more popular colors rather than to increase durability. Competitive manufacturers may often be as ignorant of the relative qualities of their products, judged by scientific tests of good service, as are average individual consumers. A producer offering inferior products at higher prices may be guilty not of calculated fraud but of following the most easily stimulated preferences of poorly informed purchasers or of employing the most effective trick of stimulation.

Some of this has been said before, but it needs restatement in the particular context of this chapter. The intelligent buyer should bear it in mind and possibly look back to it from time to time as he reads the following report on some specific advertising activities which are current or recent as of this writing, which show the advertiser and his agent at work on a variety of fronts, and which exhibit (among other things and in one way or another) that "ignorance and suggestibility" of sellers and buyers alike. It hardly needs saying that the examples given are simply representative of a large quantity of candidates, and that as these recede into advertising history others will emerge to take their place. These are interesting less for their details, which are familiar enough, than for their exemplification of the range of techniques used over and over in the continuing assault on buyers.

The Great Hollow Yell

The Ajax White Tornado has jangled television screens for some years in one of the biggest and noisiest campaigns ever for a household cleaner. The advertising has been highly successful; in advertising circles it was credited with making Colgate's New Ajax All Purpose Cleaner with Ammonia the biggest seller in its class. Consumers Union bought some Ajax, along with two competing products, Lever Brothers' New Handy Andy All-Purpose Cleaner with Ammonia and Procter & Gamble's Mr. Clean All-Purpose Cleaner. Claims were made in the advertising and on the labels of each of the three brands to the general effect that it was best for household cleaning; removing old, built-up wax from kitchen floors, for example, is the job that Ajax White Tornado has done best and most often on television. So the CU testers tried out the three cleaners full strength in standardized laboratory wax-removal tests, and on a stretch of built-up wax and dirt in an office corridor. The testers also tried out a solution they put together themselves—one cup of Tide and six fluid ounces of ammonia to a gallon of water.

In these tests it was necessary to work hard with all three of the commercial cleaners to remove the wax and dirt, and approximately as hard with one as with another. The Tide mixture was "clearly superior," according to the test report, to any of them (any other detergent of the Tide type would probably have done as well). And its cost, at 10¢ per gallon or less than 0.1¢ per fluid ounce, was less than half the cost of the others.

A question for the intelligent buyer to ponder here is whether the added value of the White Tornado on the TV screen is worth the extra cost and effort of using Ajax on the floor.

See No Evil, Speak No Evil

In the spring of 1961 Consumers Union joined with the Association for the Aid of Crippled Children to sponsor a conference on passenger car design and highway safety—because, as the introduction to the subsequent proceedings noted, "Of the three areas into which the automobile accident problem is customarily divided—the driver, the vehicle, and the highway—it seemed to us that the vehicle was receiving the least research attention."

A lot has happened since that conference took place. For one thing, the death rate per 100,000,000 vehicle miles started up the following year and continued up for three straight years (in 1965 it declined slightly, although the number of deaths was higher than ever). For another thing, the General Services Administration of the federal government issued some safety standards affecting the thousands of cars it would be buying; the standards were mainly a codification of some of the few meaningful safety measures already taken by the industry, but the simple listing by a government agency focused attention on the problem. Then, in the summer of 1965, the Senate Subcommittee on Executive Reorganization headed by Senator Abraham Ribicoff held the first Congressional hearings in sixty years on the subject of automobile safety. It was during these hearings that Senator Robert Kennedy, questioning Frederick Donner, Chairman of the Board of the General Motors Corporation, extracted (not too easily) the information that in the preceding year General Motors as a whole had spent slightly in excess of $1 million for all of its crash-safety research out of profits of $1.7 billion; that figured out to about 25¢ per GM car sold that year, and was not appreciably better or worse than the industry average.

Earlier in 1965, in its annual April automobile issue, Consumers Union had started a year of dragons for the auto industry with its strongest statement ever (I wrote it myself) on the subject of automobile safety:

> . . . It is no longer possible, either morally or in the simple context of objective reporting, to report on autos without steady reference to their death-dealing and maiming characteristics. CU does not at present know of anything it can do or say to give readers any truly meaningful guide by which to separate safe cars from unsafe. There are no safe cars. But if that is true it is also true that all cars could be made significantly safer than they are now. There is not a single car produced whose safety could not be improved to some extent, and without the expenditure of a single extra cent. Indeed, some steps in the direction of greater safety would save money. . . .

The sins of the auto industry against safety have been

ticked off, of course, many times. The auto industry has prevailed against its critics 1) by ignoring them, 2) by changing the subject, and 3) by arguing that people cause accidents and what control, after all, does the industry have over people . . . ?

The industry has failed almost completely to accept safety in car design as a prime responsibility. It has not brought to the subject anything like the technological skill or executive emphasis that it has put into the styling, production, and selling of cars. The fact is that no one can say for sure that the industry could not build far safer cars, and that the further fact is that no one can say for sure how the industry might best go about it. The industry has not really tried . . .

But even as these words appeared the industry was off on another of its horsepower races, building up the engines to deliver far more power than man and the laws of physics could control, given the soft suspension with which the high power is commonly combined. This precise combination of characteristics, one of the most dangerous possible, has been found in cars for at least as long as CU has been reporting on them.

But, while reporting such facts, even CU, like everyone else from the manufacturers to the buyers, had been affected to some degree by the general apathy that let the manufacturers get away literally with murder by ignoring safety features year after year. The need was for a sharper, more concentrated, more single-minded focusing of attention on the problem and the need was met at the beginning of 1966 with the spectacular success of Ralph Nader's *Unsafe at Any Speed*—a straight-out indictment of the automobile industry for the atrocities it had committed against the public interest by subordinating transportation values and simple safety to a pattern of styling for sales. It was the kind of indictment that the industry had had coming for a long time.

The industry's first reaction was to try to brazen out the new opening up of the subject, but this for once did not work. General Motors hired detectives to try to spy out something in Nader's life that might be used to divert attention from his well documented charges, but that didn't work either, and GM had to apologize. Thereafter, backing and filling, the nation's largest manufacturing industry took an indignant stand against federal legislation in the car safety field, then rather abjectly seemed to accept the idea, then characteristically began to hedge. In response to Senator Ribicoff's request for data on defective cars sold, the industry had to report that more than 8,000,000 cars had been called back because of defects of one kind or another (not all related to safety) in the past six years. But as of the spring of 1966 industry leaders are being quoted again in the newspapers trying to get the safety emphasis back on the drivers and away from the cars. Even so, the prospects for some constructive action are at least higher than they've been.

In all probability the buyer now will be charged extra for safety features that may not actually cost extra, but buyers are used to that. On many counts, it will be interesting to see what happens during the new attempt to bathe the long unwashed auto industry in the waters of public responsibility.

The False Front

One of the early advertisements for Micrin appeared in *Reader's Digest* under the heading: "The First Mouthwash Ever Advertised in *Reader's Digest*." The advertisement was subsequently reproduced in a curious promotional volume presenting "The Best Advertisements from *Reader's Digest*," by Julian L. Watkins, a retired advertising copywriter. This book, priced at $17.50 and full of reproductions of advertisements that Mr. Watkins found "great," "tremendous," "distinguished," and "great" again, opened with a preface in which Mr. Watkins managed to work in the word "great" fourteen times in two pages. It then proceeded to its reproductions, culled from the years 1955 to 1961. Of the Micrin advertisement Mr. Watkins wrote in his comment: "Tell me—did you ever see a more dignified, yet more powerfully effective display of a new product? . . . Everything about this ad invites your attention, is believable, *earns your respect.*" This ad came from Young & Rubicam, the source of that marvelous justification of advertising which we read in Chapter Eleven (" . . . an eminent philosopher of our times has written that great art is superior to lesser art in the degree that it is 'life-enhancing.' Perhaps something of the same thing can be claimed for the products that are sold through advertising.") In this hushed atmosphere let us examine the Micrin advertisement.

Mouthwash advertising, from the summer day in St. Louis when Gerard Lambert first heard the word halitosis and was struck by the possibilities of exploiting it to make money out of Listerine, has been one of the least dignified, least believable, least respectable of advertising's achievements. The Micrin ad is a visual improvement; the pictured bottle is handsome, the typography is clean, the layout is chaste, But on other counts the Micrin ad is standard. It makes the standard claims—that it destroys millions of germs in the mouth and throat, that it gives long-lasting results, that it keeps your breath clean. And, like most other mouthwash advertising, it vaguely implies that all this might have some meaning with respect to health. The advertisement says Micrin is "far ahead of any toothpaste or other mouthwash," the bottle label itself gives a dosage for "minor sore throats."

From years of indoctrination by this kind of advertising, the buyer is presumably supposed to think of bad breath, tooth decay, gum irritation, throat infection, and the like. But proof of effectiveness for products of this sort is hard to come by. Bacteria normally exist by the millions in the mouth and throat and are held in check by the natural defenses of the body tissues and fluids. Moreover, viruses belonging to the group known as adenoviruses probably cause upper respiratory infection more frequently than bacteria and neither Micrin nor any other oral antiseptic destroys or inhibits them. Moreover again, if a sore throat is truly minor, no mouthwash is needed for that, and if a sore throat is major, no mouthwash will help, although it might delay treatment long enough for a strep throat to lead on to rheumatic fever. Moreover once more, no mouthwash can help significantly in preventing or controlling gum disease and no mouthwash has been shown to have any effect on dental decay. As for bad breath, that is rarely if ever due to the action of any mouth or throat bacteria that might be temporarily reduced by any mouthwash. A mouthwash can, of course, cover up the smell of a bad breath with the smell of the mouthwash for a short while. Micrin, like any other mouthwash, will do this, and Micrin has a nice smell.

The intelligent buyer is referred to the trade magazine *Chemical Week*, where he could have read in the February 4, 1961, issue, the following: "Psychologists and motivational researchers . . . say the deep-seated reason for using a mouthwash is to 'wash away guilt feelings.'" This sounds as improbable as the mouthwash ads; it sounds, in fact, like the ever-ready Dr. Dichter. And sure enough, a quick check with his *Handbook of Consumer Motivations*, although it reveals nothing directly on mouthwashes, does find a text that twists and coils around the subject:

> . . . and it was found that people often blame themselves for minor upsets. This shows up most obviously in connection with hangovers. It is considered a sort of punishment, a tendency to self-condemnation; to feel that one must pay for one's pleasures by suffering is dominant. Proprietary drugs that promise relief from this guilt can secure success for themselves.

The Added Value

The label on the Clorox container is one of the wordiest on anything anywhere; it is full of directions, cautions, and claims.

At least one of the claims is a flat falsehood: "Clorox is the most effective household disinfectant of its kind." This is false because Clorox contains one active ingredient, sodium hypochlorite in a 5.25 per cent solution, and virtually all other liquid household bleaches contain the same active ingredient in the same solution. In its advertisements, Clorox is more laconic and also more circumspect. Its claim in a recent advertisement was that "no other bleach, liquid or dry, bleaches clothes cleaner, whiter than Clorox." All evidence suggests that this is true. But, of course, it is also true that many other bleaches, liquid or dry, bleach clothes as clean, as white as Clorox. In short, Clorox is an effective bleach and so are its competitors, some of which are much simpler to use and less risky as well.

The Clorox advertising is worth the intelligent buyer's consideration on other counts. It reflects to an unusual degree the common advertising problem of trying to invent differentiations where none exist, and it is an interesting refutation of the old trade belief that advertising lowers costs. In 1957, when Procter & Gamble bought out the Clorox Company, approximately two hundred other companies were manufacturing the same kind of bleach—each of them a 5.25 per cent solution of sodium hypochlorite. Despite this, Clorox had taken nearly half the market and the Federal Trade Commission found Procter & Gamble's acquisition of the company tended to create a monopoly in the bleach industry. And how had Clorox done this? It had done it at least in part by advertising at the rate of almost 10 per cent of its gross sales. And what effect had its capture of the market had on its price? It was the premium price product in the field, as it still is.

The Bridge from Nowhere

The literature of package labels, as all intelligent buyers know, is a literature somewhat divorced from the real world. Phrases like "old-fashioned goodness" turn out to mean artificial colors and flavors plus chemical additives not old enough to be old-fashioned; and red on red or dark blue on black are considered very attractive color combinations for conveying weight or size information (the type must be small enough, too). One connoisseur of package literature noted with interest the ingredients in Royal Custard Style Dessert: sugar, artificial color, artificial flavoring, and a thickening agent. The package also carried the claim: "Good for children." The connoisseur wrote Standard Brands, which makes the product, asking how they got from the ingredients to the claim. Standard Brands wrote back that, to begin with, a box of Royal Custard Style Dessert contains 250 calories (the closest equivalent to this nutritionally might be the calories in one and a half martinis). Then, said Standard Brands, the dessert is made by adding 2¼ cups of milk (you have to buy and add the milk, but it *is* good for children). Finally, Standard Brands said, its product contains no eggs and therefore is good for children who are allergic to eggs.

The Well-Guaranteed Defect

In the fall of 1963 a Consumers Union shopper bought, anonymously and at retail, a Hotpoint high-oven range with the model number RH952. The range, in its factory sealed box, was delivered to CU's laboratories, where it was duly tested. In the March, 1964, issue of the *Reports* the Hotpoint RH952 was rated Not Acceptable because "live 115-volt terminals . . . were partially exposed and would be within easy reach when the unit's built-in venting system was cleaned. Touching one of these terminals and any metal part of the grounded range simultaneously could result in a severe, even lethal, shock. Such carelessness of design, or sloppiness on the production line is, in CU's judgment, unforgivable."

The Hotpoint division of General Electric Company issued a statement to the press and wrote a long letter to Consumers Union. The story from this point on was told perfectly clearly in the June, 1964, issue of *Consumer Reports:*

Hotpoint contended it had consulted with Underwriters' Laboratories (the organization whose label on an electrical appliance indicates that its design conforms with UL standard requirements for safety) throughout the development of the line of ranges represented by the RH952 and had complied with "every one of their requests." "The range has their approval as well as our own," the company wrote, "and we think this is adequate assurance that the product is safe to use and does not represent any hazard."

Despite this judgment, however, the letter went on to state that new steps were now being taken to cover the exposed live terminals: "We have voluntarily and at our own discretion, taken extra precaution by covering these electrical terminals with a silicone compound." Hotpoint sent CU a sample of the redesigned component, which certainly would have eliminated the shock hazard in the sample tested.

CU is gratified, of course, that Hotpoint has stated that steps are being taken to eliminate the shock hazard. For without doubt there was a hazard in the sample tested. It is true that CU's standards for electrical safety sometimes are more stringent than those of UL, but in this instance the exposed terminals violated UL's safety requirements as well as CU's. When informed of this, UL replied that it would take "immediate steps" to see that future production complied with its requirements.

There was more to Hotpoint's case in its own defense. The company argued that the sample tested was "in our judgment a pre-production model supplied to New York for introductory sales and service meetings and for display purposes." In speaking to the trade press, Hotpoint apparently had put matters even more baldly, for one article said that the sample CU tested was a "hand-made model for builder display purposes only and not meant for consumer use."

Inquiry has disclosed that the store from which CU

bought its sample purchased it from the regional Hotpoint distributor, and that it came directly from a Hotpoint warehouse. Inquiry has also established the significance of the model's full designation, which included the number "107" on the sample CU bought. The New York District Manager for Hotpoint explained that the sample was made during the first production run. So it was *not* a pre-production model.

Whenever there is some question about a flaw in a product under test, CU buys at least one more sample for testing before making a final judgment. The only exception to this policy concerns products with dangerous hazards. There can be no acceptable excuse, in CU's opinion, for the marketing of even one such sample.

Nevertheless, after all the fuss had been raised, a second sample of the Hotpoint RH952 was purchased. It was obtained five months after the first one, in a different store in a different state. The second sample was found to have the very same shock hazard as the first sample.

While all of this was going on, advertising for the Hotpoint ranges in general continued, with happy promises and pretty pictures and reassurances to the buyers:

Hotpoint first with the features women want most . . . plus Hotpoint's 90-day replacement Guarantee of Satisfaction, in addition to the regular 1-year warranty against defects in materials and workmanship.

The Deceptive Differential

Rosser Reeves, in his book on *Reality in Advertising,* has an interesting chapter entitled "The Deceptive Differential." At the beginning of it he tells how the theologians at the University of Paris "refuted good sense and wore out the world's patience by debating, for years, how many angels could dance on the point of a pin." (The world is often impatient with

oddities; Mr. Reeves might at least have mentioned the speculation that calculus had one of its roots in this long debate.) He
then goes on to compare to the theologians the advertising man
"who strains over miniscule differences," and he adds:

> This is idea bankruptcy, leading to the distortion, exaggera-
> tion, fake-claims, and hucksterism that have given all ad-
> vertising a bad name.

He ends this chapter with some examples of what he considers
major differences, which lead to valid "Unique Selling Propositions"—or U.S.P.'s, as he likes to call them. The first one has to
do with the headache remedy Anacin:

> Anacin is, and in a major way, quite different from aspirin,
> or aspirin with a buffer added. It is a unique combination
> of ingredients. Any physician, any authority on analgesics,
> will tell you that the combination of these particular in-
> gredients has different effects on the human body than
> aspirin alone.

But any physician, any authority on analgesics, will not tell
you this at all, or at least will not tell you this to support Mr.
Reeves's desired meaning that Anacin is better than aspirin or
is a unique combination. Anacin is a perfectly ordinary patent
medicine of the APC type, which came on the scene first about
half a century or more ago and has appeared under a great
variety of brand names. To make any particular claims for
Anacin or any other APC product as opposed to aspirin by itself
is distortion, exaggeration, etc.

And yet, Mr. Reeves not only made particular claims for
Anacin; he mounted one of the most strident ("Fast! Fast!
Fast!") campaigns in the history of advertising for Anacin. And
for the propagation of Anacin's endlessly familiar commercial of
the three lines leading to the three symbols of the headache,
Mr. Reeves got his client, American Home Products Corp.,
to spend a total of more than 86 million dollars. As he explained to an *Advertising Age* editor interviewing him:

You take this one piece of copy. . . . A big drug company doesn't spend $86,400,000 unless they're making money on it. That money was spent on one television commercial. It cost $8,200 to produce and it made more money than "Gone With the Wind."[1]

The letters "APC" stand for aspirin, phenacetin, and caffeine. And these were the ingredients of Anacin until 1963, by which time medical reports in widely scattered parts of the world were reporting suspicions that phenacetin, in large doses and taken over a period of months, might cause fatal damage to the kidneys (Uncle Teddy, speaking of the "very vivid tonics" in Tono-Bungay, would have referred to this as "a marked action on the kidneys"). In that year, quietly and without any notice to the public, the phenacetin was dropped out of Anacin: this left aspirin and caffeine as the two active ingredients, and nobody has yet shown reliably that the addition of caffeine to an analgesic serves any rational therapeutic purpose.

[1] With all deference to the views of advertising's apologists, as set forth in Chapter Eleven, I should like to submit an advertisement of my own composition, a variation on the Anacin theme, or, more precisely, a simple reversal of that theme (which really works quite as well one way as another), plus a few added values. This advertisement is made out of whole cloth, but would seem to bear roughly the same relation to truth as the run of advertisements here discussed:

GET S-L-O-W, 1-WAY HEADACHE RELIEF WITH MOGG'S SUGGESTABS

Fast drugs sometimes speed right by the cause of many headaches. . . . Suggestabs work s-l-o-w-l-y to give their magic ingredient time to get at hard-to-reach pains of some headaches. . . . Easy does it with Suggestabs

And remember

Suggestabs cost us almost nothing to make. Each bottle you buy brings us a high profit on which we pay high taxes to keep our economy going, buy guns, fight poverty! So Suggestabs really work 2 ways! They bring s-l-o-w relief to your headache and at the same time they remove the cause of headaches by bringing quick relief to our delicately poised economy. Be proud of Suggestabs!!

OUR GUARANTEE: *Suggestabs contain no drugs. They are compounded exclusively of the miracle ingredient* suggestio falsi. *Your money back if you find anything you really need in Suggestabs.*

S-U-G-G-E-S-T-A-B-S
(A Product of Added Value Laboratories, Inc.)

But the $86,400,000 commercial went right on; three dishes of ingredients—"a combination of ingredients"—had moved from the foreground of the TV screen back into the package when there were three ingredients, and three dishes kept right on moving back. Finally, after a few months, the commercial quietly dropped the three dishes. But the "combination of ingredients" continued, as loud as ever and even more devoid of significance. With minor modifications it is still going on as of this writing; one is brought to the conclusion that the big drug company and its advertising agent are not content even with having outdone *Gone With the Wind*.

The Studied Comparison

The Federal Trade Commission sponsored a comparative study of Bayer Aspirin, St. Joseph's Aspirin, Bufferin, Excedrin, and Anacin; the *Journal of the American Medical Association* reported it. As of this writing, Bayer Aspirin has been distorting it, over TV and in print, ever since. A major finding of the study was that no appreciable difference could be found among the five products in their effectiveness in relieving pain; the least expensive products performed as well as the most expensive. Bayer rushed into print with adroit phrases intimating that the U.S. government had shown Bayer Aspirin to be best. The FTC, which had issued complaints against four major producers of analgesics, withdrew them pending a general study of analgesic advertising. The adroit Bayer claims continued.

A U. S. Court of Appeals decision turned down an FTC action to stop this exploitation; Bayer thereupon changed its copy to some extent but the point that all the brands in the test came out about the same still remained out of reach.

The best procedure for the intelligent buyer continues to be as Consumers Union's medical consultants have stated it many times over the years: "You will get as good relief from common pains and fever as is available without a prescription if you buy the least expensive U.S.P. aspirin you can find." The U.S.P., be it noted, stands, not for Unique Selling Proposition, but for United States Pharmacopoeia—and least expensive means typically about 15¢–20¢ per 100 tablets as opposed to 79¢ for 100 Bayer tablets and $1.25 for 100 Anacin tablets.

We are here in the presence of some of the mansions of the house of advertising, and by and large they are considerable mansions, although they do not seem to be mighty fortresses. Certainly not even the most pompous agency president or the most naïve trade association executive could dismiss any of the advertisers we have been talking about with "that small minority" of evil-doers, those "fly-by-nights," or any of the other easy phrases with which advertising apologists seek to avoid issues. These advertisers are among the biggest in the business, and what is the intelligent buyer to say then?

He may ask, as he may have asked before, if there is really a place in advertising's good life for him. He may wonder if it is only Dr. Dichter's cowlike satisfaction that makes him consider the mighty fortress to be more than a little patchy in spots. Can an advertiser or an advertising agent really argue that, in efforts of this sort—and certainly, in private if not in public, he must know how easy it would be to extend the list —he is "powering the economic drive-shaft"? that the "economy cannot exist" without displays like these? Do these fit among the reasons (an advertising agent might ask himself) why "anyone in the land should be proud to know us?"

Quite aside from the morality, the ethics, the simple taste, or the simple legality of what goes on in selling of this sort, it seems perfectly clear that it doesn't add up to much of anything other than a pressure to browbeat buyers into switching from Mogg's to Bogg's. Moreover, even with this limited objective, so sadly inadequate to the century's and the country's need, advertising seems to be falling off in its effect. At the International Design Conference in Aspen in 1964, it was one of advertising's leading practitioners, William Bernbach, the

president of the Doyle Dane Bernbach agency and the acknowl-
edged master of the soft sell as a copywriter (Volkswagen, Avis,
etc.), who made the point:

> Eighty-five per cent of all ads today don't get looked at.
> This statistic was just revealed in a study made by the
> 4A's.[2] This study was conducted by the advertising industry
> to find out what the public thought of advertising. We were
> worried about whether or not the public loved us. Our
> problem is they don't even hate us. The sad thing is that
> business is spending so much time and money on making
> advertising boring, and we're achieving this boredom with
> such great American efficiency. The scientific way we're
> going about it, we just can't miss. . . .
>
> With the tremendous increase in political and social pres-
> sures, with violence confronting us at every turn, with the
> fierce competition among advertisers, more and more it will
> take tremendous artistry with words and pictures to touch
> and move the reader. So exposed is he to banalities, to self-
> conscious artificial attempts to arrest his attention, that he
> looks, but he does not see; he listens, but he does not hear;
> and what is worse, he does not feel.

There is some reason to believe that the advertising man
himself is in much the same state and has been for some time,
a concept that was raised interestingly by David Riesman a
decade and a half ago in *The Lonely Crowd:*

> Why, I ask, why isn't it possible that advertising as a
> whole is a fantastic fraud, presenting an image of America
> taken seriously by no one, least of all by the advertising
> men who create it? Just as the mass media persuade people
> that other people think politics is important, so they per-
> suade people that everyone else cannot wait for his new
> refrigerator or car or suit of clothes. In neither case can
> people believe that "others" are as apathetic as they feel

[2] The American Association of Advertising Agencies.

themselves to be. And, while in the case of politics their indifference may make people feel on the defensive, in the case of advertising their indifference may allow them to feel superior.

In fact, I think that a study of American advertising during the last quarter century would clearly show that the advertising men themselves realize the consumer's loss of emotional enthusiasm. . . . In many contemporary ads the possession itself recedes into the background or is handled abstractly, even surrealistically; it no longer throws off sparks or exclamation points; and copy itself has become subtler or more matter-of-fact.

Given even the approximate truth of such views as Mr. Bernbach's or Professor Riesman's, what then? The present-day buyer can hardly ignore advertising. For one thing, it is too all-present. But for another, even with its abuses, it is a functional part of the economy under which he lives. This economy is not necessarily the only one, to be sure. As Arnold Toynbee observed in an article in *Printers' Ink* three years ago:

> The moral that I draw is that a way of life based on personal consumption, stimulated by advertising, needs changing and there are dozens of possible alternatives to it. For instance, we could still have full employment in the economically advanced countries if we gave up advertising and restricted our personal consumption to, say, the limits that present-day American monks and nuns voluntarily set for themselves, and if we then diverted our production to supply the elementary needs of the poverty-stricken three-quarters of the human race. . . .
>
> Advertising deliberately stimulates our desires, whereas experience, embodied in the teaching of the religions, tells us that we cannot be good or happy unless we limit our desires and keep them in check. . . .
>
> Therefore, let us reform a way of life that cannot be lived without advertising.

But for now the economy is as it is and advertising is an irreducible part of it. That dean of American economists, the late John Maurice Clark, examined its irreducibleness while considering the needs of the economy's growth in his most recent book, *Competition as a Dynamic Process.* The ground he led the reader to is neither high nor very solid; but it is familiar; and it turns out, under scrutiny, to be well occupied by buyers who have stopped there to rest:

> It [the avoidance of industrial contraction] calls for a combination of new products and improvements or elaborations of existing ones, the test being always whether the consumers can be persuaded to pay for the new products or the elaborations. This gives the advertising industry much work to do, because new or altered products do not command acceptance automatically. And this raises the question whether advertising might perform the function that is here in question by merely misleading the consumers into buying what industry offers, regardless of whether it gives them any net increase in service values. To this, the ultimate limit comes when consumers become too disillusioned to respond, but one must regretfully admit that consumers appear capable of absorbing large amounts of misleading salesmanship before reaching the ultimate limit of no-response. Their psychology may be like that of the gambler who was warned that the faro game he was bucking was crooked. He answered: "I know it, but it's the only game in town."

13

◄◄◄◄◄◄◄◄◄◄◄◄◄◄◄◄◄◄◄◄◄◄◄◄►►►►►►►►►►►►►►►►►►►►►►►►►►

Here's Reasoning
for You

THE "ultimate limit" comes, as Professor Clark notes at the end of Chapter Twelve, when consumers become too disillusioned with advertising to respond. Mr. Bernbach thinks, or thought as of a couple of years ago, that the advertisers' banalities and self-conscious artificial exploitations had about brought the consumer to the limit. Professor Riesman thinks, or thought as of fifteen years ago, that even the exploiters had lost all but a technician's interest in the game. And yet the game goes on, ever more fervently and with ever higher stakes. The 5 billion dollars spent on advertising when *The Lonely Crowd* first appeared in 1950 has become the 15 billion dollars plus of now. And by now the consumers' capacity to absorb misleading salesmanship has to be reckoned as well-nigh insatiable. Those rather evil-smelling mansions in the house of advertising, as opened up in the preceding chapter, hold the remains of countless consumer hopes and expectations.

Professor Clark's parallel of the gambler and the crooked faro game clarifies matters. Exploration of one other mansion of the house of advertising may clarify them further. Let us examine cigarette advertising, where the almost addictive quality of the consumer's involvement with advertising and the almost addictive quality of the smoker's involvement with the product[1] have been jointly exploited by cigarette manufacturers in what is assuredly the most scandalously immoral use of advertising in history.

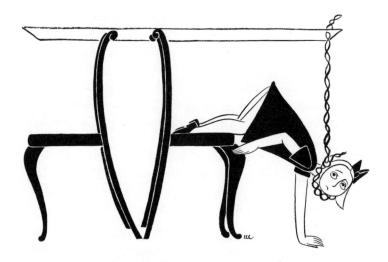

[1] Much medical opinion holds that "addiction" is too strong a word to apply to the smoking habit. The technical argument is that one cannot be considered to have been addicted to anything unless withdrawal presents specific physiological symptoms. It is probably true that, given the will, most smokers can stop smoking without showing any such symptoms. And yet most smokers are familiar, either from their own or from friends' experiences, with withdrawal miseries that seem too strong for "habit." The classic case is that of Dr. Sigmund Freud, who was advised to stop his heavy cigar smoking at the age of thirty-eight and who tried on many occasions over many years to do so; Dr. Ernest Jones's life of Freud reports numerous harrowing instances. At sixty-seven Freud developed cancer of the jaw and had the first of thirty-three operations for cancer that he endured during the sixteen remaining years of his life, which he ended with an artificial jaw and in almost constant pain. "Smoking," Freud wrote shortly after his first operation, "is accused as the etiology of this tissue rebellion." But he could never stop. As Dr. Jones observes quietly of Freud's smoking: "That it might be called rather an addiction than a habit was shown by the extent to which he suffered. . . ."

The six companies that produce the cigarettes that account for approximately 99 per cent of total sales have been, if anything, worse offenders of public decency than the pill and nostrum vendors who gave mass advertising its start in 1665 during London's great plague (see page ooo). Indeed, the record begins to show that the cigarette manufacturers are supporting and thriving upon a man-made plague more destructive to human life than the bubonic plague that took 90,000 lives in London just 300 years ago. In May of last year the Surgeon General of the United States reckoned that premature deaths from diseases associated with cigarette smoking would reach a total of 240,000 for the year, and "perhaps as many as 300,000." Lung cancer alone, a very rare disease when cigarette smoking first became popular, now takes about as many lives per year as are lost in all automobile accidents—that is, about 50,000.

The intelligent buyer may recall Pozzo's comment when Estragon and Vladimir ask why the tied and tethered Lucky, panting from exhaustion, did not put down the sand-filled bags he was carrying in *Waiting for Godot:*

> Let's try and get this clear. Has he not the right to? Certainly he has. It follows that he doesn't want to. There's reasoning for you.

This is approximately the reasoning of the cigarette advertisers, too; although to make sure that smokers would not want to put down their cigarettes the industry has increased its advertising pressure from about 50 million dollars a year in the early 1950's, when the medical evidence against cigarettes as a major health hazard first won widespread attention, to approximately a quarter of a billion dollars now that the evidence is overwhelming. The industry has also kept its public relations firms and its research fronts busy trying to undermine, or at least divert attention from, the steady enlargement of the medical evidence against its profitable product. Its conduct, in the face of the charges driven home against cigarettes by the great bulk of the medical profession, health officials of the U.S. government, government regulatory agencies, all relevant private health agencies, medical and governmental authorities of many foreign countries, and even many congressmen (despite the political power of the tobacco lobby and the numerous tobacco state representatives), is an almost unparalleled example of private interest triumphant over public good. But as Samuel Pepys said, speaking of *his* plague:

> . . . Three or four days since I saw a dead corps in a coffin lie in Close unburied; and a watch is constantly kept there night and day to keep the people in, the plague making us cruel as doggs one to another.

The basic strategy of the cigarette advertisers for many years was to face up to the health issue fearlessly whenever they felt able to exploit it and at other times to act as though it were a false issue or as though they didn't quite catch its name. Long before the full magnitude of cigarette smoking as a health menace was known, back in 1932, Lucky Strike ran an advertisement under the bold headline: "Do you inhale?" The subhead read: "What's there to be afraid of?" And the copy went on to say: "Lucky Strike meets the vital issue fairly and squarely . . . for it has solved the vital problem." It would be unfair to indict the Lucky Strike advertisers for not having known then what is now so widely known about cigarette smoking as a major health hazard. But it is not unfair to charge them with giving assurances in this advertisement that they could not support, and with arrogating to themselves an omniscience that they did not have. Most of the other cigarette advertisers did the same. Indeed, all through the 1930's and 1940's, cigarette advertising played endless variations on the idea that other brands were somehow bad for you but the brand in any given advertisement was good (or at least better) for you.

This practice reached the point of burlesquing itself about ten years after the "Do you inhale?" advertisement, when *Reader's Digest* made some comparative tests of cigarettes. The tests disclosed, and the magazine duly reported, that Old Golds had slightly less tars and nicotine than other brands. The difference, as the *Digest* also duly noted, was so slight as to be without meaning. Thereupon Old Golds took full pages in newspapers and magazines to report that they were "lowest in tars, lowest in nicotine." The impression created by the advertisements was as false as possible with so small a story. And just how small this story was has been told very well in a book already referred to, *The Advertising Smoke Screen*, by Blake Clark (who has been for many years a roving editor for *Reader's Digest*). Mr. Clark brought the reality of the *Digest*'s findings and the fantasy of the Old Gold advertising into sharp juxtaposition as he reviewed the Federal Trade Commission's complaint against the P. Lorillard Company:

> FTC points out that the advertisement omits the article's statement that the difference in nicotine content of all the brands tested was, for all practical purposes, negligible. . . . The actual difference between the average amount of nicotine in an Old Gold and in each of the other two brands tested was only 1/177,187 of an ounce! By switching to Old Golds, the person who smokes twenty cigarettes a day will subject his system to only 1/24 of an ounce less nicotine in a year's smoking. This infinitesmal fraction is the remarkable difference that P. Lorillard Company paid J. Walter Thompson and Lennen & Mitchell, Inc., thousand of dollars a week to advertise.

By the end of the 1940's cynicism concerning the industry's endless conflicting claims was widespread, and so was confusion. The advertisers said nothing concrete enough for anyone to attach a real meaning to it but the nonsense they talked was suggestive nonsense. And in 1949 a Gallup Poll on smoking found that more than half the cigarette smokers questioned thought their smoking was probably harmful in one way or another and had tried to give it up from time to time. Then, in the early 1950's, the long, slow research into the relationship between cigarette smoking and really serious lung and heart diseases began to shape itself into some of the unpleasant facts of modern life.

One of the early general discussions of cigarette smoking in this context appeared in *Consumer Reports* some thirteen years ago, in the February, 1953, issue, which said in part:

> Vital statistics show few trends more dramatic than the rise during the past thirty years in the death rate from cancer of the lung. Only a part of this increase can be attributed to aging of our population, or to improvements in diagnosis by physicians. . . . The most vigorously advocated hypothesis today is that heavy smoking (more than 20 cigarettes a day) over a period of many years is one of the most important factors, if not the most important of all. . . . It is obvious that those who can should cut their smoking to what is considered moderate levels—certainly not more than a pack a day. Those who cannot should understand that they are taking a risk of unknown dimensions, and should get an X-ray of their lungs every six months.

At the time of that warning, health appeals were much the biggest thing in cigarette advertising; Phillip Morris, Chesterfield, Camel, Pall Mall, and Old Golds specifically were all arguing then that they were less risky than other brands. And the Federal Trade Commission was trying, as it had been trying for years without much success, to get the most obviously deceptive of such appeals toned down.

In that same year five of the six major cigarette manufacturers joined together with growers associations and tobacco warehouse groups to form the Tobacco Industry Research Committee (recently renamed the Council for Tobacco Research —U.S.A.). This industry front has been the industry's voice ever since on what is known among tobacco men as "the health scare." That is, in the name of the Committee industry spokesmen sought to divert attention from, or cast doubt on, studies of the health effects of cigarettes, except for industry-financed studies seeking causes of lung and heart disease other than smoking. Year after year, while the implication of cigarette smoking as a major health hazard moved from the level of a serious suspicion to the level of statistical certainty, Committee press releases attacked the entire body of evidence in support of this implication as "one-sided," "extreme," "unsupported," "nothing new," "biased," "not convincing," "non-scientific," "pure speculation," "over-publicized," and so on. The quoted words are taken from actual Committee comments on major reports by the American Cancer Society, the British Medical Research Council, the U.S. Public Health Service, the U.S. Surgeon General, city health officials, and doctors doing research in veterans' hospitals.

So negative did the industry's record in this area become that, after some years of it, the advertising journal *Printers' Ink* called the industry to task:

> The time has come, obviously, for the TIRC (and its equally ineffectual companion, the Tobacco Institute) to drop this injured, defensive tone and say and do something more positive. The industry's current problems won't just disappear . . . by disclaiming them.

In a sharp letter to *The New York Times* John Kenneth Galbraith criticized "these unsupported denials" with which "for years now the tobacco industry has been capping careful research reports." And increasingly from the medical profession came increasingly sharp reviews of the industry's irresponsibility. But none of the criticisms had any more effect on the industry than the medical research itself seemed to have. Whatever the research showed, and whatever the critics said, the industry's answer was a public relations attack and advertising and yet more advertising. Lewis Gruber, chairman of the board of the P. Lorillard Company (Kent, Old Gold, Newport, etc.), expressed the general industry view of its advertising objective very well in 1959:

As to cigarette advertising, the pattern is indicated— heavier and more extensive advertising via print, TV, radio, billboards, point of sale, promotions, coupled with greater use of product claims and inferences of product differences. Selling advantages will be dramatically emphasized.[2]

The year before Mr. Gruber said that, his company had spent 41.9 cents a carton advertising its Newport brand, inferring with cool, clean pictures that Newports were meaningfully different from other brands, although no known objective test could substantiate the inference. In Consumers Union's 1959 laboratory tests for tars in the cigarette smoke of fifty-five U.S. brands and types, Newports came out a little above the middle of the ranking.[2]

But the exploitation of meaningless differences to get smokers to change from one brand to another is by no means the whole aim of the industry's heavy advertising. It has to attract non-smokers, too, so that it can enlarge its market and thus help to build our unique and restless economy into a mighty fortress.

At the very least, since the evidence shows that cigarette smokers die off earlier than nonsmokers, nonsmokers must steadily be recruited to maintain sales. The chief supply of nonsmokers is the nation's youth, and cigarette companies over the years naturally have lavished special attention on "the youth market."

[2] *Reader's Digest*, to its great credit, has consistently spoken out on the health hazards of cigarette smoking and on the meaningless differentiations so heavily advertised by the manufacturers. Following one *Digest* article, the American Tobacco Company (Lucky Strike, Herbert Tareyton, etc.) in 1957 asked Batten, Barton, Durstine & Osborn, the advertising agency that handled both the tobacco company's and the magazine's advertising, to give up the magazine's account. The *Digest* was then spending about $1,300,000 annually on its advertising; American Tobacco was spending about $22,000,000 with this one agency; BBD&O gave up the *Digest*. On another occasion, in 1960, a car-card advertisement for a *Reader's Digest* article entitled "The Growing Horror of Lung Cancer" was removed from New York commuter trains after cigarette advertisers objected.

In 1963, the year before the publication of the U.S. Surgeon General's report on *Smoking and Health,* cigarette advertising accounted for something like 40 per cent of the national advertising in college newspapers; and the total selling effort (including the paying of students to get other students to start smoking by giving them free samples) was estimated by the head of the Student Marketing Institute to have doubled in the five years before that. As the director of Phillip Morris' College Sales Department said:

> Students are tremendously loyal. If you catch them, they'll stick with you like glue because your brand reminds them of happy college days.

Moreover, as the advertising director of Liggett & Myers said:

> Between the time a kid is 18 and 21, he's going to make the basic decision to smoke or not to smoke. If he does decide to smoke, we want to get him.

The president of the National Association of Broadcasters not long ago deplored "the promotional impact of [cigarette] advertising designed primarily to influence young people." But, deploring that statement, the Television Bureau of Advertising and the Radio Advertising Bureau promptly circulated private memos to broadcasters, advising them to reassure cigarette advertisers that their advertising was still welcome on the air. In general, the industry has had very kindly treatment from advertising media of all kinds, particularly during the trying years in which the cigarette's health effects were being tracked down. The *New York Daily News,* for example, distinguished itself at one point with the headline, "Ciggies assailed again— Ho Hum," followed by the real hip declaration:

> Sure, the *News* takes cigarette advertising and likes it, and so what?

In return, James C. Bowling of the Tobacco Institute praised the *News* later, when cigarettes were even more deeply involved than before, for its "fine editorial stand."

But the helping hand of advertising media, while it could mitigate, could not conceal the importance of the Surgeon General's report on *Smoking and Health* issued early in 1964. With the publication of this 170,0co-word document it was no longer possible for reasonable men to deny that cigarette smoking had become one of the major health hazards of modern life. The conclusions of the report, indicting cigarette smoking for damaging health, shortening life, and raising the death rate, were doubly impressive because all ten members of the Surgeon General's Committee had agreed unanimously to them. And these ten had been approved unanimously in advance by nine organizations, including the Tobacco Institute as spokesman for the cigarette industry.

Confronted by the Surgeon General's report, the industry naturally increased its advertising. It had already changed its advertising style from the raucous days of the Tar Derby, when claims and counter-claims about whose brands offered the least tars filled the air waves and printed media alike. The Tar Derby had gone on through most of the 1950's and had been called off only when the Federal Trade Commission, unable to enforce its orders against individual companies, and the advertisers, perhaps growing wary of their constant reminders that their products were threats to health, agreed in closed-door negotiations that this particular hokum should end (nobody knew precisely what a low tar figure meant and, worse, each advertiser had his own private method of arriving at the figures). Thereafter the cigarette advertisers had regrouped and started a new kind of promotional assault on the public. It was well characterized by the Reverend Neil Hurley, just shortly before the Surgeon General's report appeared, in the magazine *America:*

The sultry woman's voice; the society setting; the rich, rough scion with the tattooed hairy hands; the attitude of complacency and apparent lack of anxiety—isn't this the typical TV approach for much cigarette advertising? It is basically a narcotic dream with an inexcusable dosage of dishonesty.

But it is in this general area that cigarette advertising continues. In 1964, hoping to head off government regulations and legislation, the industry adopted a new code and appointed an industry czar to police cigarette advertising and levy fines for violations of certain rules. The TV announcer who reported this news on the network program I listened to then went on to say:

It is not expected that cigarette advertisements will undergo much change, however.

Nor have they. Principal effects of this code to date (it became operative last year) would seem to be a reduction in the use of testimonials, omission of the word "health" from the text accompanying the healthy young models in the pictures, and a cutdown on the direct exploitation of the college market. But the problem would seem to lie elsewhere. As the Consumers Union *Report on Smoking* observed:

The work of criticizing this cigarette advertisement or that because it is false or misleading in one respect or another has been made trivial by the decade's events. The medical statistics force one to ask whether *any* kind of advertising for a product so intimately connected with disease can be condoned, and if so, then precisely what kind?

The question is as apt as ever. This past year one possible answer was proposed and the cigarette industry and its lobbyists and lawyers went to work on it and killed it. In all the annals of the endless war between buyers and sellers, the intelligent buyer will find few more instructive and sobering pictures of what he's up against than is contained in the story of the cigarette industry's well-planned triumph over buyers, Congress, and social responsibility.

The story starts with the specific warning in the Surgeon General's report that "cigarette smoking is a health hazard of sufficient importance in the United States to warrant appropriate remedial action." The Federal Trade Commission, acting on that warning, within days of the report's appearance adopted a trade practice rule requiring that all cigarette labels and all cigarette advertising carry a notice that "cigarette smoking is dangerous to health and may cause cancer and other diseases." The industry, also acting on the warning, put together a strategy committee of leading Washington lawyers and representatives of each of the six big companies. The committee's major objective was to block the FTC or any other similar ruling—that is, to stop or dilute the "appropriate remedial action" that the medical evidence called for. There were other objectives, too: to divert any state legislatures that might contemplate actions in the consumer's health interest; and even to use the situation to achieve some hedge by which companies could be protected in years to come from damage suits by smokers who developed lung cancer.

This was quite an array of objectives, but it was a very high-level committee (Abe Fortas, personal attorney to President Johnson and subsequently his choice for the Supreme Court, was active in its work). And, quietly and steadily, professionalism prevailed over the simplicities of cause and effect, ordinary reason, and the amateurish responsibility of man to man. So carefully did the tobacco lobby do its work that all but the most informed were hardly aware that its committee was meeting regularly, that strings were being pulled all over Washington, and that its strategy was working, item by item and week by week.

As early as October of 1964, *Consumer Reports* urged consumers to beware:

Strange as it may seem, the cigarette industry might welcome a warning requirement—if it could write the warning itself. This is true for two reasons. First there is a considerable likelihood that state legislatures and city councils may require warning labels if national action is not taken. Congressional committees, with the help of cigarette lobbyists, could readily draft a Federal law that, in addition to requiring only a modest and unalarming "warning," would in legal terms "pre-empt the field" and thus block states and localities from requiring stronger warnings. A spokesman for the cigarette industry, indeed, made this suggestion to a House committee in June.

Second, the cigarette industry faces, and will no doubt continue to face, multiple lawsuits seeking millions of dollars of damages for the wrongful death of men who have contracted lung cancer after smoking Brand A or Brand B. So far the companies have been winning these suits—on the ground that they could not have foreseen, years ago, the medical evidence now available that cigarettes cause death from lung cancer. But this defense is wearing thinner and thinner. Sooner or later a court is likely to decide that the industry has knowledge enough to make it liable for damages. A mild warning on the label might help the companies win such cases indefinitely; for they could allege that they had shifted the burden to smokers by printing the warning.

Thus the stage is set for the passage by Congress of a new law that, though purporting to be a public health measure, would actually serve the ends of the cigarette industry and fail to accomplish any significant public health advance.

Six months later the *Wall Street Journal* reaffirmed that this was what was happening:

Tobacco lobbyists shove for "health hazard" labeling of cigarette packs. The angle: Legislation they're backing would block the Federal Trade Commission's far tougher plan to require warnings in ads as well as labels. A Federal law could also foreclose action by states. Fine print on

the packs could even help protect companies from future
lung-cancer lawsuits by smokers.

And three months later it had happened. Against all the
evidence, the Cigarette Labeling and Advertising Act of 1965
was passed by Congress during the summer. Senator Warren
Magnuson, Democrat, of Washington, called it "a forthright,
historic step towards the responsible protection of the health
of this nation's citizens," and Representative Oren Harris,
Democrat, of Arkansas, called it a "legislative approach in which
we can take some degree of pride." These two sponsors of the
legislation, outmaneuvered and badly used by the industry,
presumably had to say something, although they might have
had the delicacy to avoid such words as "responsible" and
"pride." The record shows that their legislation was a profound
defeat for the nation's health and the interests of consumers,
and a major relief for the cigarette industry in precisely the
way that *Consumer Reports* had predicted.

Elizabeth Brenner Drew, a former member of the *Congressional Quarterly*, reviewed the record for the *Atlantic Monthly*
in September 1965 under the title, "The Quiet Victory of the
Cigarette Lobby," and the subhead, "How it found the best
filter yet—Congress." The substance of the industry victory she
put as follows:

> Behind the façade of a requirement for printing a warning
> on cigarette packages (which is not expected to deter
> smoking much), Congress tied the hands of the Federal
> Trade Commission by forbidding it to proceed with its own
> plans to apply much more stringent regulations. Had it
> not been for Congress, the FTC, which is charged with
> preventing unfair and deceptive trade practices, would have
> required a warning both on cigarette packages *and in cigar-
> ette advertising.* The effect of the advertising regulation is
> what the cigarette industry most feared; Congress obliged
> by forbidding it for at least four years.
>
> In another remarkable provision, the law prohibits state

and local governments from taking any action on cigarette labeling or advertising. It is one thing for Congress to prohibit the states from enacting legislation which overlaps and is inconsistent with its own requirements, but it is a far different thing for Congress to refuse to act, and to prohibit the states from acting, as in the case of cigarette advertising.

The tobacco industry's success at winning from Congress what it wanted while still providing the lawmakers with an opportunity to appear to be all in favor of health was a brilliant stroke.

It was all the more brilliant because the routed forces of public health were not without representation. Indeed, the representation was far stronger than is usual in contests of this sort. It was headed by the National Inter-Agency Council on Smoking and Health, established by the American Cancer Society, American Dental Association, American Heart Association, American Pharmaceutical Association, American Public Health Association, National Congress of Parents and Teachers, National Tuberculosis Association, and other equally respected groups, including the U.S. Public Health Service, U.S. Children's Bureau, and U.S. Office of Education.[3] They were all outmaneuvered, partly because the Council blundered into early support of a compromise bill that the industry lobby subsequently got amended to serve the ends set forth by Mrs. Drew; and partly because the lobby pulled in the newspaper and radio-TV industries to work on its side. The cigarette companies and their strategists accomplished this by letting it be known that,

---

[3] One organization conspicuously missing from this list is the American Medical Association. It was invited to join the Council when the other organizations got together in the summer of 1964, but declined. Possibly it felt that it should not join since it had accepted 10 million dollars from the cigarette manufacturers only a few months before to do some research—an act for which it has been much criticized by doctors, medical societies, and others, including Congressman Frank Thompson, Jr., of New Jersey, who charged that "the AMA is siding with the tobacco industry . . . in return for tobacco state support in its fight against medicare. . . ." The AMA denied this.

if they had to put any warning notices in their advertising, they might well cut down on their advertising or even stop it altogether.

Every member of Congress has TV and radio stations in his district or home state, and newspapers whose support would be nice in his next campaign—many members of Congress, for that matter, are tied up with the ownership of stations and newspapers. Pretty soon after the cigarette lobby had scared the media with its hint of withdrawal of business, letters to the appropriate Senate and House committees began arriving; they came from the Advertising Federation of America, the American Newspapers Publishers Association, the Magazine Publishers Association, the National Association of Broadcasters. . . . Nobody wrote an editorial in praise of the cigarette; nobody launched a campaign specifically demanding the freedom to die of lung cancer. But the letters sufficed. When the vote was taken on the preemption amendment in the seventeen-member Senate Commerce Committee, the two Senators from the tobacco states had picked up seven allies.

This was not good enough for the cigarette lobby; there were further negotiations, some compromises, and finally a unanimous committee vote on a bill that forbade the FTC and all states, and cities as well, to require any health warning in cigarette advertising for a period of three years. In that form the bill passed the Senate. The House passed a bill calling for permanent preemption, which was a little showy as an affront to consumers, the nation's health, and the rights of states. But the provision was useful in getting the Senate-House conference to extend the final bill's protection of the industry's advertising from three years to four.

Cigarette advertising has now been established as a kind of favored ward of Congress—an unprecedented achievement for a lobby—and the guardianship may go on for even longer than the four years voted. We may end this sorry chronicle with a word from that twentieth-century Domesday Book called *Supermarket News*, the very recorder of seller's tricks with which we began in Chapter One. Concerning the great victory of the cigarette lobby, *Supermarket News* is as down-to-earth as it was about short-weighting back on page 6:

> While the ban on FTC action is due to expire in 4 years, the agency has estimated it would take a further four to make the industry comply with any rules it might impose ... and 8 years is a long time for an industry with as many friends in Congress as this one has.

Or, as the classical scholar Gilbert Murray once wrote, using somewhat different words:

> The enemy has no definite name, though in a certain degree we all know him. He who puts always the body before the spirit, the dead before the living; who makes things only in order to sell them; who has forgotten that there is such a thing as truth, and measures the world by advertisement or by money; who daily defiles the beauty that surrounds him and makes vulgar the tragedy.

14

‹‹‹‹‹‹‹‹‹‹‹‹‹‹‹‹‹‹‹‹‹‹‹‹‹‹‹‹›››››››››››››››››››››››››››

Confessions
of Another
Advertising Man

MY own career in advertising has gone unre-
marked by historians of the business; and no one, least of all
myself, could find any fault in this. Still, I have had a career
in advertising; in fact, I have had a couple of careers in advertising. And the reader, in his own interest, will now have to
bear with me while I bring a recital of certain events from
these careers to bear on the subject at hand. Two reasons make
this evil necessary: for one thing, it is relevant; for another, it
is a counter to the advertising industry's common but stultifying
feeling, often articulated in very strong language, that nobody
undertakes a critical evaluation of the business except from the
outside. It may be held by some that this very volume, this
search for light and this redressing of balance, is a critical evaluation of a kind to elicit that familiar response. And so, to the
objectivity of the preceding pages, let me append the subjec-
tivity of the following.

My first career began when I was twenty-one and went to
work for *Time* upon graduating from the University of Chi-

cago. I went to *Time* because, having edited two magazines at the university, I had decided that *Time* needed me; and so I had instructed my friend who ran the university's job-placement bureau to make whatever arrangements were necessary with *Time*. It turned out that, in *Time*'s view, no arrangements were necessary, and they told me so by an unimaginative form letter. However, I had also had the wit to tell my friend and teacher, Thornton Wilder, of my intentions, and had urged him to tell his friend, Henry Luce, the editor and publisher of *Time*, that I was ready. Mr. Wilder had graciously done so, and Mr. Luce's grudging letter of acceptance arrived on the very day that the form letter of rejection arrived. I chose the former and proceeded to New York, where a man named Roy Larsen greeted me in a friendly way and then disappeared. I have not seen him since.

But I was at once put to work in a kind of twilight zone between *Time*'s editorial department and promotion department, where I wrote book reviews and small paragraphs for inconspicuous departments of the magazine, along with *Time* house ads for a publication called *Tide*. This was a monthly house organ distributed to advertisers and agents, and after two or three months I found myself installed as its editor, everybody else being preoccupied with the beginnings of *Fortune* and the triumph of *Time*. I was editing *Tide* when Raymond Rubicam decided he wanted to be a publisher and bought *Tide* to build on; he didn't want to be an editor, though, and so I went along as a part of the package. It would probably have to be called a deceptive package; Mr. Rubicam had never published anything, I had never edited anything except the two magazines at the university I had just left, and on the day the Tide Publishing Company was incorporated there was not yet a working staff.

It is necessary to view this preposterous adventure in its context. The great market crash was still resounding, the depression was closing in, and there were at least three strong publications with which *Tide* would be competing as a trade journal of advertising and marketing. Furthermore, Mr. Rubicam's colleagues at the vigorously growing Young & Rubicam advertising agency were fully appreciative of his importance to them and made no bones of their resentment of this diversion. "They think I'm crazy," he told me early; I was inclined to agree, although I also thought him farseeing, audacious, and, increasingly, a good publisher. Having made his gamble, he stuck with it; he was always available and he neither interfered nor imposed.

We worked closely together, arguing and reasoning at late dinners or after hours in his office or even mine, talking about life and work in general more than we discussed the specifics of *Tide*. We did this fairly regularly for five years, after three of which *Tide* was making money, and practically every advertising agent and most of the advertisers and media men were reading it. It had the best editorial staff in the business, including Mildred Edie (the Brady came later), who even then held highly articulate ideas about the buyer-seller relationship, and with her Mr. Rubicam argued even more (although to less avail) than he did with me.

It would be impossible to spend five years in close association with a man so knowledgeable, so articulate, and so close to what was going on in the advertising world without learning something about it. Moreover, in addition to editing *Tide*, I spent much time on my own making the rounds of agencies and companies for material. I had a long and fascinating discussion with a well-known advertising man about the importance of certain hieroglyphs on an Egyptian pyramid; he was surprised that I planned to spend the summer of 1934 in New York City since the hieroglyphs indicated that this might be a dangerous time. I also had an interesting talk with the president of the Lydia E. Pinkham Company, who told me that their experiments with other types of copy had not paid off and they were going back to what he described as "a straight uterine basis."

Most of the time, of course, I encountered no such fascinations as these; most of the time I interrupted people who were working more or less hard in more or less orthodox ways.

I went to all the advertising conventions and with my own ears heard the call for greater Truth in Advertising. I talked to the advertising agent for a drug that had the American Medical Association's Seal of Approval at that time and who lamented this because it inhibited him in writing the advertising copy. I spent much time with account executives, media men, copywriters, art directors, and others of the fraternity discussing aspects of advertising, and I wrote and published stories about most of these aspects. While learning, I think, a fair amount about the workings of advertising, I came to believe increasingly from what I learned that the values served by advertising as a going institution and the standards generally observed in its practice were seriously inadequate. On top of that, after five years it dawned on me that I could no longer work up an honest interest in the details of a new campaign for toilet paper, cigarettes, or even a new car. And so, after five years, I resigned.

It seemed to me that when Raymond Rubicam was in the room one could think of advertising as a profession; but Raymond Rubicam wasn't always in the room, and too often advertising was only another trade, and all too often not a very high-grade one. The relevant point here is that I came to my conclusions not from the outside but from the inside, and despite a close and rewarding association with one of the industry's most able and respected members. (I can recall a small deception that can be charged to him, however. This happened one lunchtime—my depression salary was often eked out with elegant lunches and dinners provided by Mr. Rubicam. On our way to the restaurant Mr. Rubicam asked me if I had ever tasted Postum. I said I had not. He said that we were meeting someone from General Foods for lunch; in fact, he said, the man we were meeting was the advertising manager for Postum, a Young & Rubicam account. "This fellow," said Mr. Rubicam, "doesn't run into many people who drink Postum. Would you mind ordering Postum? It's not really so bad. Would you mind? I think he'd get a kick out of actually hearing somebody order it." I thought this a touching deception and readily agreed to share in it; but I found that he *had* rather overstated the case for Postum.)

This was my first career in advertising. My second stretches over the eighteen years I have spent, off and on, with Consumers Union. Consumers Union is—although most of the advertising people I know seem totally unaware of it (that's the trouble with outsiders)—an active advertiser. It has been a steady user of direct mail, even printing its own mailing pieces by the millions, since the very first year, which is when I joined the staff. One of my early responsibilities when Consumers Union was in its infancy was to write the direct mail promotion. All along, as editor, publications director, assistant director, and finally director of Consumers Union, I took part in the planning and preparation of most of this material, and I supervised all of it for a number of years. The first issue of the *Reports* went out to about 3,000 people and the issues for quite a few years now have been going out to nearly 300 times that number.

Is Consumers Union, then, a great unsung advertising success and am I a genius of at least one kind of advertising? It is not and I am not. If there ever were a genius at Consumers Union, it was Arthur Kallet, its founding director, who put the organization together to begin with, raised its standards high and held them there, drove the organization on for twenty years before leaving it—and had, among fifty other talents more important, one whereby he could tell a bad piece of direct mail from a good one at a glance. Certainly the organization benefited from all this, but even all this doesn't explain the organization's success; Arthur Kallet explained that when he pointed out a long time ago that what was good for the country, so to speak, was good for Consumers Union.

Specifically, when consumer goods production goes up, as in general it has for many years, the direct mail generally works fine, and Consumers Union's circulation goes up, too; and when production falls off, the mail returns generally fall off and so does circulation. Advertising men like to think that advertising increases production, which is often true enough on a small scale; the big-scale reality, however, is that production increases advertising.

Consumers Union's experience is, in fact, not different from that of other advertisers; but advertising men are very often blind to economic truisms. The present one is well stated in, of all places, Rosser Reeves's *Reality in Advertising*, where Mr. Reeves tries to argue more involved economics of advertising with John Kenneth Galbraith, and comes off so horribly that I will not review his disaster here. But he does see this particular economic truth, and he states it very well:

> Advertising was born with the industrial revolution, when personal selling for mass goods became an impossibility; it grew with the industrial revolution, as improvements in technology spewed out still more goods; it became immense, as production became immense; but it was always an effect —and never a cause.

That is a perfectly sensible statement on the general economics of advertising, one of the few I have encountered in a book by an advertising man. It doesn't fit all cases; advertising is often a cause, of course, with respect to certain individual products, such as the cosmetic that is dreamed up specifically to provide the excuse for an advertising push. And in this area one might better invoke that economic doctrine enunciated by Sinclair Lewis, as quoted in *The New York Times* more than twenty years ago:

> Advertising is a valuable economic factor because it is the cheapest way of selling goods, particularly if the goods are worthless.

Consumers Union got into direct mail advertising because the newspapers and magazines of the 1930's (and of the 1940's and well into the 1950's as well) would not accept its space advertising; and I learned something about advertising from this, too. I remember a talk I had one summer afternoon with the late Colonel (subsequently General) Julius Ochs Adler of *The New York Times*, which had accepted several advertisements from Consumers Union, all of which had been very effective, and then had refused to accept more. My purpose in calling on Colonel Adler was to find out why. His explanation, as nearly as I can recall it from this distance, ran as follows. *The New York Times*, he said, had an advertising policy whereby one advertiser was not allowed to use its columns to attack another advertiser. In effect, our Not Acceptable ratings of products could be considered attacks on advertisers. Our advertising for *Consumer Reports*, which carried such ratings, urged people to subscribe to the magazine. Such advertising, therefore, used the columns of the *Times* to urge people to read attacks on advertising, and this, Colonel Adler concluded, was the same thing as using the columns for the attacks themselves, and hence was a violation of *The New York Times* advertising policy. I was quite dazzled by this, and I am sure the intelligent buyer will admire its artistry, too.

Over a span of two or three years, from 1937 to 1939 or thereabouts, we received rejections from more than sixty newspapers and magazines. The letters ran a considerable range, from the extreme of one which said flatly and honestly, "We cannot run your advertising because our other advertisers would object to it," to any number which rang some variant of the theme, "Your advertising does not seem consistent with our standards of suitability." And so we took to direct mail.

But there was much more to be learned about advertising from Consumers Union than could be learned from participation in its functioning as an advertiser. The real education came from the products that we bought, tested, and compared not only with each other but with their advertising claims. The novelty and potential of product testing in relation to the

uses of advertising have made up the subject matter of any
number of speeches that many of us at Consumers Union have
given over the years to any number of audiences of advertising
men. The point of view has not instantly converted all members
of these not always attentive audiences, but, if nothing else,
its frequent statement has served to clarify our own understanding. Here is the rough essence of fifty such statements:

> We have never really understood the need on your part to
> avoid the actual product the way you so often do in your
> advertising copy. We are fascinated with the product. We
> spend literally months in tests and retests, descriptions and
> further descriptions, and writing and rewriting to be as accu-
> rate as we can about how some of these very complicated,
> highly complex products behave. And furthermore, for these
> long, detailed, and, in your terms, dull descriptions of prod-
> ucts, we find that our members not only pay what it costs us
> to provide them but do read the dull descriptions in detail.
> We find no need to search for the psychological quirks or
> the frustrated instincts or the neurotic substitutes to provide
> a basis for interest in a description of what is going on in
> the world of products. We also find that we do not need
> the cynical and murky complications of the Dichter sub-
> conscious to comprehend the disparities between product
> performances and advertising claims—which usually out-
> run the disparities between products—or to talk about
> goods to consumers.
>
> We find that the whole truth, so far as we can deter-
> mine it, is much more interesting than half-truths. We find
> that the qualifications imposed by reality on the perform-
> ance of a product enrich the information rather than
> deplete it. We find that only rarely are superlatives valuable
> or interesting. We find, rather, that the matter-of-fact,
> work-a-day behavior of goods in use is a meaningful revela-
> tion of the degree to which man has adapted, or failed to
> adapt, the rich potentiality of the technology of our times

to the public good; and that the vague and fanciful presentations of this behavior in advertising are a meaningful revelation of the degree to which man has affronted the public good.

It is true enough. The intelligent buyer should also take notice that one of the interesting distinctions between the seller as a producer and the seller as an advertiser is intimated here. The stereotype of the producing seller as a man who can't talk about anything except what he makes is very apt to be true, but (if he knows anything else) it is possible for him to be rewarding, stereotype or not. But the advertising seller is a different sort. With him the product tends to get lost under overlays and puffed out with talk around the fringes. The product itself may be a sorry thing, cheapened in quality, overpriced for what it is, possibly hazardous, and designed for promotion rather than use. Still, it is one thing to the man who makes it and generally —one cannot say always—another to the man who puts together the advertising for it.

Since Consumers Union neither makes, nor advertises, the products it tests, they probably represent something different to its staff than they do to either of these others. What is one to think, for example, of the Montgomery Ward gas range with a control panel made of plastic and so positioned that the heat of some of the range's burners could melt it? It was, of course, bad design and corrupt as well because it set out to cozen the buyer with the look of efficiency and ended up exploiting him. And the Mirro-Matic electric skillet with neat little handles that could not be held without making the fingers touch hot metal was a stupid design.

We encountered these products just in recent tests, and we have encountered plenty of others like them. For most of them there is the pretty little tag or booklet with the fatuous beginning of the "Congratulations! you are now the proud owner of . . ." variety. And for most there is the good-looking advertisement, as well designed as the product is not, putting best feet forward all over the place and leaving it up to the buyer to find out on his own time and money that the range will devour itself and the skillet burn him. We are no longer surprised by such disparities between the advertisement and the thing advertised, but most of us still feel a small sense of shock, a frisson of outrage, muted by the years but discernible none the less.

We feel something more when we come across an electric toothbrush that sets up a lethal shock hazard under reasonable conditions of use. Why such a product is put on the market in the first place, I suppose, is that it is an example of designing for sale. Our problem was how to get it off the market. The name of this product was Vibra-dent; it was made by the Chase Manufacturing Company of New York; and our shoppers found it in a store only a couple of weeks after it was put on sale. The advertising literature accompanying it featured a child happily cleaning her teeth with the device. But the device was so constructed that, if it were accidentally or playfully dropped into a basin of water, anyone atempting to retrieve it could be electrocuted if he happened to be touching a ground, such as a water faucet.

This seemed to us a most serious hazard and we informed both the U.S. Food and Drug Administration and the manufacturer, and then issued a public warning in the form of a news release. The press generally ignored the release; one radio station in New York (WABC) and one newspaper, the *New York Post,* carried the story. The Chase Manufacturing Company informed CU that it intended to redesign the product. The Food and Drug Administration began an investigation.

But the old Vibra-dent, the one that could kill you under not unreasonable conditions of use, remained on sale. More than that, a full-page Vibra-dent ad in *Life* pictured this model more than a month after CU's public warning; and the same model continued to be promoted as a cut-price feature with large posters in the windows of a number of chain drugstores, even after the manufacturer discontinued production of the model. The Food and Drug Administration eventually seized

some samples in the stores; the Underwriters' Laborat
revised its standards for electric toothbrushes; and eventually,
I suppose, the promotional advertising got rid of the stock on
hand to all the happy little children.

It may be necessary to point out that one of the rewards of
disinterested product testing is the finding of products that
won't kill you, are well made, fill an actual need, and aren't
too wildly misrepresented by their advertising. This happens
quite regularly. It also happens quite often that the tests disclose
relatively inexpensive products good enough to be better made
than high-priced competitors, lightly advertised products that
perform better than their heavily advertised competitors, and
private brands that outperform either.

From the perspective of the tests—which give no more "insight into the foundations or the constraining force of law and
order" than advertising itself does, both being tools to be used
—advertising is not meretricious but simply unreliable. From
the perspective of the tests, the common protestation of advertising men that inferior products cannot be foisted on buyers is
simply untrue. And at least in the spirit of the tests, the once
shining tenet of the advertising fraternity that advertising lowers
costs runs afoul of the very common finding that the most
heavily advertised products are seldom the least expensive of
their kind and are often the most expensive.

The intelligent buyer should note that sellers have changed
their views on advertising and costs in recent years. The old
argument, once as real to advertising men as Santa Claus to
a small child, ran to the effect that advertising lowered the
cost of products by providing a mass market to accommodate
the volume to bring unit costs down. That was an argument
left over from the twenties, when advertising was thought
to be a sure thing, as noted many pages back. The change
came in with some of the recessions following World War II,
and the reasoning now runs rather more discreetly: a mass
market is needed to maintain the productive system and advertising helps to build a mass market. That's about as far as

goes; nothing is said of lower prices or
omy. Advertising is admitted to be a cost
the products, but is held to be a justifiable

nan justifying an advertising cost can be a
and his justifications ever so elastic. He can
ng cost amounting to 100 per cent or more
rtion which is quite routine for the introduction of a new drug or cosmetic or food—on the grounds
that, if he can knock over the competition by spending that
much, he will have a good thing going and can make money
thereafter. (I would not argue with him over the good thing,
although this is somewhat removed from the good life that he
talks about at other times.) Gleem toothpaste had a budget of
15 million dollars for the advertising campaign with which it
set out to get a toehold in that market; and David Ogilvy observed in his *Confessions* book that a 10-million-dollar budget
was cutting it pretty thin for putting a detergent on the market.
The high price of market entry in these times of ever higher
advertising costs, and the consequent tendency to monopoly
situations, seems clear enough.

In five years nearly 7 million dollars was spent on the advertising of Brylcreem, a hair dressing, and during those five years the
sales totaled 12 million. As *Advertising Age* noted, it was "a
successful campaign"; the measure of success was that Brylcreem "increased its share-of-market" from 2.6 per cent to 10 per
cent. This would seem to fall somewhere short of a cause for
particular fierce pride on the one side and short of the general
hum of destruction on the other. Indeed, it is in this generally
hospitable area that most justifications of advertising costs
come to rest, evocative of both extremes and somewhat remote
from the reality still most familiar to most of us.

The advertising mentality moves very slowly in the presence
of an economic concept, and adjusts to reality with infinite
circumspection; so the old thesis of advertising as a sure thing
still crops up in advertisers' talk. One way to tell an old-type

advertiser is to test his reaction to what some of the company financial reports of recent years have said about advertising. Thus a National Biscuit Company report, in which it was written that "our profits were adversely affected . . . by heavy advertising and promotion expenses." Thus a Coty, Inc., report, in which a loss was credited to "an increase in advertising and selling expense." Thus a news report such as this:

> In spite of Max Factor & Company's increased emphasis on promotion and advertising, which includes three nation-wide television shows, earnings for the six months ended June 30th went up by 31%. . . .

That "in spite of" clause would never have issued from an advertising man's lips some years ago.

Over the years at Consumers Union, a kind of nonprofit institution for the study of advertising and selling, I have changed my views some, too. I confess there was a time, in the early stages of my discovery that advertising claims did not necessarily bear any meaningful relationship to a product's performance, when I invested the simple technique of advertising with institutional powers of evil that I no longer think it has. What it does have might be described as an institutional power to call forth evil, in the form of the seamiest motivations of its practitioners. The combination of petty objectives and gross means that characterizes the great bulk of advertising calls to mind those badly sprung and overpowered automobiles that contribute to the hazards of American life. And while in theory advertising can be made to serve fair and useful ends (indeed, Stuart Chase once observed that advertising "sanely" employed could "remake the world"), in fact its lack of standards and controls means that it thrives in the hands of the simply greedy, the morally inept, and the socially backward. One of the steady hopes of such moralists as myself is that these practitioners may come to count too much on the buyer's lack of sophistication and protective devices. But the lack, God knows, is a big one; a major contribution of Consumers Union may have been to reduce it, at least to some degree, and still it is there.

Unfortunately, Consumers Union has reached least those low-income consumers who are precisely the ones most and worst victimized by the needless costs that flow from advertising's ceaseless brand-switching drives. These people, of whom one must say that they stand in least need of the false hopes and obscurantisms peddled by the adman, are steadily preyed on also by the door-to-door salesmen, whose activities are beyond even the modest controls exercised over advertising. Their functioning among low-income families in some low-cost public housing projects in New York City has been set forth to some extent in David Caplovitz's book entitled *The Poor Pay More,* written with the help of a grant from Consumers Union. Many of the details reported are simply pathetic, such as this excerpt from an interview:

> When I first moved, the man who said he was the manager asked me to sign some papers. It turned out I signed for encyclopedias thinking I was signing some housing authority forms as a new tenant. . . . My husband was threatened with a garnishee by the encyclopedia company.

And so on; about 40 per cent of the families studied had been involved in some serious exploitation. Let Mr. Caplovitz summarize the situation:

> The numerous accounts of exploitation fall under several general headings. Some reveal the high-pressure sales techniques to which these families are subjected. Others relate to the misrepresentation of the price of goods. And still others refer to the substitution of inferior goods for those ordered. Included here are accounts of the sale of reconditioned goods as new.
>
> The repetitiveness of the incidents is quite striking. Some families were victimized by unethical television repairmen, a few by the same company. Another group were victims of

the pots-and-pans salesmen; encyclopedia salesmen show up in several of the accounts, as do the peddlers selling sink attachments.

As we shall see, the incidents touch upon a number of themes. These include the role of the mass media in setting off the chain of events with alluring ads; the anonymity of many of the credit transactions to the point where the consumer is not sure who the merchant is; the bewilderment of the consumer in the face of powerful forces brought into play by the merchant; and the hopelessness, frustration, and resignation of many in the face of exploitation.

The commercial spirit is pervasive, of course. The well-to-do buyer, the one who lives in the pleasant suburbs or the high-priced apartment, gets exploited on most of these counts, too. The ads seduce him; most of the time—if he buys on installment, as more and more people at all income levels do—he doesn't know where he fits into what credit structure; he faces the same forces from the merchant, although he may go to a store which does not choose to use them on him; and certainly there are few buyers left who have not experienced hopelessness, frustration, and resignation somewhere in the complex of the buying-selling relationships which fill these times. But it all bears hardest, by far, on the low-income consumers, on the 40,000,000 or more Americans whose less-than-$4,000 annual incomes have little or no leeway in them. The non-poor buyer has his extra income to maintain his bank balance if not his self-respect. But in Watts, at a certain point, that cushion being absent (see page ooo), there was a riot.

Probably in accordance with the widely held belief that everything which has grown to be big is respectable because advertising must have made it so, Consumers Union's advertising is no longer objectionable to newspapers and magazines. I made the discovery about eight years ago, when I hired a small advertising agency to institute inquiries among some of the media about the current acceptability of Consumers Union advertisements. The agent asked several of them what their feelings were, and all but one said they didn't think they wanted any. I thought about this for some months and finally decided that the approach had been a bad one. So I had some regular copy prepared and regular insertion orders sent out to ten newspapers, just as though we were General Motors or Lydia E. Pinkham or even Anacin.

Nine of the ten ads were accepted without any ado at all; and Consumers Union has been running space advertising off and on ever since. No advertiser has gone out of business because of this advertising, at least none I ever heard of. It is possible that the advertisers and their agents, busy spending their billions of dollars, haven't even noticed.

Meantime, Consumers Union, or rather the Consumers Union idea, has spread into a number of other countries, where the pressure of commercialism has had effects similar to those it has had here. The International Organization of Consumers Unions, with headquarters at The Hague, has meetings every two years to which representatives of consumer testing organizations in more than twenty countries come for discussions; and, in between, joint test programs are undertaken.

The English organization, which got its start about eight years ago with a small grant of money from Consumers Union and a large investment of time and effort from a variety of Britishers, has grown to be much the biggest and most active of the foreign groups. With a circulation of about 400,000, its publication *Which?* is, indeed, already larger in relation to England's population than *Consumer Reports* is in relation to this country's. In part, this may be because the media of communication there have treated the idea of consumer testing far less fearfully than the media did here when Consumers Union was getting started. It was even possible for *Which?* to get on British TV with a program on which actual products were actually tested; a Consumers Union effort to get any one of the three big U.S. commercial networks to make room for a similar program in this country failed.

The *Manchester Guardian* took notice of the spread of consumer testing in England with a stirring call for defense of the Fifth Freedom by columnist Michael Frayne. Mr. Frayne gets into dangerous waters and it is really not my place to advance his notions; but, in the spirit of fair play which has animated this book throughout, here is his report on how to stop the consumer testing conspiracy:

Those of us who have the sacred liberty of the individual at heart (*said Rollo Swavely, the well-known public relations consultant*) are gravely concerned about the spread of this dangerous fashion for consumer research and consumer advisory services. And now that they've managed to inveigle support from BBC Television—well, frankly, old boy, the time has come for all men of goodwill to band together and say: "It's just not on."

Now look, Mike, I wouldn't try to hide anything from an old friend like you, and anyway you've probably heard that I've got the account for the newly formed Fair Play for Manufacturers movement. (No, no—doing it for love, old boy, I assure you.) Anyway, I know I couldn't move your stony heart with the manufacturers' sufferings—though, by God, Mike, some of the fully authenticated cases I've got in my files of real hardship inflicted by consumer research reports—some of the sheer misery I've seen our chaps suffering, just because they've made one little slip like putting an inflammable ingredient into their fire-extinguishers. . . .

No, Mike, it's not the manufacturers I'm thinking of at the moment. I'm buying you lunch today not as a public relations man, but simply as a disinterested private citizen who feels he can no longer stand idly by and watch the terrible inroads consumer research is making into the personal liberty of the ordinary man in the street.

You see, I know you liberals—or radicals, or socialists, or what have you. I mean, God knows, I'm one myself. I know your heart's in the right place, but the trouble with you is you're all a bit woolly-minded. You look at *"Which?"* and the rest of them, and you think in your fuzzy, imprecise way that they're somehow on your side against the wiles of the manufacturers.

But it's not like that, you see Mike. These organizations are actually *reducing* your right of choice. Instead of letting you choose goods for yourself, they appoint snoopers to chose them for you. And these snoopers don't know you, or anything about you—they don't know the little fads and fancies that go to make up the quintessential you. Their cold, impersonal criteria don't take any account of the housewife who actually wants a slightly less inhumanly efficient foodmixer, or the fellow who expresses his personality by actually *choosing* to pay more for the identical formula of shaving-soap. They're making life soulless and impersonal. What is a man, when all's said and done, but the sum of his consumer choices?

And in the end, Mike, they're going to destroy your choice altogether. They're going to force the models they've set their minds against off the market—drive the manufacturers who fall foul of their petty-minded preconceptions about what you ought to like out of business. You start off by going along with their advice voluntarily—but you'll finish up buying the best goods whether you want them or not—because there won't be any bad or indifferent products to be had! Could police-state tyranny be carried further? And what do you think's going to become of the advertising industry if there's only one brand of each product?

But the real point, Mike, is the basic constitutional one. The faceless men behind consumer research are trying to deprive people of what I call the Fifth Freedom—the absolutely fundamental and inalienable right of man to be influenced by advertising.

What can ordinary chaps like you and me do to stop them? Well, Mike, this is where you come in. I don't often ask you a favor, but for the sake of our precious heritage, for the sake of the Western way of life, I am asking you just to make one appeal to your readers. Just five little words, Mike, but they could nip the whole conspiracy in the bud. As a matter of fact, it's the slogan of the Fair Play for Manufacturers movement. I'll write it down for you, Mike:

MAKE A BAD BUY TODAY!

‹‹‹‹‹‹‹‹‹‹‹‹‹‹‹‹‹‹‹‹‹‹‹‹‹‹‹››››››››››››››››››››››››››

Postscript:
The Cool Wind
from the Future

THE factual framework of anything is the first part of it to go, along with the meanings of the words that define the framework. And the specifics of these pages are not the important things for the intelligent buyer or anyone else to remember. Certainly, as of this moment, no one can foresee the factual framework for the commercial spirit of the future, even defining the future as no more than a generation or so ahead. Assuredly one of the major revolutions in the history of man is taking place before our eyes in the spread of electronic communication around the world and into space. The effects of this revolution can only be profound, and that will be true even in the relatively small world of man's goods and of such endless activities as man undertakes to move them at a profit. The commercial drive will have to take different forms and shapes on this side of Early Bird than it did on the other. The challenge, of course, is enormous. For, as Arthur Clarke wrote twenty years or more ago, three communications satellites properly stationed could link all the world's people—and if that is done, he said, "ours will be the last century of the savage and for all mankind the stone age will be over."

It must be added that this is the hope, the dream, and the theoretical possibility. But it is important to know in what state of grace, with what values, and with what achievements from the past and present we are approaching the unknown future. These matters, on a small scale, have been the underlying concern of this book. And the news from this front—as opposed to the always good news from advertising—seems not so good. Neither the direction nor the content of things seems quite appropriate to the great new vistas.

We can almost see ourselves in a recent report by Maya Pines of some work being done with seriously disturbed children. One of these children, a six-year-old boy named Jackie, was autistic; he lived within himself, spoke only in gibberish, and could hardly be spoken to without flying into a tantrum. Communication with him, for all practical purposes, was non-existent. And several psychiatrists had made the conventional recommendation that he be put away in an institution. But one doctor sat Jackie down in front of a new and interesting research machine called ERE (for Edison Responsive Environment). This machine presents a private environment of sounds and sights which a child completely controls and modifies through a typewriter keyboard. In numerous experiments the machine has been found to draw forth responses and actions from children otherwise unreachable, and this was the case with Jackie. He sat in front of the machine, alone in a closed booth, and after a while began tapping out words, and the words read: IVORY LIQUID CLOROX ARRID DEODORINT MR CLEAN—and the list went on (the spelling is Jackie's).

Little Jackie would seem to be compelling evidence that the marketplace is no longer the "place set apart" that Diogenes Laertius called it. It is not possible to know what ARRID DEODORINT, for example, means to Jackie, but it is plainly one of the fixed points that he has found in his brief exposure to this society; and, for that matter, it is one of the fixed points

from which the sellers, plying their trades in what *could* be the
last century of the savage, speak to all of us. One may pay tribute
to the influence of this advertising that penetrated the consciousness of little Jackie, whose consciousness forbade entry
to so many other things. But still one must ask: what has really
penetrated little Jackie's consciousness?

It is very hard to say—perhaps only words that have lost
their meaning; or perhaps words blown in on the cool wind
from the future, bringing back the commercial good news before
we are even there.

It may be that they are the same, the lost words and the
cool commercial words. The trouble is that we can no longer
endure either. "When words lose their meaning, the people
will lose their liberty"; but our loss in communication is perilous
even beyond that. The ships of the old explorers moved slowly
and erratically; the maps were crude and inaccurate; and the
explorers could tolerate both. At 2,300 miles an hour, to pick a
perfectly reasonable number more or less at random, any lack
of precision in the design of any part, any breakdown in its quality, or any minute gap in the communication between producer
and user means death. At higher figures, on more ranging trips,
we do not know what might happen; that is, we are not sure of
the precise nature of the death.

Our penetrations of time, of space, and increasingly of matter,
coupled with the seemingly endless increase in ourselves, have
moved contemporary civilization, for better or for worse, beyond the real comprehension or actual reach of all generations
but one. That generation may be described as the one which can
think of a light year, for example, in personal terms; which
can imagine, for example, a fire of 15,000,000 degrees; and which
knows that from now on all wars are civil wars.

None of these thoughts, in the world of today, can be held
very long without threatening many other thoughts with absurdity. Planning and criteria that were designed for the relatively simplified constructions of the eighteenth and nineteenth
centuries do not work for the period of the rise of the biologic

sciences, the searching of the subatomic mass, and the dissipation of distance as a meaningful concept. The danger is that the absurdity will come to tinge all planning and all criteria.

And the danger is real. For we have been badly prepared for the breath-taking show we face. Perhaps there has not been enough time or perhaps we are too slow. But simple speculation framed in lost or meaningless words can no longer serve us adequately, any more than Newtonian mechanics, which are not ultimately precise, can serve us adequately in the nuclear realm. A task imposed on all generations now is to seek out as well as possible the true fixed points of the turning world, as many as can be found, and it must be remembered all the time that these fixed points sometimes are masked, and that string-operated imitations (*vide* ARRID DEODORINT) dot the landscape. Still, the real ones must be sought for such guidance as they can provide. They must be sought through the trivilization and the falsification of meanings, and through the slow spread of waste and the withering of our resources.

It is precisely in this quest that the spirit of the modern seller fails us most. For he has aspired to the power without the glory, and he is, as the creature of his function thus conceived, the trivializer, the falsifier, the spreader, and the witherer. He sets the beautiful and the useful in opposition, as though there were no alternative to that, and he confuses the useful and the useless as though there were no difference. His trimmings and transgressions do not usually constitute calamities, but the values from which they evolve are hospitable to calamity, being one with such values—to take a very immediate example—as governments must draw on when they have to force-sell actions that do not in themselves command respect.

Such values have been at work in the government's efforts to rationalize even the most repugnant aspects of this country's interventions in the affairs of the Vietnamese. Whatever the aims and justifications of these adventures, our actions plainly have involved us in the support of military dictatorships that could not command the support of their own people, in indiscriminate bombings of civilians, and in varied transgressions of international law. Much of the press of the world, including the best of our own, has documented such actions a hundred times over, and many voices have deplored them. But official doctrine, in somewhat the tone of voice of the advertising agent who announced that "we did no more and no less than an advertising agency is required to do," has discounted all criticism, has proclaimed our ends to be noble, and has found justification of the offensive deeds in the proclaimed intention. This is the spirit of the seller at work; it involves the government in the defense of ignoble exploits, and the defenses often have been of a piece with, say, the cigarette industry's efforts to extricate itself from responsibility for the health hazards of its products by pointing at its tax returns. (And what *is* one to think of our label of "defoliation" for our destruction of the Vietnamese countryside and food supply? Surely, few things could be closer to the essence of *suppressio veri* than that.)

This is, after all, the country in which the spirit of the seller has reached its finest flowering and the gaudy blooms touch our values everywhere. One might even find a fairly precise commercial equivalent to the Vietnamese adventure; it would be, for example, the mighty effort of the Ford Motor Company to force-sell, with great supplies of money and rationalizations, the hopelessley ill-begotten Edsel. The Vietnam war, as this country has been pushing it, is an Edsel-type war—a heavily-financed undertaking, proceeding from outdated surveys, ingrown committee thinking, and naive and arrogant assumptions with respect to supposed beneficiaries. After two years of trying to justify its wrong guesses with the Edsel, the Ford company took its quarter-of-a-billion dollar loss and called it quits. Robert S. McNamara was one of those in charge at the time. As things turned out, he lost no face and the company continued doing business with its honor as intact as ever. The clear achievement of the Mustang, introduced with much less money than the Edsel but with a far better appreciation of what people were willing and able to accept, soon followed. It is an interest-

244) *Part Three:* PRIDE AND PREJUDICE

ing parallel, and one wonders whether, as Secretary of Defense, Mr. McNamara has ever stopped to think of it.

It is not necessary to make too much of such parallels, but they should not be ignored, either. The point here, at all events, is a simple one, though basic: it is that the modern seller is not likely to be our best source of thoughts that can help us, or himself either, when he turns to larger matters.

And there is simply ceasing to be room, in a world of three and a half billion people going on six, all within a few hours of each other, for the divisive act at any level of life. The antics of the sellers, viewed so long and so broadly as a kind of mischievous fun and games, have come to be not only boring in that light but alarming in stronger lights. What the German economist said years ago—"Search out the customer and attack him"— has loomed ever larger in the modern seller's mind, albeit without the economist's irony; the seller's own reiterations of such an outlook, as set forth in some small part throughout this book, bear witness.

"Search out the customer and attack him." But the customer, attacked endlessly, cannot always be counted on not to attack back. It was partly the antics of the seller, it is worth noting, that the residents of the Watts district of Los Angeles rioted against in the summer of 1965. As everyone in the low-income ghetto of Watts knew, including the merchants, the seller's exploitation of the buyer there was more intense—the products worse, the prices higher—than elsewhere in Los Angeles. "You see," said a witness before the commission investigating the riots afterwards, "you see, before the riots owners of stores in this community didn't do a thing for us. They didn't care about this community. They robbed the people. And also we would find that most of the goods here were seconds and thirds. And you know they're going to lay a high interest rate on you. That's Watts, man, before the riots."

And that is why, or partly why—although the newspapers and the television stations said little about it—the residents of Watts burned and looted the supermarkets and the credit clothiers and the small-loan offices and other such businesses, but did not touch a Goodwill Industries outlet, for example, right next door.

"Search out the customer and attack him." It is a rather shabby sentiment with which to try to move out of the last century of the savage; it goes better with the hum of destruction than with a new creative climate; it is a fit slogan for a blind force that does not mean us well. As I said on page 6, a sentiment of this sort falls "rather harshly on the ear so early in the game, and the reader will not be asked to dwell on it at this stage." But I think the time has come to dwell on it, now and for the future.

The time has come, in short—if indeed it is not running out —to ask some questions of this blind force that stares at us from the TV screens and from advertisements in the newspapers and magazines and gives us our instructions 1,600 times a day. Like the love which came to Professor Guildea in Robert Hitchen's chilling story, something smothering and irrational has taken possession of our lives and our only hope is to belay it with questions. Questions, as always, are more important than the answers; for we will not get the right answers unless and until we ask the right questions and ask them over and over and over.

Howard Gossage, a thoughtful and articulate advertising man on the West coast, asks whether advertising in its present form —he characterizes it as a 15-billion-dollar sledge hammer to drive a 49-cent economy-size thumbtack—has any right to exist at all; it does so, he points out, only because the media have allowed financial control to shift from the audience to the advertiser. Jules Henry, in his *Culture Against Man*, proceeds from the same point to a different end down another street:

> It is common knowledge that advertising firms and their clients, in bending the mass media almost exclusively to pecuniary ends, have come to play an important regulatory role and have, therefore, usurped the functions of federal regulatory agencies. The least the government can do is to

treat advertising as a public utility, and regulate it accordingly.

Dr. Henry also suggests that we might send advertisers and advertising agents to a truth school where, "under the direction of wise and benevolent philosophers of the old tradition, they would have classes in the difference between pecuniary and traditional truth, the nature of values and their social function, the nature of human dignity, etc."

There is no dearth of answers; I have indicated some of my own back at the end of Part Two of this book. But, as I say, the answers are less important than the questions. The next time you steal a glimpse at your television screen, think of those questions of Hillel:

If I am not for myself, who will be?
But if I am for myself alone, what do I amount to?
If not now, when?

Index

◄◄◄◄◄◄◄◄◄◄◄◄◄◄◄◄◄◄◄◄◄◄◄►►►►►►►►►►►►►►►►►►►►►►►►

A NOTE ABOUT THE AUTHOR

DEXTER MASTERS was for six years the director of Consumers Union and for many years the editor of Consumer Reports; he now serves CU as consulting editor while also working on his own as an editorial consultant and writer. His novel, *The Accident*, has appeared in more than a dozen foreign editions since Alfred A. Knopf, Inc., published it ten years ago and was recently issued in a new American edition with a foreword by Milton Mayer. Mr. Masters has contributed to *The New Yorker*, *The Saturday Evening Post*, *Fortune*, *Book Week*, and other magazines. Before joining CU in its first year, he was the editor of *Tide*, then one of the leading journals of advertising and marketing. A radio series written by Mr. Masters won a Peabody Award in Educational Broadcasting. In addition, he has served as a staff member of the Radiation Laboratory of the Massachusetts Institute of Technology and as a consultant to several publishing houses. Mr. Masters, a native of Springfield, Illinois, and a graduate of the Choate School and the University of Chicago (Ph.B., 1930), is married and is the father of a newly born son. He makes his home in New York.

A NOTE ON THE TYPE

THE text of this book is set in Electra, a typeface designed by W(illiam) A(ddison) Dwiggins for the Mergenthaler Linotype Company and first made available in 1935. Electra cannot be classified as either "modern" or "old style." It is not based on any historical model, and hence does not echo any particular period or style of type design. It avoids the extreme contrast between "thick" and "thin" elements that marks most modern faces, and is without eccentricities which catch the eye and interfere with reading. In general, Electra is a simple, readable typeface which attempts to give a feeling of fluidity, power, and speed.

W. A. Dwiggins (1880–1956) was born in Martinsville, Ohio, and studied art in Chicago. In 1904 he moved to Hingham, Massachusetts, where he built a solid reputation as a designer of advertisements and as a calligrapher. He began an association with the Mergenthaler Linotype Company in 1929, and over the next twenty-seven years designed a number of book types, of which Metro, Electra, and Caledonia have been used very widely. In 1930 Dwiggins became interested in marionettes, and through the years made many important contributions to the art of puppetry and the design of marionettes.